ENGLISH FOR INTERNATIONAL FINANCE STUDIES

国际金融英语

顾维勇　编著

东南大学出版社
SOUTHEAST UNIVERSITY PRESS
·南京·

内容提要

本书按照国际货币体系发展、国际金融机构以及枢要货币等专题,较为详细地介绍了国际货币体系的形成、发展以及在国际经济活动中的作用,重点介绍了国际货币基金组织 IMF(GAB,SDRs 等)、世界银行、亚洲发展银行等主要国际金融机构的溯源、变迁以及在现代国际金融体系中的重要功能,详述了美国联邦储备体系及美元、欧元体系及欧元、人民币和香港、澳门、台湾地区的货币的来源及发展过程,力图帮助学习者了解国际货币体系的概貌、相关金融机构的功能及在现代政治和经济生活中的作用、主要货币的发展变化及其在国际金融体系中的重要作用。本书选材专业,时效性强,易教易学,且辅之以翻译练习和阅读材料以拓展专题知识。本书适用于金融、外经贸等专业的学生,也可供从事金融工作的人员作为辅助读物使用。

图书在版编目(CIP)数据

国际金融英语/顾维勇编著. —南京:东南大学出版社,2015.12(2022.6 重印)
 ISBN 978-7-5641-6238-2

Ⅰ.①国… Ⅱ.①顾… Ⅲ.①国际金融—英语 Ⅳ.①H31

中国版本图书馆CIP数据核字(2015)第316148号

国际金融英语

编　　著	顾维勇	责任编辑	刘　坚
电　　话	(025)83793329/83790577(传真)	电子邮箱	liu-jian@ seu.edu.cn
出版发行	东南大学出版社	出 版 人	江建中
地　　址	南京市四牌楼2号	邮　　编	210096
销售电话	(025)83794561/83794174/83794121/83795801/83792174　83795802/57711295(传真)		
网　　址	http://www.seupress.com	电子邮箱	press@ seupress.com
经　　销	全国各地新华书店	印　　刷	江苏凤凰数码印务有限公司
开　　本	787mm×1092mm　1/16	印　　张	18	字　　数	470 千字
版　　次	2015 年 12 月第 1 版		
印　　次	2022 年 6 月第 2 次印刷		
书　　号	ISBN 978-7-5641-6238-2		
定　　价	45.00 元		

* 未经许可,本书内文字不得以任何方式转载、演绎,违者必究。
* 本社图书若有印装质量问题,请直接与营销部联系,电话:025-83791830。

前　言

作为商务英语、金融及贸易等课程体系中的重要组成部分,《国际金融英语》的主要目的在于通过得当的选材和丰富的专题阅读,让学习者能够了解涉及国际金融的基础知识,熟悉相关专业词汇和表述,为进一步深入学习专业课程奠定坚实的基础。笔者于2010年编写并出版了《新编国际金融英语教程》,得到了同行专家的关注和好评,并被国内多家院校选用,且于2012年获得了南京市"第十一届哲学社会科学优秀成果三等奖"。

本教材《国际金融英语》是在广泛征集使用者的意见的基础上,结合笔者近几年的研究成果和最新的国际金融发展状况修订而成的,主要包括:国际货币体系发展、国际金融机构以及枢要货币等专题。国际货币体系发展专题涉及金本位制、弹性汇率、布雷顿森林体系以及欧洲货币体系等,较为详细地介绍了国际货币体系的形成及发展以及在国际经济活动中的作用;国际金融机构重点介绍国际货币基金组织 IMF(GAB,SDRs 等)、世界银行、亚洲发展银行等,重点介绍了各组织的溯源及变迁以及在现代国际金融体系中的重要功能;枢要货币专题重点介绍美国联邦储备体系及美元、欧元体系及欧元、人民币和香港、澳门、台湾地区的货币的来源及发展过程。通过这三个部分的学习,学习者能够了解国际货币体系的概貌、相关金融机构的功能及在现代政治和经济生活中的作用、主要货币的发展变化及在国际金融体系中的重要作用。相较于同类图书,本书的鲜明特色在于:

1. 选材紧扣专业方向。世界货币体系的发展、世界主要金融机构、枢要货币,中国货币单元除了介绍人民币外还介绍了港币、澳币及台币,这些专题内容都涉及相关专业学生必备的专业基础知识。

2. 内容既具有专业性,也具有较好的适时性。大部分内容为市面上教材中所未涉及的,语言地道。

3. 设计风格生动活泼。有的章节配备了图片,让读者欣赏图案的同时学习相关的英语知识。

4. 编排体例新颖,实用性强,易教易学。内容中涉及的背景知识均专项列出,为教学提供了方便。难度较大的句子尽量排在翻译专项练习中。配备的拓展阅读材料与课文材料相关以拓展该专题知识。

本教程建议用40课时左右学完。使用者可根据教学实际,考虑各校安排的课时量,对教程进行有选择的使用,亦可补充新的内容充实教学或替换旧的材料。教学过程中建议师生充分利用网络资源,采用多媒体手段,拓展阅读视野,对课文中出现的相关术语,语言点或背景知识多查阅资料或工具书等,力求完全准确的理解。

全书由顾维勇教授统筹大纲、目录及选材,孙维林和刘源老师分别负责国际金融机构及枢要货币单元的编写,全书最终由顾维勇教授统稿。《国际金融英语》获得了江苏省教育厅重点教材建设立项,东南大学出版社编审刘坚博士后在本书出版过程中精心审稿,提出了不少有益的建议,在此谨致谢忱!

由于时间仓促,加之笔者专业知识有限,本书中差错在所难免,欢迎同行专家及使用者不吝赐教!

顾维勇
2015 年 9 月于南京

Contents

PART I	**EVOLUTION AND OPERATION OF THE INTERNATIONAL MONETARY SYSTEM**	
	CHAPTER 1 THE GOLD STANDARD ERA, 1870—1914	/2
	FURTHER READING GOLD STANDARD	/10
	CHAPTER 2 THE INTER-WAR PERIOD (1918—1939) AND THE BRETTON WOODS SYSTEM (1944—1973)	/15
	FURTHER READING THE LATE BRETTON WOODS SYSTEM THE U.S. BALANCE OF PAYMENTS CRISIS (1958—1968)	/31
	CHAPTER 3 MANAGED FLOATING SINCE 1973 AND THE EUROPEAN MONETARY SYSTEM	/38
	FURTHER READING FIXED OR FLEXIBLE? GETTING THE EXCHANGE RATE RIGHT IN THE 1990s	/48
PART II	**ORGANIZATIONS**	
	CHAPTER 4 THE INTERNATIONAL MONETARY FUND (IMF)	/62
	FURTHER READING PROMOTING A MORE SECURE AND STABLE GLOBAL ECONOMY—IMF ANNUAL REPORT 2013 (Overview)	/75
	CHAPTER 5 THE WORLD BANK	/79
	FURTHER READING THE WORLD BANK: THE ROLES OF IBRD AND IDA	/97
	CHAPTER 6 ASIAN DEVELOPMENT BANK	/101
	FURTHER READING PEOPLE'S REPUBLIC OF CHINA, ASIAN DEVELOPMENT OUTLOOK 2014	/114
PART III	**CURRENCIES**	
	CHAPTER 7 THE FEDERAL RESERVE SYSTEM	/124
	FURTHER READING THE FEDERAL RESERVE SYSTEM	/155
	CHAPTER 8 THE EUROPEAN CENTRAL BANK & THE EUROSYSTEM	/175
	FURTHER READING THE EUROSYSTEM	/209
	CHAPTER 9 HISTORY OF RENMINBI (RMB)	/228
	FURTHER READING HK DOLLAR, MACANESE PATACA, NEW TAIWAN DOLLAR	/255
	KEY TO THE EXERCISES	/271

Part I

EVOLUTION AND OPERATION OF THE INTERNATIONAL MONETARY SYSTEM

CHAPTER 1

THE GOLD STANDARD ERA, 1870—1914

Learning Objectives

1. The concept of gold standard and its origins;
2. The rules of gold standard;
3. The operation of the gold standard.

Origins of the Gold Standard

The gold standard had its origin in the use of gold coins as a medium of exchange, unit of account, and store of value. While gold has been used in this way since ancient times, the gold standard as a legal institution dates back to 1819, when the British Parliament passed the Resumption Act. The Resumption Act marks the first adoption of a true gold standard because it simultaneously repealed long-standing restrictions on the export of gold coins and bullion from Britain.

Later in the nineteenth century, Germany, Japan, and other countries also followed suit. The U.S. effectively joined the gold standard in 1879 and institutionalized the dollar-gold link through the U.S. Gold Standard Act of 1900. With Britain's preeminence in international trade and the advanced development of its financial system, London naturally became the center of the international monetary system built on the gold standard.

The Gold Standard Rules

The gold standard regime has conventionally been associated with three rules of the game. The first rule is that in each participating country the price of the domestic currency must be fixed in terms of gold. Since the gold content in one unit of each currency was fixed, exchange rates were also fixed. This was called the mint parity. The second rule is that there must be a free import and export of gold. The third rule is that the surplus country, which is gaining gold, should allow its volume of money to increase while the deficit country, which is losing gold, should allow its volume of money to fall.

The first two rules together ensure that exchange rates between participating countries are fixed within fairly narrow limits. With the price of any two currencies fixed in terms of gold the implied exchange rate between the two currencies is also fixed and any significant deviation from this fixed rate will be rapidly eliminated by arbitrage operations.

The third rule, requiring the volume of money to be linked in each participating country to balance of payments developments, provides an "automatic" mechanism of adjustment which ensures that, ultimately, any balance of payments disequilibria will be corrected.

The Automatic Adjustment Mechanism under the Gold Standard

The gold standard contains some powerful automatic mechanisms that contribute to the simultaneous achievement of balance of payments equilibrium by all countries. The most important of these was the price-specie-flow mechanism (precious metals were referred to as "specie"). Hume's description of this mechanism has been translated into modern terms. Assume that Britain's current account surplus is greater than its non-reserve capital account deficit. In this case, foreigners' net imports from Britain are not being financed entirely by British loans. The balance must be matched by flows of international reserves that is, of gold—into Britain. The gold inflows into Britain automatically reduce foreign money supplies and increase Britain's money supply, driving foreign prices downward and British prices upward. As a result, the demand for British goods and services will fall and at the same time the British demand for foreign goods and services will increase. Eventually, reserve movements stop and both countries reach balance of payments equilibrium. The same process also works in reverse, eliminating an initial situation of foreign surplus and British deficit.

However, the response of central banks to gold flows across their borders furnished another potential mechanism to help restore balance of payments equilibrium. Central banks experiencing persistent gold outflows were motivated to contract their domestic asset holdings for the fear of becoming unable to meet their obligation to redeem currency notes. Thus domestic interest rates were pushed up and capital would flow in from abroad. Central banks gaining gold had much weaker incentives to eliminate their own imports of the metal. The main incentive was the greater profitability of interest-bearing domestic assets compared with "barren" gold. Central banks that were accumulating gold might be attempted to purchase domestic assets, thereby increasing capital outflows and driving gold abroad. These domestic credit measures, if undertaken by central banks, reinforced the price-specie-flow mechanism in pushing all countries toward balance of payments equilibrium. Because such measures speeded up the movement of countries toward their external balance goals, they increased the efficiency of the automatic adjustment processes inherent in the gold standard.

However, research has shown that countries often reversed the steps mentioned above and sterilized gold flows, that is, sold domestic assets when foreign reserves were rising and bought domestic assets as foreign reserves fell. Government interference with private gold exports also undermined the system. The picture of smooth and automatic balance of payments adjustment before World War I therefore did not always match reality.

Given the prices of currencies fixed in terms of gold, the price levels within gold standard countries did not rise as much between 1870 and 1914 as over the period after World War II, but national price levels moved unpredictably over shorter horizons as periods of inflation and deflation followed each other. What is more, the gold standard does not seem to have done much to ensure full employment. A fundamental cause of short term internal instability under the pre-1914 gold standard was the subordination of economic policy to external objectives. Internal policy objectives were only emphasized after World War I as a result of the worldwide economic instability of the interwar years, 1918—1939. To understand how the post-World War II international monetary system tried to reconcile the goals of internal and external balance, we need to examine the economic events of the period between the two world wars.

WORDS AND EXPRESSIONS

- *unit of account* 计算单位；记账单位
- *a legal institution* a legal system 合法的制度
- *repeal* /rɪˈpiːl/ *v.* to revoke or rescind, especially by an official or formal act 撤销,废止
- *long-standing* /ˈlɔŋstædɪŋ/ *adj.* of long duration or existence 长时间的；经久不衰的；长期存在的
- *follow suit* follow the example, imitate 效仿
- *institutionalize* /ˌɪnstɪˈtjuːʃənəlaɪz/ *vt.* to make into, treat as, or give the character of an institution to 制度化；to make part of a structured and usually well-established system 使机构化
- *preeminence* /priːˈemɪnəns/ *n.* 卓越,杰出
- *regime* /reɪˈʒiːm/ *n.* social system; a form of government 体制；政体,政权制度
- *in terms of* 依……，据……；从……方面；从……角度来讲；换算,折合；以……为单位；关于,在……方面,就……来说
- *surplus country* the country who has favorable balance of trade/active trade balance/active balance/trade surplus 顺差国
- *deficit country* a country who has adverse balance of trade/trade deficit 逆差国
- *deviation from* 偏离

Part I EVOLUTION AND OPERATION OF THE INTERNATIONAL MONETARY SYSTEM

- *arbitrage operations* arbitration procedures 仲裁程序
- *disequilibria* /dɪsiːkwɪˈlɪbrɪə/ *pl.* of disequilibrium /ˌdɪsˌiːkwɪˈlɪbrɪəm/ *n.* loss or lack of stability or equilibrium 不均/平衡,不安定
- *price-specie-flow mechanism* 价格—货币—流动机制
- *capital account* an account stating the amount of funds and assets invested in a business by the owners or stockholders, including retained earnings 资本账户,股本账户记录企业所有者或股东投资于这个企业的资金和资产数量的账户,包括净利润的记录。
- *meet one's obligation* 履行某人的职责
- *redeem* /rɪˈdiːm/ *vt.* pay off, compensate, to convert into cash 兑换成现金
- *incentive* /ɪnˈsentɪv/ *n.* encouragement, inducement, motive, stimulus 刺激
- *barren* /ˈbærən/ *adj.* unproductive, unfertile, unprofitable 没有收益的,无利息的
- *central bank* an institution which—by way of a legal act—has been given responsibility for conducting the monetary policy for a specific area. 央行

BACKGROUND KNOWLEDGE

1 *gold standard n.* A monetary standard under which the basic unit of currency is equal in value to and exchangeable for a specified amount of gold. 金本位制：一种货币制度,在此制度下,通货基本单位与一定数量的黄金价值相同,并可与之兑换。

Gold standard is a monetary system formerly used by many countries, under which the value of the standard unit of currency was by law made equal to a fixed weight of gold of a stated fineness. Thus the rates of exchange between various gold-standard countries remained fixed, which helped international trade, but the system limited the power of the monetary authorities to control the supply of money in fighting inflation and unemployment. Under a full gold-standard system, such as existed in Britain from the 1870s to 1914, gold coin and bullion (bars of gold) could be freely imported and exported; gold coins circulated freely; and the central bank bought and sold gold in any quantity at the fixed price. The system was set up again by 1928 in limited form but it broke down in the 1930s. After the Second World War some countries in Europe agreed to make their currencies freely convertible into gold for international payments only, thus forming a gold standard that was entirely external. Variations of the gold standard are: gold bullion standard; gold exchange standard. 金本位是过去许多国家采用的货币制度,在这种制度下,货币标准单位的价值由法律规定等于固定重量的既定纯度黄金。这样,各个不同的金本位制国家之间的汇率保持固定,有助于国际贸易。但这种制度限制了财政当局控制货币供应数量以抑制通货膨胀及失业的力量。在完全金本位制下,如在19世纪70年代至1914年间的英国,金币和金条/块可以自由输出输入,金币自由流

通,中央银行按固定价格收购及出售任何数量的黄金。1928年这一制度以有限的形式重新建立,但在20世纪30年代垮台。"二战"后,有些欧洲国家同意其货币可以自由兑换黄金,但只限于国际支付,这样就形成了完全对外的金本位。金本位的不同形式有:金块本位制;金汇兑本位制。(引自杨佑方主编,《外贸经济英语用法词典》,2002:PP618—619)

2 *the Resumption Act* 纸币收回条例

3 *mint parity = mint par of exchange, par rate of exchange*: It is the rate of exchange between two currencies that are on the gold standard, i. e. when the gold value of their standard currency unit has been fixed by law. The rate between any pair of gold standard currencies is always directly related to the amount of gold in a unit of each currency. 铸币平价汇率是两种金本位之间的汇率,即标准货币单位的黄金值已由法律固定时的汇率。任何两种金本位之间的汇率总是直接与每种货币一个单位的金含量有关。

4 *balance of payments* 国际收支

It is the balance of a national account in which are recorded all the international dealings resulting in payment of money during certain period. Unlike the balance of trade, which includes only visible dealings (articles of trade, and gold and silver bars and coins), the balance of payments takes note of invisible imports and exports (payments for banking, insurance, transport, and other services), interest payments and movements of capital. The balance is said to be in deficit, adverse, passive or unfavorable if it shows that the country pays or owes more than it receives or is owed; and in surplus, active or favorable if the opposite is true. 国际收支是一个国家记录一定时期内发生支付货币的所有国际交易的账户上的余/差额。与贸易差额只包括有形交易(贸易商品、金条银条及硬币)不同,国际收支着重于无形进出口(银行、保险、运输及其他服务)、利息支付及资本的流动。如其差额表示一个国家支付与欠人多于收入与人欠,则为逆差,反之则为顺差。

5 *currency notes* 流通券,国库券

Currency notes are notes issued as money by the British Treasury during the war of 1914—1918 and after, of two values, £1 and 10s, later amalgamated (1928) with Bank of England notes. 流通券是在1914—1918战争期间及战后英国财政部发行作货币使用的票据,有两种面值:1英镑和10先令,之后于1928年与英格兰银行票据合并。[同]Treasury notes. 此文中指"通货券,流通券",并非特指英国的"流通券"。

NOTES

1 *current account* 经常项目:国际收支差额一个分类,包括商品进出口及劳务项目收支,其差额大小与方向对一个国家的国际收支有重大影响。(注:在不同的语境下,此词还有下列意义:往来账户;经常账户;活期存款账户)

Part I EVOLUTION AND OPERATION OF THE INTERNATIONAL MONETARY SYSTEM

例：The immediate causes of the fall of the Canadian dollar are a current account deficit of $4 billion and a sharp drop in Canadian borrowing abroad. 加元下跌的直接原因是,40亿加元的经常项目赤字和加拿大从国外借款的急剧减少。

2 *sterilize* /ˈsterɪlaɪz/ vt. [Economics] to place (gold) in safekeeping so as not to affect the supply of money or credit 【经济学】使(黄金)封存而不起作用

sterilization of gold（黄金冲销）：在金本位制下,黄金的输入使通货供给量增加,导致通货膨胀物价上升。为了防止此通货膨胀,必须阻止黄金流入对通货及物价上升的影响。此种做法称为黄金冲销(sterilizing of gold)

注：本课中出现了大量的英语复数形式词,需要学习者特加注意,（参见2007第5期《中国翻译》"商务英语复数形式词语的翻译"）如：reserves, movements, holdings, flows, outflows, loans 等。在金融英语里及商务英语中,复数形式是一种常见的语法现象,但它们与通常的复数形式有所不同,它们常常是有所指的,常用来表示"量",或"金额"、"额"。又如：

单数词与词义	复数词与词义
import 进口	imports 进口量
export 出口	exports 出口量
damage 损坏	damages 损坏赔偿金
loss 灭失	losses 损失额/金
sale 销售	sales 销售额
stock 库存(货)	stocks 库存量
reserve 储存	reserves 储量
shipment 装船	shipments 装船的货
holding 持有	holdings 持有量
payment 付款	payments 付款额

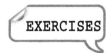

Ⅰ. Translate the following expressions into Chinese.

1. the international monetary system built on the gold standard
2. participating country
3. significant deviation from this fixed rate
4. automatic mechanism of adjustment
5. achievement of balance of payments equilibrium
6. the response of central banks to gold flows across their borders

7. meet their obligation to redeem currency notes
8. ensure full employment
9. subordination of economic policy to external objectives
10. tried to reconcile the goals of internal and external balance

II. **Give the Chinese meaning of the following plurals.**

1. international reserves
2. gold flows
3. net imports
4. capital outflows
5. domestic assets

III. **Translate the following paragraphs into Chinese.**

1. However, research has shown that countries often reversed the steps mentioned above and sterilized gold flows, that is, sold domestic assets when foreign reserves were rising and bought domestic assets as foreign reserves fell. Government interference with private gold exports also undermined the system. The picture of smooth and automatic balance of payments adjustment before World War I therefore did not always match reality.

2. The gold standard regime has conventionally been associated with three rules of the game. The first rule is that in each participating country the price of the domestic currency must be fixed in terms of gold. Since the gold content in one unit of each currency was fixed, exchange rates were also fixed. This was called the mint parity. The second rule is that there must be a free import and export of gold. The third rule is that the surplus country, which is gaining gold, should allow its volume of money to increase while the deficit country, which is losing gold, should allow its volume of money to fall.

3. Central banks experiencing persistent gold outflows were motivated to contract their domestic asset holdings for the fear of becoming unable to meet their obligation to redeem currency notes. Thus domestic interest rates were pushed up and capital would flow in from abroad. Central banks gaining gold had much weaker incentives to eliminate their own imports of the metal. The main incentive was the greater profitability of interest-bearing domestic assets compared with "barren" gold.

4. Given the prices of currencies fixed in terms of gold, the price levels within gold standard countries did not rise as much between 1870 and 1914 as over the period after World War II, but national price levels moved unpredictably over shorter horizons as periods of inflation and deflation followed each other.

Part I EVOLUTION AND OPERATION OF THE INTERNATIONAL MONETARY SYSTEM

IV. Read the passage and fill in the blanks with the words or phrases given below.

bonds; payments; dividends; record; broking; financial transactions; bank advances; net overflow; immediate transactions; an overall balance; capital account; investment purposes; visible account; non-commercial items; net errors and omissions

Balance of payments is the total movement of goods, services and (1) _____ between one country and the rest of the world; the term commonly used for the (2) _____ of such movements. In money terms, therefore, the balance of payments is the total of all receipts from abroad, and of all (3) _____ to recipients abroad. All receipts and payments of whatever nature are included, whether they be payments and receipts for non-commercial purposes, such as legacies and for pensions; for goods sold or services rendered; for (4) _____; on behalf of government; or of private persons and agencies.

The balance of payments record or account is conventionally divided into the current account, or payments and receipts for (5) _____, such as the sale of goods and rendering of services; and the (6) _____, or the money movements not immediately devoted to trade, such as investment. The current account is subdivided into the merchandise, or (7) _____ (often also termed the trade account), comprising the movement of goods; and the invisible account, comprising the movement of services, transfers and investment incomes. Services comprise transport, travel, banking, insurance, (8) _____ and other activities; transfers comprise money movements for the transmission of legacies, pensions and other (9) _____; investment income consists of the interest, profits and (10) _____ deriving from capital placed abroad.

The capital account is normally divided into long-term and short-term capital, the former relating to capital employed for investment purposes, the latter to (11) _____, trade credit and the like. Long-term capital is again subdivided into direct investment capital, or capital employed for the establishment of commercial premises and industrial plant, and portfolio investment capital(证券投资资本), or capital employed for the purchase of (12) _____ and shares.

A balance of payments account will normally resolve the various subordinate accounts into balances or net receipts and payments, summing these to (13) _____, subject to a balancing item (UK), (14) _____, or statistical discrepancy (US), against which the (15) _____ from or net inflow into the country's reserves is noted. The balance of payments account is also referred to as the external account of a nation.

(*FROM*: *International Dictionary of Finance* P. 18)

FURTHER READING

GOLD STANDARD
by Michael D. Bordo

The gold standard was a commitment by participating countries to fix the prices of their domestic currencies in terms of a specified amount of gold. National money and other forms of money (bank deposits and notes) were freely converted into gold at the fixed price. England adopted a **de facto**(事实上的) gold standard in 1717 after the master of the mint, Sir Isaac Newton, overvalued the silver **guinea**(几尼:英国的旧金币,等于一镑一先令) and formally adopted the gold standard in 1819. The United States, though formally on a **bimetallic** (gold and silver 金银复本位) standard, switched to gold de facto in 1834 and **de jure**(权利上的) in 1900. In 1834 the United States fixed the price of gold at \$20.67 per ounce, where it remained until 1933. Other major countries joined the gold standard in the 1870s. The period from 1880 to 1914 is known as the classical gold standard. During that time the majority of countries adhered (in varying degrees) to gold. It was also a period of unprecedented economic growth with relatively free trade in goods, labor, and capital.

The gold standard broke down during World War I as major **belligerents**(交战国) resorted to inflationary finance and was briefly reinstated from 1925 to 1931 as the Gold Exchange Standard. Under this standard countries could hold gold or dollars or pounds as reserves, except for the United States and the United Kingdom, which held reserves only in gold. This version broke down in 1931 following Britain's departure from gold in the face of massive gold and capital outflows. In 1933 **President Roosevelt**(罗斯福总统) nationalized gold owned by private citizens and abrogated contracts in which payment was specified in gold.

Between 1946 and 1971 countries operated under the Bretton Woods system. Under this further modification of the gold standard, most countries settled their international balances in U.S. dollars, but the U.S. government promised to redeem other central banks' holdings of dollars for gold at a fixed rate of \$35 per ounce. However, persistent U.S. balance-of-payments deficits steadily reduced U.S. gold reserves, reducing confidence in the ability of the United States to redeem its

Part I EVOLUTION AND OPERATION OF THE INTERNATIONAL MONETARY SYSTEM

currency in gold. Finally, on August 15, 1971, President Nixon announced that the United States would no longer redeem currency for gold. This was the final step in abandoning the gold standard.

Widespread dissatisfaction with high inflation in the late seventies and early eighties brought renewed interest in the gold standard. Although that interest is not strong today, it strengthens every time inflation moves much above 6 percent. This makes sense. Whatever other problems there were with the gold standard, persistent inflation was not one of them. Between 1880 and 1914, the period when the United States was on the "classical gold standard," inflation averaged only 0.1 percent per year.

How the Gold Standard Worked

The gold standard was a domestic standard, regulating the quantity and growth rate of a country's money supply. Because new production of gold would add only a small fraction to the accumulated stock, and because the authorities guaranteed free convertibility of gold into non-gold money, the gold standard assured that the money supply and, hence, the price level would not vary much. But periodic surges in the world's gold stock, such as the gold discoveries in Australia and California around 1850, caused price levels to be very unstable in the short run. The gold standard was also an international standard—determining the value of a country's currency in terms of other countries' currencies. Because adherents to the standard maintained a fixed price for gold, rates of exchange between currencies tied to gold were necessarily fixed.

Because exchange rates were fixed, the gold standard caused price levels around the world to move together. This co-movement occurred mainly through an automatic balance-of-payments adjustment process called the price-specie-flow mechanism. Here is how the mechanism worked: Suppose a technological innovation brought about faster real economic growth in the United States. With the supply of money (gold) essentially fixed in the short run, this caused U.S. prices to fall. Prices of U.S. exports then fell relative to the prices of imports. This caused the British to demand more U.S. exports and Americans to demand fewer imports. A U.S. balance-of-payments surplus was created, causing gold (specie) to flow from the United Kingdom to the United States. The gold inflow increased the U.S. money supply, reversing the initial fall in prices. In the United Kingdom the gold outflow reduced the money supply and, hence, lowered the price level. The net result was balanced prices among countries.

The fixed exchange rate also caused both monetary and nonmonetary (real) shocks to be transmitted via flows of gold and capital between countries. Therefore, a shock in one country affected the domestic money supply, expenditure, price level, and real income in another country.

An example of a monetary shock was the California gold discovery in 1848. The newly produced gold increased the U.S. money supply, which then raised domestic expenditures, nominal income, and ultimately, the price level. The rise in the domestic price level made U.S. exports more expensive, causing a deficit in the U.S. balance of payments. For America's trading partners the same forces necessarily produced a balance of trade surplus. The U.S. trade deficit was financed by a gold (specie) outflow to its trading partners, reducing the monetary gold stock in the United States. In the trading partners the money supply increased, raising domestic expenditures, nominal incomes, and ultimately, the price level. Depending on the relative share of the U.S. monetary gold stock in the world total, world prices and income rose. Although the initial effect of the gold discovery was to increase real output (because wages and prices did not immediately increase), eventually the full effect was on the price level alone.

For the gold standard to work fully, central banks, where they existed, were supposed to play by the "rules of the game." In other words, they were supposed to raise their discount rates—the interest rate at which the central bank lends money to member banks—to speed a gold inflow, and lower their discount rates to facilitate a gold outflow. Thus, if a country was running a balance-of-payments deficit, the rules of the game required it to allow a gold outflow until the ratio of its price level to that of its principal trading partners was restored to the par exchange rate.

The exemplar of central bank behavior was the Bank of England, which was played by the rules over much of the period between 1870 and 1914. Whenever Great Britain faced a balance-of-payments deficit and the Bank of England saw its gold reserves declining, it raised its "bank rate" (discount rate). By causing other interest rates in the United Kingdom to rise as well, the rise in the bank rate was supposed to cause holdings of inventories to decrease and other investment expenditures to decrease. These reductions would then cause a reduction in overall domestic spending and a fall in the price level. At the same time, the rise in the bank rate would stem any short-term capital outflow and attract short-term funds from abroad.

Most other countries on the gold standard—notably France and Belgium—did not, however, follow the rules of the game. They never allowed interest rates to rise enough to decrease the domestic price level. Also, many countries frequently broke the rules by "sterilization"—shielding the domestic money supply from external disequilibrium by buying or selling domestic securities. If, for example, France's central bank wished to prevent an inflow of gold from increasing its money supply, it would sell securities for gold, thus reducing the amount of gold circulating.

Yet the central bankers' breaches of the rules must be put in perspective. Although exchange rates in principal countries frequently **deviated from par**(偏离面值), governments rarely debased their currencies or otherwise manipulated the gold standard to support domestic economic activity. Suspension of convertibility in England (1797—1821, 1914—1925) and the United States (1862—1879) did occur in wartime emergencies. But as promised, convertibility at the original **parity**(等值) was resumed after the emergency passed. These resumptions **fortified**(加强) the credibility of the gold standard rule.

Performance of the Gold Standard

As mentioned, the great virtue of the gold standard was that it assured long-term price stability. Compare the aforementioned average annual inflation rate of 0.1 percent between 1880 and 1914 with the average of 4.2 percent between 1946 and 1990. (The reason for excluding the period from 1914 to 1946 is that it was neither a period of the classical gold standard nor a period during which governments understood how to manage monetary policy.)

But because economies under the gold standard were so vulnerable to real and monetary shocks, prices were highly unstable in the short run. A measure of short-term price instability is the coefficient of variation, which is the ratio of the standard deviation of annual percentage changes in the price level to the average annual percentage change. The higher the coefficient of variation, the greater the short-term instability. For the United States between 1879 and 1913, the coefficient was 17.0, which is quite high. Between 1946 and 1990 it was only 0.8.

Moreover, because the gold standard gives government very little discretion to use monetary policy, economies on the gold standard are less able to avoid or offset either monetary or real shocks. Real output, therefore, is more variable under the gold standard. The coefficient of variation for real output was 3.5 between 1879 and 1913, and only 1.5 between 1946 and 1990. Not coincidentally, since the government could not have discretion over monetary policy, unemployment was higher during the gold standard. It averaged 6.8 percent in the United States between 1879 and 1913 versus 5.6 percent between 1946 and 1990.

Finally, any consideration of the **pros and cons**(赞成与反对) of the gold standard must include a very large negative: the resource cost of producing gold. Milton Friedman estimated the cost of maintaining a full gold coin standard for the United States in 1960 to be more than 2.5 percent of **GNP** (Gross National Product 国民生产总值). In 1990 this cost would have been $137 billion.

Conclusion

Although the last vestiges of the gold standard disappeared in 1971, its appeal is still strong. Those who oppose giving discretionary powers to the central bank are attracted by the simplicity of its basic rule. Others view it as an effective anchor for the world price level. Still others look back longingly to the fixity of exchange rates. However, despite its appeal, many of the conditions which made the gold standard so successful vanished in 1914. In particular, the importance that governments attach to full employment means that they are unlikely to make maintaining the gold standard link and its corollary, long-run price stability, the primary goal of economic policy.

(*FROM*: http://www.econlib.org/library/Enc/GoldStandard.html)

balance-of-payments deficit = *external deficit*; *trade deficit* 国际收支赤字

When the total value of imports is greater than the total value of exports, the difference is a balance-of-payments deficit. 进口总额大于出口总额的差额即国际收支赤字。

Part I EVOLUTION AND OPERATION OF THE INTERNATIONAL MONETARY SYSTEM

CHAPTER 2 THE INTER-WAR PERIOD (1918—1939) AND THE BRETTON WOODS SYSTEM (1944—1973)

Learning Objectives

1. The monetary system in the interwar period;
2. Bretton Woods System: establishment, evolution and collapse.

Governments effectively suspended the gold standard during World War I and financed part of their massive military expenditures by printing money. Moreover, labor forces and productive capacity had been reduced sharply through war losses. Consequently price levels were very high everywhere at the war's conclusion in 1918. Between 1918 and 1924, exchange rates also fluctuated wildly, and this led to a desire to return to the stability of the gold standard. The U.S. returned to gold in 1919. In 1922, Italy, Britain, France, and Japan agreed on a program calling for a general return to the gold standard and cooperation among central banks in attaining internal and external objectives. In 1925 Britain returned to the gold standard by pegging the pound to gold at the prewar price. To return the pound price of gold to its prewar level, the Bank of England was thus forced to follow contractionary monetary policies that contributed to severe unemployment. British stagflation in the 1920s accelerated London's decline as the world's leading financial center. The United Kingdom had lost a great deal of its competitiveness and attempted to contain its deficits when the balance of payments deficits and inflation were serious. On the other hand, France faced large balance of payments surpluses after the franc was stabilized at a depreciated level in 1926. As short term capital shifted from London to Paris and New York, the United Kingdom was forced in September 1931 to suspend the convertibility of the pound into gold, devalued the pound, and the gold exchange standard came to an end.

The causes of the collapse of the gold exchange standard lay in the lack of an adequate adjustment mechanism, the huge destabilizing capital flows and the outbreak of the Great Depression. This also was a period when nations imposed very high tariffs and other serious import restrictions. According to Nurkse, the interwar experience clearly indicated the prevalence of destabilizing speculation and the instability of flexible exchange rates.

Since a full recovery from the Great Depression of 1929—1933 did not take place until the onset of World War II, the conditions for a formal reorganization of the international financial order were not present. The depression had provided an environment in which self interested beggar-thy-neighbor policies encouraged competitive devaluation and increased tariff protection—followed the model established earlier by France. Since no long lasting effective devaluations were possible and the great interruption of world trade eliminated the gains from international trade, such an environment hindered global economic growth: all countries could not simultaneously devalue by raising gold prices, with collective action doing nothing more than devaluing money by causing inflation. When the war replaced the depression, cooperation became impossible. All countries would have been better off in a world with free international trade, provided international cooperation had helped each country preserve its external balance and financial stability without sacrificing internal policy objectives. It was this realization that inspired the blueprint for the post war international monetary system, the Bretton Woods system.

In July 1944 representatives from the United States, the United Kingdom, and 42 other nations meeting at Bretton Woods, New Hampshire, drafted and signed the Articles of Agreement of the International Monetary Fund (IMF). Even as the war continued, the allied countries were looking forward to economic needs of the post-war world, hoping to establish an international monetary system that would foster full employment and price stability while allowing individual countries to attain external balance without imposing restrictions on international trade.

Goals and Structure of the IMF

The system devised at Bretton Woods called for fixed exchange rates against the U. S. dollar and unvarying dollar price of gold— $35 per ounce. Member countries held their official international reserves largely in the form of gold or dollar assets and had the right to sell dollars to the Federal Reserve for gold at the official price. The system was thus a gold exchange standard, with dollar as its principal reserve currency. The inter-war experience had convinced governments that full employment was their primary responsibility and floating exchange rates were a cause of speculative instability and were harmful to international trade. The IMF agreement therefore tried to incorporate sufficient flexibility to allow countries to attain external balance in an orderly fashion without sacrificing internal objectives or fixed exchange rates.

Generally, the goals of the IMF were: (1) to promote international monetary cooperation by providing the means for members to consult on international monetary issues; (2) to facilitate the growth of international trade and foster a multilateral system of international payments; (3) to promote exchange-rate stability and seek the elimination of exchange restrictions that disrupt international trade; (4) To establish a system of multilateral payments; and (5) to make short-term financial resources available to member nations on a temporary basis so as to allow them to correct payments disequilibria without resorting to measures that would destroy national prosperity.

Operation of the Bretton Woods System

While the Bretton Woods system allowed flexibility in exchange rates in cases of fundamental disequilibrium, in practice industrial countries were very unwilling to change their par values until they were forced to do so. They thought devaluation was a sign of national weakness and a revaluation would reduce the competitiveness of a country. As a result, from 1950 until August 1971, the United Kingdom devalued only in 1967; France devalued only in 1957 and 1969; West Germany revalued in 1961 and 1969; and the United States, Italy, and Japan never changed their par values. Meanwhile, Canada (defying the IMF rules) had fluctuating exchange rates from 1950 to 1962 and then reinstituted them in 1970. Developing nations, on the other hand, devalued all too often.

The unwillingness of industrial nations to change their par values as a matter of policy when in fundamental disequilibrium had two significant effects. First, it robbed the Bretton Woods system of most of its flexibility and the mechanism for adjusting balance of payments disequilibria. Second, and related to the first point, the reluctance of industrial nations to change their par value when in fundamental disequilibrium gave rise to huge destabilizing international capital flows by providing an excellent one-way gamble for speculators.

The IMF articles also called for convertibility on current account transaction only because the designers of the Bretton Woods system hoped to facilitate free trade while avoiding the possibility that private capital flows might tighten the external constraints faced by policymakers. The convertibility of the dollar into gold resumed soon after World War II. The major European currencies became convertible for current account purposes in 1958 and formally in 1961. In spite of these restrictions, the post-war era witnessed huge destabilizing capital flows, which became more frequent and more disruptive, culminating in the collapse of the Bretton Woods system in August 1971.

Evolution of the Bretton Woods System

Over the years, the Bretton Woods system evolved in several important aspects in response to the world's changing conditions. In 1962, the IMF negotiated the General Arrangements to Borrow up to $6 billion from the so-called "Group of Ten" most important industrial nations (the U.S., the United Kingdom, West Germany, Japan, France, Italy, Canada, the Netherlands, Belgium, and Sweden). GAB was renewed and expanded in subsequent years. The resources that the IMF could borrow under GAB have been increasing greatly with time.

Starting in the early 1960s, member nations started to negotiate stand-by arrangements, referring to advance permission for future borrowings by the nation in IMF. Nations negotiated these arrangements for defense against anticipated destabilizing hot money flows. National central banks also began to negotiate so-called swap arrangements to exchange each other's currency to be used to intervene in foreign exchange markets to combat hot money flows.

By 1968, the run on gold was of such a scale that at a March meeting in Washington, D. C., a two-tier gold pricing system was established. While the official U. S. price of gold was to remain at $35 per ounce, the private market price of gold was to be allowed to find its own level. These steps were taken to prevent depletion of U. S. gold reserves.

The most significant change introduced into the Bretton Woods system during the 1947—1971 period was the creation of Special Drawing Rights (SDRs) to supplement the international reserves of gold, foreign exchange, and the reserve position in the IMF. Sometimes called paper gold, SDRs are accounting entries in the books of the IMF. SDRs are not backed (supported) by gold or any other currency but represent genuine international reserves created by the IMF. SDRs can only be used in dealings among central banks to settle balance of payments deficits and surpluses and not in private commercial dealings. A charge of 1.5 percent (subsequently increased to 5 percent and now based on market rates) was applied on the amount of SDRs allocated to it. The reason for this was to put pressure on both deficit and surplus nations to correct balance of payments disequilibria. The value of SDRs was originally set equal to one U. S. dollar but rose above $1 as a result of the devaluations to the dollar in 1971, and 1973. Starting in 1974, the value of SDRs was tied to a basket of currencies (the U. S. dollar, German mark, Japanese yen, French franc, and British pound). Basket valuation was intended to provide stability for the SDR's value under a system of fluctuating exchange rates, making the SDR more attractive as an international reserve asset. Because the movements of some currencies could be offset by the movements of other currencies, the value of SDRs in terms of a group of currencies was likely to be relatively stable.

Over the years, membership in the IMF has increased to include most nations of the world. Despite the shortcomings of the Bretton Woods system, the postwar period until 1971 was characterized by world output growing quite rapidly and international trade growing even faster. On the whole, it can be said that the Bretton Woods system served the world community well, especially until the mid 1960s.

Collapse of the Bretton Woods System

From 1945 to 1949, the U. S. ran huge balance of payments surpluses with Europe and the extended Marshall Plan aid to European reconstruction. With the economic recovery of European countries more or less complete by 1950, the U. S. balance of payments turned into deficit. The U. S. settled its deficits mostly in dollars. Surplus nations were willing to accept dollars for the reasons: (1) the U. S. stood ready to exchange dollars for gold at the fixed price of $35 an ounce; (2) the dollar acted as an international currency to be used to settle international transactions with any other nation; and (3) dollar deposits could earn interest while gold could not.

Furthermore, the sharp increase in capital outflows (FDI in Europe) and the high U. S. inflation rate (connected with the excessive money creation during the Vietnam War period) worsened the U. S. deficits as well. Because of the international currency position of the dollar, the U. S. felt unable to devalue the dollar to correct its balance of payments deficits. Alternative policies were adopted but resulted in very limited success. They included the increase of short-term interest rates to discourage short-term capital outflows, the decrease of the long-term interest rates to stimulate domestic production, interventions in foreign exchange markets, and a number of direct controls over capital outflows. The U. S. also failed to persuade surplus nations to devalue their currencies (e. g. West Germany and Japan). The expectation then became prevalent that the U. S. sooner or later would devalue its currency—the dollar. This led to huge destabilizing capital movements outside dollars and into stronger currencies. On August 15, 1971, the United States responded to a huge trade deficit by making the dollar inconvertible into gold. A 10 percent surcharge was placed on imports, and a program of wage and price controls was introduced. The Bretton Woods system was really dead.

Among the more skeptical holders of dollars was France, which began in 1962 to exchange dollars for gold despite the objection of the United States. Not only were the French doubtful about the future value of the dollar, but they also objected to the prominent role of the United States in the Bretton Woods system. Part of this distaste for a powerful United States was political, and part was based on the seigniorage gains that France believed accrued to the United States by virtue of the U. S. role as the world's banker. Seigniorage is the profit accruing to a nation from issuing the currency or when its currency is used as an international currency. The U. S. paid a high cost for its seigniorage privilege. Not only was it unable to devalue the dollar, but also its use of monetary policy was more constrained than in other nations.

On August 15, 1971, the United States made it clear that it was no longer content to support a system based on the U. S. dollar. The costs of being a reserve currency country were perceived as having begun to exceed any benefits in terms of seigniorage. The 10 largest countries were called together for a meeting at the Smithsonian Institution in Washington, D. C. As a result of the Smithsonian Agreement, the United States raised the price of gold to $38 per ounce. Each of the other countries in return revalued its currency by an amount of about 10 percent. The dollar devaluation was insufficient to restore stability to the system. U. S. inflation had become a serious problem. By 1973 the dollar was under heavy selling pressure even at its devalued or depreciated rates, and in February 1973, the U. S. was forced to devalue the dollar again by about 10 percent, and the price of gold was raised from $38 to $42.22 per ounce. By the next month most major currencies were floating. This was the unsteady state of the international financial system as it approached the oil crisis in the fall of 1973.

In short, the immediate cause of the collapse of the Bretton Woods system was the huge balance of deficits of the United States in the early 1970s and the inability of the U. S. to devalue the dollar. Thus, the Bretton Woods system lacked an adequate adjustment mechanism that nations would be willing and able to use as a matter of policy. Consequently the U. S. balance of payments deficit persisted and this undermined the confidence in the dollar. Therefore, the fundamental cause of the collapse of the Bretton Woods system is to be found in the interrelated problems of adjustment, liquidity, and confidence.

WORDS AND EXPRESSIONS

• *suspend* /səˈspend/ *vt.* defer or delay (an action, event, or judgment) 延期；延迟（行动，事件，判决）

• *pegging* /ˈpegɪŋ/ *n.* the fixing of the value of a country's currency on foreign exchange markets 外汇钉住

• *stagflation* /stægˈfleɪʃn/ *n.* stag (nation) + (in) flation: sluggish economic growth coupled with a high rate of inflation and unemployment 通货滞胀：不景气状况下之物价上涨

• *short term capital*: capital raised for a short period to cover an exceptional demand for funds over a short period; A bank loan, rather than a debenture/bond, is an example of short term capital. 短期资金

• *prevalence* /ˈprevələns/ *n.* the condition of being prevalent 流行，盛行

• *speculation* /ˌspekjʊˈleɪʃn/ *n.* a commercial or financial transaction involving speculation 投机

• *self-interested* /ˌselfˈɪntərɪstɪd/ *adj.* motivated by one's personal interest or advantage, especially without regard for others 自私自利的

• *beggar-thy-neighbor adj.* （外交政策等）损人利己的；课文中仿拟了 beggar-my-neighbor 一词，同义词有"损人利己"，"以邻为壑"（use the neighbor's field as an outlet for one's overflow; use one's neighbor's field as a drain——shift one's troubles onto others; dump rubbish in the neighbor's yard）

• *hinder* /ˈhɪndə(r)/ *v.* create difficulties for (someone or something), resulting in delay or obstruction 阻碍，打扰

• *provided* /prəˈvaɪdɪd/ *conj.* （常与 that 连用）假若；倘若；倘使

例：You may keep the book a further week provided (that) no one else requires it. 倘若这本书没有其他人想借的话，你可以再续借一个礼拜。（亦作：providing）

• *preserve* /prɪˈzɜːv/ *vt.* to maintain in safety from injury, peril, or harm; protect 保

Part I EVOLUTION AND OPERATION OF THE INTERNATIONAL MONETARY SYSTEM

护; to keep in perfect or unaltered condition; maintain unchanged 保存

- **safeguard**: stresses protection against potential or less imminent danger and often implies preventive action 强调保护不遭受潜在的或不那么迫近的危险,常含有防御性行动的意思

  例: The *Bill of Rights* safeguards our individual liberties. 《人权法案》保护我们的个人自由。

- **foster** /ˈfɒstə(r)/ vt. to promote the growth and development of; cultivate 促进,抚育,培养,鼓励

- **devise** /dɪˈvaɪz/ vt. designed or contrived, created, made up, planned, established 设计,发明,图谋,作出(计划),想出(办法)

- **par values**: n. the value imprinted on a security, such as a stock certificate or bond, used to calculate a payment, such as a dividend or interest, face values 面值;也叫 nominal value

- **defy** /dɪˈfaɪ/ vt. to oppose or resist with boldness and assurance 反抗,违抗

  to refuse to submit to or cooperate with 不服从,不合作

  to challenge or dare (someone) to do something 挑战,刺激

- **swap arrangement** n. 交换协定,互换货币协定

- **seigniorage** /ˈsiːnjərɪdʒ/ n. revenue or a profit taken from the minting of coins, usually the difference between the value of the bullion used and the face value of the coin 铸造利差:通过铸造硬币所获的收益或利润,通常是指所使用的贵金属内含值与硬币面值之差

- **interrelate** /ˌɪntərɪˈleɪt/ v. to place in or come into mutual relationship 相互联系

BACKGROUND KNOWLEDGE

1 the gold exchange standard It is an international monetary agreement according to which money consists of fiat national currencies that can be converted into gold at established price ratios. 金汇兑本位制为一国际货币协定,根据此协定,各国法定货币可以按照确定的比价兑换成黄金。

It is a limited form of gold standard used from 1925 to 1931 by some of the smaller countries, esp. the group of Scandinavian countries, under which the central bank would exchange the currency of its own country for a fixed amount of the currency of a particular country which was on the gold standard, and not for gold. Gold coins did not circulate, and reserves were held, not of gold but of the particular gold-standard currency chosen. 金汇兑本位制是1925年至1931年有些小国,特别是斯堪的那维亚国家集团采用的有限形式金本位制。在此制度下,中央银行用本国货币与另一特定的金本位制国家定量兑换其货币,但不是兑换黄金。金币不流通,储备要保持,但不是黄金储备,而是选定的特定金本位货币储备。

2 the Great Depression The Great Depression was a severe worldwide economic depression in the decade preceding World War II. The timing of Great Depression varied across nations, but in most countries it started in about 1929 and lasted until the late 1930s or early 1940s. 经济大萧条,指 1929—1933 年由美国股市全面崩溃引发的国际资金流动大幅减缓、世界各国工业产量锐减而造成的世界性经济危机。

3 *Bretton Woods Agreement* It is the result of a conference of 44 nations held in 1944 at Bretton Woods, U. S. A. , to plan better cooperation in world trade and currency matters. The International Monetary Fund and the International Bank for Reconstruction and Development (the World Bank) were started under the control of the United Nations, with the aim of raising world incomes, encouraging international trade and investment, and making steadier the exchange rates between currencies. 《布雷顿森林协定》是 1944 年在美国布雷顿森林举行的有 44 个国家参加的(布雷顿森林)会议的产物,会议对世界贸易及货币事务制定更好的合作方案。国际货币基金及国际复兴开发银行(世界银行)在联合国的管理下开设,目的在于提高世界收益,鼓励国际贸易及投资,使各国货币之间的汇率较为稳定。

4 *International Monetary Fund* is a fund set up in 1944 at the Bretton Woods conference as a specialized agency of the United Nations, mainly to encourage monetary cooperation between nations and to increase international trade. Its offices are in Washington and its members number more than 120 states. Each member deposits, mainly in its own currency, an amount determined by the size of its national income, international trade and currency reserves. A member in temporary difficulty with its balance of payments may use its Regular and Special Drawing Rights and can get further help if necessary. The Fund is essentially a bank from which a borrower uses its own currency to buy the foreign currency it needs. The work of the Fund in rebuilding confidence in currencies that are in temporary difficulty has been valuable. 国际货币基金组织是 1944 年在布雷顿森林会议上建立的基金,作为联合国专门机构,主要为促进国家之间的货币合作,以扩大国际贸易。其总部在华盛顿,成员国有 120 多个。每个成员国用其本国货币存入一笔按其国民收入、国际贸易及货币储备的大小而决定的金额。国际收支有暂时困难的成员国可以使用其正常及特别提款权,可以得到必要的进一步援助。基金主要发挥银行作用/功能,借款人可以用其本国货币购买所需外汇。基金对遇到临时困难的货币重建信心非常有价值。

5 *General Arrangements to Borrow* (G. A. B. , GAB《借款总安排》) It is the name of a document containing an agreement made in 1961 by ten countries to provide standby credits extra to those obtainable under the standby arrangements of the International Monetary Fund. Such credits are ready of use in an emergency and they form one of the means by which members of the I. M. F. can be helped if they get into temporary difficulty with their balance of payments. 《借款总安排》是一个文件的名称,它包括 1961 年由 10 个国家签订的一项协议,协议提供国际货币基金组织备用(信贷)安排可以得到的信贷之外的备用信贷,这项信贷准备用于紧急情况,并构成国际货币基金组织成员国在国际收支遇到暂时困难时可以得到的援助的手段之一。

Part Ⅰ EVOLUTION AND OPERATION OF THE INTERNATIONAL MONETARY SYSTEM

6 *Group of Ten* was established in Dec. 1961 in Paris by ten relatively rich industrial countries which set up a credit fund of $6 billion for the member countries to borrow of the IMFO on the condition that the approval of seven members of the Group is obtained and repayment will be made within five years. The ten members are: Belgium, Canada, France, Italy, Japan, the Netherlands, Sweden, Germany, the U. K. and U. S. A. They inaugurated Special Drawing Rights. Switzerland, although not a member of the IMF, is a party to the *General Arrangements to Borrow*, which the G10 countries established to provide additional credit facilities. 十国集团于1961年12月由10个相对来说富裕的工业国家在巴黎成立,十国集团建立一笔60亿美元的信贷基金,供国际货币组织成员国借用,条件是须得到七个集团成员国同意及在五年内归还。十个成员国是比利时、加拿大、法国、意大利、日本、荷兰、瑞典、德国、英国、及美国。它们赋予了特别提款权。瑞士虽然不是国际货币基金组织成员国,但它是《借款总安排》的成员,《借款总安排》由十国集团设立用以提供额外的贷款便利。

7 *hot money* n. Money that is moved by its owner quickly from one form of investment to another, as to take advantage of changing international exchange rates or gain high short-term returns on investments. It is the money attracted from abroad by high interest rates or to find a relatively safe place in a time of political trouble. Since it may be quickly transferred elsewhere, it can greatly upset a country's balance of payments. 游资,(为追求高额利润而流动的)短期投机资金:游资为利用不断变化的国际汇率或获得高额短期投资利润而被所有者迅速从一种投资形式转移到另一种形式的资金。游资是以高利率从国外吸收来的资金,或由于在政治动乱时想找安全地点投放的资金。因为这种资金可很快转移到其他地方,所以对一个国家的国际收支造成很大混乱。同 refugee capital。

8 *special drawing rights* n. It is a standard unit of account used by the International Monetary Fund (IMF). In 1970 members of the IMF were allocated SDRs in proportion to the quotas of currency that they had subscribed to the fund on its formation. There have since been further allocations. SDRs can be used to settle international trade balance and to repay debts to the IMF itself. On the instructions of the IMF a member country must supply its own currency to another member, in exchange for SDRs, unless it already holds more than three times its original allocation. The value of SDRs was originally expressed in terms of gold, but since 1974 it has been valued in terms of its members' currencies. SDRs provide a credit facility for IMF members in addition to their existing credit facilities (hence the name); unlike these existing facilities they do not have to be repaid, thus forming a permanent addition to members' reserves and functioning as an international reserve currency. (Compare European Currency Unit 比较"欧洲货币单位","欧元"的前身). It is also called "paper gold". (国际货币基金组织的)特别提款权,国际货币基金组织使用的标准计算单位。1970年国际货币基金组织成员国按该组织成立时各成员国所交货币配额而得到的相应特别提款权份额。此后有了进一步的分配。特别提款权可以用来稳定国际贸易差额并偿还所欠国际货币基金组织的债务。根据国际货币基金组织的指示,在兑换特别提款权时某成员国必须将其本国的货币提供给另一成

员国,如果它已拥有其原始分配额的三倍以上则除外。特别提款权的价值原先是以黄金为单位的,但 1974 年以来它折算成成员国的货币单位。特别提款权给国际货币基金组织成员国提供了现有信贷资金以外的信贷资金,因此而得名。与现存的信贷资金不同的是,该资金是不需偿还的,因此它成了对成员国储备的永久性的追加款,具有国际货币储备的功能,也称为纸黄金,"币黄金"。

9 *reserve position in the IMF* 在国际货币基金组织储备净额

If there is still a balance after deducting the national currencies held by the Fund and subscriptions receivable of a member country from the quota it paid to the Fund and the loans it obtained from the Fund, it is called the reserve position in the Fund of the member country. 如果从国际货币基金组织会员国交纳的基金份额及该国从基金组织获得的贷款中,减去基金组织持有的该国货币及该国认购部分应收额之后,仍有余额,此余额即为该会员国在国际货币基金组织的储备净额。也可称为"在国际货币基金组织的储备头寸/准备金"。头寸:(1) 中国旧时指银行钱庄等所拥有的款项。收多付少叫头寸多,收少付多叫头寸缺,结算收付差额叫轧头寸,借款弥补差额叫拆头寸。(2) 现金,货币供应量指市场上货币流通数量,即银根。如银根松说头寸松,银根紧也说头寸紧。

10 *Marshall*(*Aid*)*Plan n.* Marshall (Aid) Plan consists of economic help given by the U. S. A. mainly to countries in Europe to help to rebuild their economics after the Second World War. The three-year plan was administered in the U. S. A. by the E. C. A. (European Cooperation Administration) and in Europe by the O. E. E. C. (Organization for European Economic Cooperation). The help was in the form of money, goods and technical advice and was directed to increasing industrial and agricultureal production rebuilding internal finances and encouraging international trade. 马歇尔(援助)计划是美国主要给予欧洲国家的经济援助,以帮助他们在"二战"后重建经济。这一计划在美国由欧洲合作总署(E.C.A.)管理,在欧洲由欧洲经济合作组织(O.E.E.C.)管理。援助形式有货币、商品、技术咨询,作用为增加工农业生产、重建国内财政及促进国际贸易。

1 *reserve currency* It is a foreign currency that is held by a government because it has confidence in its stability and intends to use it to settle international debts. The US dollar and the pound sterling fulfilled this role for many years. 储备货币:因确信其稳值性而由政府储备用来偿付国际债务的外国货币。美元及英镑曾长期担当此角色。

2 By 1968, the run on gold was of such a scale that at a March meeting in Washington, D. C., a two-tier gold pricing system was established. 截至 1968 年,由于黄金被大量抢购,所以 3 月的华盛顿会议上建立了黄金双价制。

注意句中 run 的用法。

3 *a basket of currencies* 一揽/篮子货币

They are a group of selected currencies used to establish a value for some other unit of currency. The European Currency Unit's value is determined by taking a weighted average of a basket of European currencies. 挑选一组货币用作某种货币的币值。如欧洲货币单位的币值是采用一揽子欧洲货币的加权平均值来确定的。(weighted：adjusted to reflect value or proportion 加权的,经过调整可反映其价值或比例的；a weighted average 加权平均数)

4 Basket valuation was intended to provide stability for the SDR's value under a system of fluctuating exchange rates,……一揽子定价是为在浮动汇率体系下,稳定特别提款权价格而设计的,……

5 *FDI foreign direct investment*

The IMF definition of FDI includes as many as 12 different elements, namely：equity capital, reinvested earnings of foreign companies, inter-company debt transactions, short-term and long-term loans, financial leasing, trade credits, grants, bonds, non-cash acquisition of equity, investment made by foreign venture capital investors, earnings data of indirectly held FDI enterprises and control premium, non-competition fee, and so on.

外商直接投资,国外直接投资,指一个国内企业在国外建厂或拥有国外企业资产的所有权,而不是在证券市场上购买国外企业的股份。国际货币基金组织对FDI的定义包括多达12个不同要素,即：股本,外国公司再投资收益,公司间债务交易,短期和中长期贷款、金融租赁、贸易信贷、赠款、债券、非现金收购股权、外资创投、间接拥有外国直接投资企业的收益数据、控制权溢价、非竞争费,等等。

Ⅰ. **Answer the following questions according to the text.**

1. What did the UK face in the 1920s?
2. From which country did beggar-thy-neighbor policies originate?
3. Under the gold exchange standard system, what was the form of international reserves?
4. Why were industrial nations reluctant to change their par values? What were the consequences of the reluctance?
5. What had happened by 1950s? What did the US do to correct its deficits?

Ⅱ. **Translate the following expressions into Chinese.**

1. financed part of their massive military expenditures
2. accelerated London's decline as the world's leading financial center
3. be forced to follow contractionary monetary policies
4. to suspend the convertibility of the pound into gold

5. in the lack of an adequate adjustment mechanism
6. allowed flexibility in exchange rates in cases of fundamental disequilibrium
7. witnessed huge destabilizing capital flows
8. started to negotiate stand-by arrangements
9. referring to advance permission for future borrowings by the nation in IMF
10. be used to intervene in foreign exchange markets to combat hot money flows
11. ran huge balance of payments surpluses with Europe
12. settled its deficits mostly in dollars
13. led to huge destabilizing capital movements outside dollars and into stronger currencies
14. raised the price of gold to $38 per ounce
15. under heavy selling pressure even at its devalued or depreciated rates

III. Translate the following paragraphs into Chinese.

1. They thought a devaluation was a sign of national weakness and a revaluation would reduce the competitiveness of a country.

2. The unwillingness of industrial nations to change their par values as a matter of policy when in fundamental disequilibrium had two significant effects. First, it robbed the Bretton Woods system of most of its flexibility and the mechanism for adjusting balance of payments disequilibria. Second, and related to the first point, the reluctance of industrial nations to change their par value when in fundamental disequilibrium gave rise to huge destabilizing international capital flows by providing an excellent one-way gamble for speculators.

3. The IMF articles also called for convertibility on current account transaction only because the designers of the Bretton Woods system hoped to facilitate free trade while avoiding the possibility that private capital flows might tighten the external constraints faced by policymakers.

4. The most significant change introduced into the Bretton Woods system during the 1947—1971 period was the creation of Special Drawing Rights (SDRs) to supplement the international reserves of gold, foreign exchange, and the reserve position in the IMF. Sometimes called paper gold, SDRs are accounting entries in the books of the IMF.

5. Alternative policies were adopted but resulted in very limited success. They included the increase of short-term interest rates to discourage short-term capital outflows, the decrease of the long-term interest rates to stimulate domestic production, interventions in foreign exchange markets, and a number of direct controls over capital outflows.

6. In short, the immediate cause of the collapse of the Bretton Woods system was the huge balance of deficits of the United States in the early 1970s and the inability of the U.S. to devalue the dollar. Thus, the Bretton Woods system lacked an adequate adjustment

Part I EVOLUTION AND OPERATION OF THE INTERNATIONAL MONETARY SYSTEM

mechanism that nations would be willing and able to use as a matter of policy. Consequently the U. S. balance of payments deficit persisted and this undermined the confidence in the dollar. Therefore, the fundamental cause of the collapse of the Bretton Woods system is to be found in the interrelated problems of adjustment, liquidity, and confidence.

IV. Read the following passage and answer the questions.

The Bretton Woods system of international monetary management established the rules for commercial and financial relations among the world's major industrial states. The Bretton Woods system was the first example of a fully negotiated monetary order intended to govern monetary relations among independent nation-states.

Preparing to rebuild the international economic system as World War II was still raging, 730 delegates from all 44 Allied nations gathered at the Mount Washington Hotel in Bretton Woods, New Hampshire for the United Nations Monetary and Financial Conference. The delegates deliberated upon and signed the Bretton Woods Agreements during the first three weeks of July 1944.

Setting up a system of rules, institutions, and procedures to regulate the international monetary system, the planners at Bretton Woods established the International Bank for Reconstruction and Development (IBRD) (now one of five institutions in the World Bank Group) and the International Monetary Fund (IMF). These organizations became operational in 1946 after a sufficient number of countries had ratified the agreement.

The chief features of the Bretton Woods system were an obligation for each country to adopt a monetary policy that maintained the exchange rate of its currency within a fixed value—plus or minus one percent—in terms of gold; and the ability of the IMF to bridge temporary imbalances of payments. In the face of increasing strain, the system collapsed in 1971, following the United States' suspension of convertibility from dollars to gold.

Until the early 1970s, the Bretton Woods system was effective in controlling conflict and in achieving the common goals of the leading states that had created it, especially the United States.

Origins

The political bases for the Bretton Woods system are in the confluence of several key conditions: the shared experiences of the Great Depression, the concentration of power in a small number of states, and the presence of a dominant power willing and able to assume a leadership role in global monetary affairs.

The Great Depression

A high level of agreement among the powerful on the goals and means of international economic management facilitated the decisions reached by the Bretton Woods Conference. The foundation of that agreement was a shared belief in capitalism. Although the developed countries' governments differed somewhat in the type of capitalism they preferred for their national economies (France, for example, preferred greater planning and state intervention, whereas the United States favored relatively limited state intervention.), all relied primarily on market mechanisms and on private ownership.

Thus, it is their similarities rather than their differences that appear most striking. All the participating governments at Bretton Woods agreed that the monetary chaos of the interwar period had yielded several valuable lessons.

The experience of the Great Depression, when proliferation of foreign exchange controls and trade barriers led to economic disaster, was fresh on the minds of public officials. The planners at Bretton Woods hoped to avoid a repeat of the debacle of the 1930s, when foreign exchange controls undermined the international payments system that was the basis for world trade. The "beggar-thy-neighbor" policies of 1930s governments—using currency devaluations to increase the competitiveness of a country's export products in order to reduce balance of payments deficits—worsened national deflationary spirals, which resulted in plummeting national incomes, shrinking demand, mass unemployment, and an overall decline in world trade. Trade in the 1930s became largely restricted to currency blocs (groups of nations that use an equivalent currency, such as the "Sterling Area" of the British Empire). These blocs retarded the international flow of capital and foreign investment opportunities. Although this strategy tended to increase government revenues in the short run, it dramatically worsened the situation in the medium and longer run.

Thus, for the international economy, planners at Bretton Woods all favored a liberal system, one that relied primarily on the market with the minimum of barriers to the flow of private trade and capital. Although they disagreed on the specific implementation of this liberal system, all agreed on an open system.

The rise of governmental intervention

The developed countries also agreed that the liberal international economic system required governmental intervention. In the aftermath of the Great Depression, public management of the economy had emerged as a primary activity of governments in the developed states. Employment, stability, and growth were now important subjects of public policy. In turn, the role of government in the national economy had become associated with the assumption by the state of the responsibility for assuring of its citizens a degree of economic well-being. The welfare state grew out of the Great Depression, which created a popular demand for governmental intervention in the economy, and out of the theoretical contributions of the Keynesian school of economics, which asserted the need for governmental intervention to maintain an adequate level of employment.

At the international level, these ideas evolved from the experience of the 1930s. The priority of national goals, independent national action in the interwar period, and the failure to perceive that those national goals could not be realized without some form of international collaboration resulted in "beggar-thy-neighbor" policies such as high tariffs and competitive

Part I EVOLUTION AND OPERATION OF THE INTERNATIONAL MONETARY SYSTEM

devaluations which contributed to economic breakdown, domestic political instability, and international war.

To ensure economic stability and political peace, states agreed to cooperate to regulate the international economic system. The pillar of the U. S. vision of the postwar world was free trade. Free trade involved lowering tariffs and among other things a balance of trade favorable to the capitalist system.

Thus, the more developed market economies agreed with the U. S. vision of postwar international economic management, which was to be designed to create and maintain an effective international monetary system and foster the reduction of barriers to trade and capital flows.

The rise of U. S. hegemony

International economic management relied on the dominant power, the United States, to lead the system. The concentration of power facilitated management by confining the number of actors whose agreement was necessary to establish rules, institutions, and procedures and to carry out management within the agreed system.

The United States had emerged from the Second World War with the strongest economy, experiencing rapid industrial growth and capital accumulation. The U. S. had remained untouched by the ravages of World War II and had built a thriving manufacturing industry and grown wealthy selling weapons and lending money to the other combatants; in fact, U. S. industrial production in 1945 was more than double that of annual production between the prewar years of 1935 and 1939. In contrast, Europe and East Asia were militarily and economically shattered.

As the Bretton Woods Conference convened, the relative advantages of the U. S. economy were undeniable. The U. S. held a majority of investment capital, manufacturing production and exports. In 1945, the U. S. produced half the world's coal, two-thirds of the oil, and more than half of the electricity. The U. S. was able to produce great quantities of machinery, including ships, airplanes, vehicles, armaments, machine tools, and chemicals. Reinforcing the initial advantage—and assuring the U. S. unmistakable leadership in the capitalist world—the U. S. held 80% of gold reserves and had not only a powerful army but also the atomic bomb.

The U. S. stood to gain more than any other country from the opening of the entire world to unfettered trade. The U. S. would have a global market for its exports, and it would have unrestricted access to vital raw materials. In addition, U. S. capitalism could not survive without markets and allies. William Clayton, the assistant secretary of state for economic affairs, was among myriad U. S. policymakers who summed up this point: "We need markets—big markets—around the world in which to buy and sell".

There had been many predictions that peace would bring a return of depression and unemployment, as war production ceased and returning soldiers flooded the labor market. Compounding the economic difficulties was a sharp rise in labor unrest. Determined to avoid another economic catastrophe like that of the 1930s, U. S. President Franklin D. Roosevelt saw the creation of the postwar order as a way to ensure continuing U. S. prosperity.

Design

Free trade relied on the free convertibility of currencies. Negotiators at the Bretton Woods conference, fresh from what they perceived as a disastrous experience with floating rates in the 1930s, concluded that major monetary fluctuations could stall the free flow of trade.

The liberal economic system required an accepted vehicle for investment, trade, and payments. Unlike national economies, however, the international economy lacks a central government that can issue currency and manage its use. In the past this problem had been solved through the gold standard, but the architects of Bretton Woods did not consider this option feasible for the postwar political economy. Instead, they set up a system of fixed exchange rates managed by a series of newly created international institutions using the U. S. dollar (which was a gold standard currency for central banks) as a reserve currency.

The Bretton Woods system of fixed exchange rates

The Bretton Woods system sought to secure the advantages of the gold standard without its disadvantages. Thus, a compromise was sought between the polar alternatives of either freely floating or irrevocably fixed rates—an arrangement that might gain the advantages of both without suffering the disadvantages of either while retaining the right to revise currency values on occasion as circumstances warranted.

The rules of Bretton Woods, set forth in the articles of agreement of the International Monetary Fund (IMF) and the International Bank for Reconstruction and Development (IBRD), provided for a system of fixed exchange rates. The rules further sought to encourage an open system by committing members to the convertibility of their respective currencies into other currencies and to free trade.

The "pegged rate" or "par value" currency regime

What emerged was the "pegged rate" currency regime. Members were required to establish a parity of their national currencies in terms of gold (a "peg") and to maintain exchange rates within plus or minus 1% of parity (a "band") by intervening in their foreign exchange markets (that is, buying or selling foreign money).

The "reserve currency"

In practice, however, since the principal "reserve currency" would be the U. S. dollar, this meant that other countries would peg their currencies to the U. S. dollar, and—once convertibility was restored—would buy and sell U. S. dollars to keep market exchange rates within plus or minus 1% of parity. Thus, the U. S. dollar took over the role that gold had played under the gold standard in the international financial system.

Meanwhile, in order to bolster faith in the dollar, the U. S. agreed separately to link the dollar to gold at the rate of $35 per ounce of gold. At this rate, foreign governments and central banks were able to exchange dollars for gold. Bretton Woods established a system of payments

Part I EVOLUTION AND OPERATION OF THE INTERNATIONAL MONETARY SYSTEM

based on the dollar, in which all currencies were defined in relation to the dollar, itself convertible into gold, and above all, "as good as gold." The U. S. currency was now effectively the world currency, the standard to which every other currency was pegged. As the world's key currency, most international transactions were denominated in dollars.

The U. S. dollar was the currency with the most purchasing power and it was the only currency that was backed by gold. Additionally, all European nations that had been involved in World War II were highly in debt and transferred large amounts of gold into the United States, a fact that contributed to the supremacy of the United States. Thus, the U. S. dollar was strongly appreciated in the rest of the world and therefore became the key currency of the Bretton Woods system.

Member countries could only change their par value with IMF approval, which was contingent on (视……而定) IMF determination that its balance of payments was in a "fundamental disequilibrium."

(FROM: http://www.answers.com/topic/bretton-woods-system)

Answer the following questions.

1. Which country was the leading country under the Bretton Woods system?
2. After the Great Depression, what lesson did the developed countries yield?
3. After the WW II, how did Americans create their economic hegemony?
4. Why did the policymakers of the Bretton Woods system accept free floating fixed rates unwillingly? How did they solve this problem?
5. In fact, what was the role of the US dollar under the Bretton Woods system? And what was its main function?

FURTHER READING

THE LATE BRETTON WOODS SYSTEM
THE U. S. BALANCE OF PAYMENTS CRISIS (1958—1968)

After the end of World War II, the U.S. held $26 billion in gold reserves, of an estimated total of $40 billion. As world trade increased rapidly through the 1950s, the size of the gold base increased by only a few percent. In 1958, the U.S. balance of payments swung negative. The first U.S. response to the crisis was in the late 1950s when the **Eisenhower**(艾森豪威尔,美国第三十四任总统) administration placed import **quotas**(配/限额) on oil and other restrictions on trade outflows. More drastic measures were proposed, but not acted on. However, with a mounting recession that began in 1959, this response alone was not sustainable. In 1960, with **Kennedy**'s election(肯尼迪,美国第35任总统), a decade-long effort to maintain the Bretton Woods System at the $35/ounce price was begun.

The design of the Bretton Woods System was that only nations could enforce gold convertibility on the anchor currency—the United States'. Gold convertibility enforcement was not required, but instead, allowed. Nations could forgo converting dollars to gold, and instead hold dollars. Rather than full convertibility, it provided a fixed price for sales between central banks. However, there was still an open gold market, 80% of which was traded through London, which issued **a morning "gold fix,"**(上午议定金价,伦敦黄金市场于每天上午及下午由五家经营黄金业务的大商号根据上一交易情况及供需变化所商定的金价,但实际买卖价格仍由买卖双方自行商定,议定金价仅供参考。) which was the price of gold on the open market. For the Bretton Woods system to remain workable, it would either have to alter the peg of the dollar to gold, or it would have to maintain the free market price for gold near the $35 per ounce official price. The greater the gap between free market gold prices and central bank gold prices, the greater the temptation to deal with internal economic issues by buying gold at the Bretton Woods price and selling it on the open market.

However, keeping the dollar because of its ability to earn interest was still more desirable than holding gold. In 1960 **Robert Triffin**(罗伯特·特里芬,美国耶鲁大学经济学教授) noticed that the reason holding dollars was more valuable than gold was because constant U.S. balance of payments deficits helped to keep the system liquid and fuel economic growth. What would be later known as Triffin's Dilemma was predicted when Triffin noted that if the U.S. failed to keep running deficits the system would lose its liquidity, not being able to keep up with the world's economic growth, thus bringing the system to a halt. Yet, continuing to incur such payment deficits also meant that over time the deficits would erode confidence in the dollar as the reserve currency creating instability.

The first effort was the creation of the "London Gold Pool." The theory of the pool was that spikes in the free market price of gold, set by the "morning gold fix" in London, could be controlled by having a pool of gold to sell on the open market, which would then be recovered when the price of gold dropped. Gold's price spiked in response to events such as the Cuban Missile Crisis, and other smaller events, to as high as $40/ounce. The Kennedy administration began drafting a radical change of the tax system in order to spur more productive capacity, and thus encourage exports. This would culminate with his tax cut program of 1963, designed to maintain the $35 peg.

In 1967 there was an attack on the pound, and a **run on**(挤兑,抢购) gold in the "**sterling area**",(英镑区,1939年成立的以英镑为中心的国际货币集团) and on November 17, 1967, the British government was forced to devalue the pound. U.S. President **Lyndon Baines Johnson**(林顿·贝恩斯·约翰逊,美国第36任总统) was faced with a brutal choice, either he could institute protectionist measures, including travel taxes, export subsidies and slashing the budget—or he could accept the risk of a "run on gold" and the dollar. From Johnson's perspective: "The world supply of gold is insufficient to make the present system workable—particularly as the use of the dollar as a reserve currency is essential to create the required international liquidity to sustain world trade and growth." He believed that the priorities of the United States were correct, and that, while there were internal tensions in the Western alliance, that turning away from open trade would be more costly, economically and politically, than it was worth: "Our role of world leadership in a political and military sense is the only reason for our current embarrassment in an economic sense on the one hand and on the other the correction of the economic embarrassment under present monetary systems will result in an untenable position economically for our allies."

While West Germany agreed not to purchase gold from the U.S., and agreed to hold dollars instead, the pressure on both the Dollar and the Pound Sterling continued. In January 1968 Johnson imposed a series of measures designed to end gold outflow, and to increase American exports. However, to no avail: on March 17, 1968, there was a run on gold, the London Gold Pool was dissolved, and a series of meetings began to rescue or reform the system as it existed. However, as long as the U.S. commitments to foreign deployment continued, particularly to Western Europe, there was little that could be done to maintain the gold peg.

The attempt to maintain that peg collapsed in November 1968, and a new policy program was attempted: to convert Bretton Woods to a system where the enforcement mechanism floated by some means, which would be set by either fiat, or by a restriction to honor foreign accounts.

Structural changes underpinning the decline of international monetary management

Return to convertibility

In the 1960s and 70s, important structural changes eventually led to the breakdown of international monetary management. One change was the development of a high level of monetary interdependence. The stage was set for monetary interdependence by the return to convertibility of the Western European currencies at the end of 1958 and of the Japanese yen in 1964. Convertibility facilitated the vast expansion of international financial transactions, which deepened monetary interdependence.

The growth of international currency markets

Another aspect of the internationalization of banking has been the emergence of **international banking consortia**(国际银行公会). Since 1964 various banks had formed international syndicates, and by 1971 over three quarters of the world's largest banks had become shareholders in such syndicates. Multinational banks can and do make huge international transfers of capital not only for investment purposes but also for hedging and speculating against exchange rate fluctuations.

These new forms of monetary interdependence made possible huge capital flows. During the Bretton Woods era countries were reluctant to alter exchange rates formally even in cases of structural disequilibria. Because such changes had a direct impact on certain domestic economic groups, they came to be seen as political risks for leaders. As a result official exchange rates often became unrealistic in market terms, providing a virtually risk-free temptation for speculators. They could move from a weak to a strong currency hoping to reap profits when a revaluation occurred. If, however, monetary authorities managed to avoid revaluation, they could return to other currencies with no loss. The combination of risk-free speculation with the availability of huge sums was highly destabilizing.

The decline of U.S. hegemony

A second structural change that undermined monetary management was the decline of U.S. hegemony. The U.S. was no longer the dominant economic power it had been for almost two decades. By the mid-1960s Europe and Japan had become international economic powers in their own right. With total reserves exceeding those of the U.S., with higher levels of growth and trade, and with per capita income approaching that of the U.S., Europe and Japan were narrowing the gap between themselves and the United States.

The shift toward a more pluralistic distribution of economic power led to increasing dissatisfaction with the privileged role of the U.S. dollar as the international currency. As in effect the world's central banker, the U.S., through its deficit, determined the level of international liquidity. In an increasingly interdependent world, U.S. policy greatly influenced economic conditions in Europe and Japan. In addition, as long as other countries were willing to hold dollars, the U.S. could carry out massive foreign expenditures for political purposes—military activities and foreign aid—without the threat of balance-of-payments constraints.

Dissatisfaction with the political implications of the dollar system was increased by **détente**(缓解政策) between the U.S. and the Soviet Union. The Soviet threat had been an important force in cementing the Western capitalist monetary system. The U.S. political and security umbrella helped make American economic domination palatable for Europe and Japan, which had been economically exhausted by the war. As gross domestic production grew in European countries, trade grew. When common security tensions lessened, this loosened the transatlantic dependence on defense concerns, and allowed latent economic tensions to surface.

The decline of the dollar

Reinforcing the relative decline in U.S. power and the dissatisfaction of Europe and Japan with the system was the continuing decline of the dollar—the foundation that had underpinned the post-1945 global trading system. The Vietnam War and the refusal of the administration of U.S. President Lyndon B. Johnson to pay for it and its Great Society programs through taxation resulted in an increased dollar outflow to pay for the military expenditures and rampant inflation, which led to the deterioration of the U.S. balance of trade position. In the late 1960s, the dollar was overvalued with its current trading position, while the Deutsche Mark and the yen were undervalued; and, naturally, the Germans and the Japanese had no desire to revalue and thereby make their exports more expensive, whereas the U.S. sought to maintain its international credibility by avoiding devaluation. Meanwhile, the pressure on government reserves was intensified by the new international currency markets, with their vast pools of speculative capital moving around in search of quick profits.

In contrast, upon the creation of Bretton Woods, with the U.S. producing half of the world's manufactured goods and holding half its reserves, the twin burdens of international management and the Cold War were possible to meet at first. Throughout the 1950s Washington sustained a balance of payments deficit in order to finance loans, aid, and troops for allied regimes. But during the 1960s the costs of doing so became less tolerable. By 1970 the U.S. held under 16% of international reserves. Adjustment to these changed realities was impeded by the U.S. commitment to fixed exchange rates and by the U.S. obligation to convert dollars into gold on demand.

In sum, monetary interdependence was increasing at a faster pace than international management in the 1960s, leading up to the collapse of the Bretton Woods system. New problems created by interdependence, including huge capital flows, placed stresses on the fixed exchange rate system and impeded national economic management. Amid these problems, economic cooperation decreased, and U.S. leadership declined, and eventually broke down.

The paralysis(瘫痪) of international monetary management
"Floating" Bretton Woods (1968—1972)

By 1968, the attempt to defend the dollar at a fixed peg of $35/ounce, the policy of the Eisenhower, Kennedy and Johnson administrations, had become increasingly untenable. Gold outflows from the U.S. accelerated, and despite gaining assurances from Germany and other nations to hold gold, the "dollar shortage" of the 1940s and 1950s had become a dollar glut. In 1967, the IMF agreed in Rio de Janeiro to replace the **tranche**(国际货币基金贷款划分的"部分") division set up in 1946. Special Drawing Rights were set as equal to one U.S. dollar, but were not usable for transactions other than between banks and the IMF. Nations were required to accept holding SDRs equal to three times their allotment, and interest would be charged, or credited, to each nation based on their SDR holding. The original interest rate was 1.5%.

The intent of the SDR system was to prevent nations from buying pegged dollars and selling them at the higher free market price, and give nations a reason to hold dollars by crediting interest, at the same time setting a clear limit to the amount of dollars which could be held. The essential conflict was that the American role as military defender

Part I EVOLUTION AND OPERATION OF THE INTERNATIONAL MONETARY SYSTEM

of the capitalist world's economic system was recognized, but not given a specific monetary value. In effect, other nations "purchased" American defense policy by taking a loss in holding dollars. They were only willing to do this as long as they supported U.S. military policy, because of the Vietnam war and other unpopular actions, the pro-U.S. **consensus**(多数人的意见,舆论,一致同意) began to evaporate. The SDR agreement, in effect, monetized the value of this relationship, but did not create a market for it.

The use of SDRs as "paper gold" seemed to offer a way to balance the system, turning the IMF, rather than the U.S., into the world's central banker. The US tightened controls over foreign investment and currency, including mandatory investment controls in 1968. In 1970, U.S. President Richard Nixon lifted import quotas on oil in an attempt to reduce energy costs; instead, however, this exacerbated dollar flight, and created pressure from petro-dollars now linked to gas-euros resulting the 1963 energy transition from coal to gas with the creation of the Dutch Gasunie. Still, the U.S. continued to draw down reserves. In 1971 it had a reserve deficit of $56 Billion dollars; as well, it had depleted most of its non-gold reserves and had only 22% gold coverage of foreign reserves. In short, the dollar was tremendously overvalued with respect to gold.

(*FROM*: http://www.answers.com/topic/bretton-woods-system)

NOTES

1 *London gold pool* 伦敦黄金总汇,指 1960 年 10 月美元危机(dollar crisis)爆发后,伦敦黄金价格上涨至一盎司 41 美元。各国为了保卫美元的地位,于 1961 年 11 月缔结《黄金总汇协定》。该协定于 1962 年 6 月生效,由美、英、前西德、法、意、荷、瑞士、比利时等八国提供总数相当于 2.7 亿单位黄金给英格兰银行,使该银行有足够的黄金在伦敦自由市场依官价出售或买入,借此稳定黄金价格。但 1965 年以后,先有法国的退出,继有英镑贬值再度引发抢金潮,致无法继续出售黄金,只好于 1968 年 3 月停止黄金总汇操作,改行黄金两价制(two-tier price system of gold),即自由市场金价由市场供需决定,但美国对各国央行,仍以每盎司 35 美元出售黄金,而私人黄金交易仍可在自由市场进行,故金价分为市场及官价两种。该制度直到 1971 年 8 月美国实施新经济政策方停止。

2 *sterling area* 英镑区:1939 年成立的以英镑为中心的国际货币集团。

3 *tranche* (国际货币基金借款划分的)部分。

CHAPTER 3 MANAGED FLOATING SINCE 1973 AND THE EUROPEAN MONETARY SYSTEM

Learning Objectives

1. Managed floating;
2. European Monetary System;
3. Summary of Part 1.

The Present System

Since March 1973, the world has had a managed floating exchange rate system under which nations' monetary authorities are entrusted with the responsibility to intervene in foreign exchange markets to smooth out short run fluctuations in exchange rates. This could be achieved by a policy of "leaning against the wind". This system was imposed on the world by the collapse of the Bretton Woods system in the face of chaotic conditions in foreign exchange markets and huge destabilizing speculation. The essential difference between this system and the Bretton Woods system is that governments are not compelled to intervene in foreign exchange markets. They intervene because they choose to do so.

In the early days of the managed floating system, serious attempts were made to devise specific rules for managing the float to prevent competitive exchange rate depreciations (which nations might use to stimulate their exports); thus possibly returning to the chaotic conditions of the 1930s. However, as the worst fears of abuses did not materialize, all of these attempts failed. Indeed, the 1976 Jamaica Accords formally recognized the managed floating system and allowed nations the choice of foreign exchange regime as long as their actions did not prove disruptive to trade partners. Between the period of 1974—1977 and 1981—1985, the United States generally followed a policy of benign neglect by not intervening in foreign exchange markets to stabilize the value of the dollar.

Part I EVOLUTION AND OPERATION OF THE INTERNATIONAL MONETARY SYSTEM

At the same time, there has been a movement away from a gold-based international monetary system. The role of gold has diminished as a result of the Jamaica Accords. The official price of gold was abolished. One-sixth of the gold paid into the IMF in quotas was to be returned to members, one-sixth to be auctioned by the IMF to private buyers with the proceeds being used to benefit the developing countries. The IMF was to retain the remaining two-thirds. Finally, gold was no longer to be the unit of account of the system. Since 1974, the IMF has measured all reserves and other official transactions in terms of SDRs instead of U. S. dollars.

The Future

The economic hegemony enjoyed by the United States at the end of World War II has been eroded by the phenomenal economic performance for South-East Asian regions, most particularly Japan, and the Four Little Dragons—Hong Kong, Singapore, Taiwan, and Republic of Korea and also by the growing strength of an increasingly integrated Europe. The change in the balance of economic power means that we can no longer predict important economic changes, such as changes in the nature of the international financial system, simply by studying the preferences of any one country. In any situation involving three players who can form coalitions, outcomes are notoriously difficult to predict. One clear consequence of the new balance of power is a need for each party to consult with the others. It seems likely that with increasing financial and economic interdependence, the evolving international financial system will involve even closer cooperation. One of the consequences of the more even sharing of economic power is the potential emergence of three trading blocs of currencies, a dollar bloc based on the Americas, a yen bloc centered around Japanese trade, and a Euro bloc centered on the place of European trade.

Trade imbalances have become larger and more persistent as some countries suffered deficit while others enjoyed surplus. We can expect increased bilateral bargaining outside of international trade organizations such as the World Trade Organization if bilateral trade imbalances persist.

While the natural environment and international finance might appear to be disconnected, the two matters come together around the actions of another important international financial institution, the World Bank, which was co-established with the IMF in the Bretton Woods in 1944. Also known as the International Bank for Reconstruction and Development, the World Bank has been assisting developing nations since its creation but its lending has contributed to environmental and social damage on a massive scale so that it has been accused of assisting widespread global environmental destruction. The role of IMF has also been questioned for not taking into account the social needs of debtor nations and the political consequences of its demands, and that its policies being "all head and no heart". Partly in response to this, the IMF has become more flexible in its lending activities in recent years and has begun to grant even medium-term loans to overcome structural problems (something that has been traditionally done only by the World Bank). And the argument about the degree of exchange rate flexibility is continued. The arguments seem bound to circulate continuously as debate continues over the "ideal" system. It should become clear that each system has its weaknesses.

The European Monetary System

The European Monetary System (EMS) began in March 1979 with eight of the nine members of the European Community (all but Great Britain) participating in its Exchange Rate Mechanism (ERM) as part of its aim toward greater monetary integration among its members, including the ultimate goal of creating a common currency and a community-wide central bank. The main features of the EMS are: (1) The European Currency Unit (ECU), defined as the weighted average of the currencies of member nations, was created. (2) The currency of each EU member was allowed to fluctuate by maximum of 2.25 percent on either side of its central rate or parity (6 percent for the British pound and Spanish peseta; Greece and Portugal were to join later). The EMS was created as a fixed but adjustable exchange rate system and with currencies of member nations floating jointly against the dollar. Starting in September 1992, however, the system came under attack and since August 1993 the range of allowed fluctuation was increased from ±2.25 percent to ±15 percent. (3) The establishment of the European Monetary Cooperation Fund (EMCF) to provide short- and medium-term balance of payments assistance to its members.

When the fluctuation of a member nation's currency reaches 75 percent of its allowed range, a "threshold of divergence" has been reached, and the nation is expected to take a number of corrective measures to prevent its currency from fluctuating outside the allowed range. Member nations were assigned a quota into the EMCF, 20 percent to be paid in gold and the remainder in dollars, in exchange for ECUs.

Eleven realignments occurred in the EMS between 1979 and 1987 in an effort to offset ongoing inflation rate differentials. Inflation rate differentials narrowed across Europe by the mid 1980s and by 1987 most capital controls were lifted.

In June 1989, a committee headed by Jacque Delors, the president of the European Commission, recommended a three-stage transition to the single currency. The first stage included widening the membership of the ERM. The second stage involved narrowing exchange rate bands as well as shifting control over some macroeconomic policies from national control to control by a central European Authority. The third stage would establish a European System of Central Banks to replace national central banks and replace national currencies with a single European currency. The Maastricht Treaty, signed at the end of 1991, set up a timetable for this process, with stage 3 starting no later than January 1, 1999. As planned later, on January 1 of 2002, Euro notes and coins would begin circulating alongside national currencies (It came true as a matter of fact). By July 1, 2002, changeover to Euro should be completed.

The Maastricht Treaty requires convergence of inflation rates and long-term interest rates among countries joining EMU, as well as exchange rate stability and debt reduction. An important political reality is the process leading up to European Monetary Union is the strong support it has enjoyed among the leaders of Europe. A similar level of support is not to be found among the citizens of European countries.

The main benefits of a single currency include: reducing costs of trading one currency for another, reducing exchange rate uncertainty, preventing competitive devaluations, and preventing speculative attacks. The benefits of switching a single currency do not come without costs. Probably the biggest cost is that each country cedes its right to set monetary policy to respond to domestic economic problems. In addition, exchange rates between countries can no longer adjust in response to regional problems. Whatever the costs of EMU, mechanism other than domestic monetary or exchange rate policy will have to bear the burden of economic adjustment after adoption of the single currency. Barriers to movements of labor have been removed, which encourages that adjustment process. Further labor market reforms may be necessary to increase labor markets' speed of adjustment. In addition, member countries may find it necessary to institute international tax and redistribution policies through growth of the European Union's budget to allow regional differences in policy stimulus or restraint.

Summary

In this unit, we examined the operation of the international monetary system from the gold standard period to the present. A good international monetary system is one that maximizes the flow of international trade and investments, and leads to an equitable distribution of the gains from trade among nations.

The gold standard functioned from about 1870 to the outbreak of World War I in 1914. The adjustment was mainly carried out through stabilizing short-term capital flows and induced income changes, rather than through induced changes in internal prices, as postulated by the price-specie-flow mechanism. The period from 1919 to 1924 was featured by wildly fluctuating exchange rates. Starting in 1925, an attempt was made by Britain and other nations to re-establish the gold standard. But this attempt failed with the deepening of the Great Depression in 1931. The Bretton Woods system came into existence in 1944, which called for the establishment of the International Monetary Fund. This system aimed to have nations follow a set of agreed rules of conduct in international trade and finance and provide nations with borrowing facilities to correct their temporary balance of payments disequilibrium. This was a gold-exchange standard with gold and convertible currencies (only the U. S. dollar at the beginning) as international reserves. Exchange rates were allowed to fluctuate by only 1 percent above and below established par values. Par values were to be changed only in cases of fundamental disequilibrium. Each member was assigned a quota into the Fund. The immediate cause of the collapse of the Bretton Woods system was the huge trade deficits in the U. S. and the destabilizing speculation in 1971. The fundamental cause of this collapse was the lack of an adequate adjustment mechanism. From March 1973 until now, the world has operated mainly under a managed float. In March 1979, the European Monetary System was formed with plans to create a single currency and a central bank in 1999. The single currency in the European monetary System has posed new opportunities and challenges to the world monetary system. The hegemony of the U. S. dollar under the Bretton Woods system has been replaced by a triple-hegemony represented by the U, S. dollar, Euro, and Japanese yen.

WORDS AND EXPRESSIONS

- *chaotic* /keɪˈɒtɪk/ *adj.* confused or disorderly 混乱的,无秩序的
- *proceeds* *n.* Money received through a sale or loan. The term sometimes refers to net proceeds (after any commissions, fees or other charges are deducted), and sometimes refers to gross proceeds (before such deductions). (出售……/贷款所得)款额
- *benign* /bɪˈnaɪn/ *neglect* 善意的忽略
- *hegemony* /hɪˈdʒemənɪ/ *n.* the predominant influence of one state over others 霸权/主,统治权
- *coalition* /ˌkəʊəˈlɪʃn/ *n.* an alliance, especially a temporary one, of people, factions, parties, or nations 联盟:人民、派别、政党或国家的联合,尤指暂时联合

  a combination into one body; a union 联/结合体:结为一体;联盟
- *notorious* /nəʊˈtɔːrɪəs/ *adj.* known widely and usually unfavorably; infamous 声名狼藉的,恶名昭彰的
- *threshold of divergence* the upper and lower limits of the fluctuation of the exchange rate 汇率波动的上下限
- *equitable* /ˈekwɪtəbl/ *adj.* marked by or having equity; just and impartial 公正的,公平的,不偏袒的
- *defy* /dɪˈfaɪ/ *vt.* to oppose or resist with boldness and assurance 反抗,违抗

  to refuse to submit to or cooperate with 不服从,不合作

  to challenge or dare (someone) to do something 挑战;刺激

BACKGROUND KNOWLEDGE

1 *European Monetary System* (EMS) It is a system of exchange-rate stabilization

Part I EVOLUTION AND OPERATION OF THE INTERNATIONAL MONETARY SYSTEM

involving the countries of the European Union, which began operations in 1979. There are two elements: the **Exchange Rate Mechanism** (ERM 汇率机制), under which participating countries commit themselves to maintaining the values of their currencies within agreed limits, and **a balance of payments support mechanism**, organized through the European Monetary Cooperation Fund. The ERM operates by giving each currency a value in ECUs(欧洲货币单位) and drawing up **a parity grid**(制定一份平价网图) giving exchange values in ECUs for each pair of currencies. In practice, the Deutschmark has replaced the ECU as the anchor currency(稳/固定的货币). If market rates differ from the agreed parity by more than a permitted percentage (currently 2.25% or 6% depending on the currency), the relevant governments have to take action to correct the disparity. Two currencies, the UK pound and the Italian lira were forced out of the ERM in 1992 and some of the currencies remaining in it are now allowed 15% fluctuations. The ultimate goal of the EMS is also controversial. To some its function is to facilitate monetary cooperation; to others, it is the first step towards European Monetary Union (EMU 欧洲货币联盟), with a single European currency and a European central bank. The decision to create a single currency was part of the *Maastricht Treaty* in 1991, provided that the participants fulfill certain conditions. Countries that fulfill the conditions for EMU will be named in 1998. Their currencies will be locked together in 1999, enabling the common European currency (the euro) to be in circulation by 2002.

2 European Monetary Cooperation Fund

It is a fund organized by the European Monetary System in which members of the European Union deposit reserves to provide a pool of resources to stabilize exchange rates and to finance balance of payments support. In return for depositing 20% of their gold and gross dollar reserves, member states have access to a wide variety of credit facilities, denominated (titled) in ECU, from the fund.

3 *weighted average*
In statistical calculation, weighted average is an arithmetical mean that gives each item its proper weight or importance. 统计计算中,加权平均数/值是一种数学方法,它把适当的权数或重要性给予每个项目。

For example, if a person buys a commodity on three occasions, 100 tons at $70 per ton, 300 tons at $80 per ton, and 50 tons at $95 per ton, his purchases total 450 tons; the simple average price would be (70 + 80 + 95) ÷ 3 = $81.7. The weighted average, taking into account the amount purchased on each occasion, would be [(100 × 70) + (300 × 80) + (50 × 95)] ÷ 450 = $79.4 per ton.

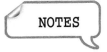

NOTES

1 *Managed Floating*
In fact, the floating exchange rate is "intervened" by the

central bank in a country, not floating freely in exchange market. So it is really managed floating. 实际上,浮动汇率是由一个国家的中央银行"干预",而不是任其在外汇市场自由浮动,故实际是管理的浮动。

亦称 **managed currency**: A currency in which the government controls, or at least influences, the exchange rate. This control is usually exerted by the central bank buying and selling in the foreign-exchange market. 政府控制的货币,或至少对外汇汇率产生影响的货币。中央银行通过在外汇市场的买卖行为实施这种控制。

亦称 **clean floating**: A government policy allowing a country's currency to fluctuate without direct intervention in the foreign-exchange markets. In practice, clean floating is rare as governments are frequently tempted to manage exchange rates by direct intervention by means of the official reserves, a policy sometimes called managed floating (see also managed currency). However, clean floating does not necessarily mean that there is no control of exchange rates, as they can still be influenced by the government's monetary policy. 清洁浮动:政府允许国家货币在外汇市场的浮动而不加以直接干预的政策。实际上,清洁浮动很罕见,各国政府经常以官方储备通过直接干预来管理汇率(有时也称作"管理浮动",参见 managed currency)。然而,清洁浮动并不一定意味着对汇率的不控制,因为汇率仍会受到政府货币政策的影响。

比较 **dirty floating**: It is the state that the float of exchange rate is actually controlled and interfered by the government. 肮脏浮动,不自由浮动:是指汇率的浮动实际由政府控制干预的情况。

2 *Four Little Dragons* "四小龙",指亚洲新兴工业国家或地区,常写作"Four Dragons"。如:

例: Japan's chasers are the new industrialized "dragons"—Taiwan, Singapore, Korea and Hong Kong. 紧追日本之后的是新兴的工业化"小龙"——台湾、新加坡、韩国、香港。

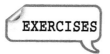
EXERCISES

Ⅰ. **Decide whether the following statements are true(T) or false(F).**

1. Since 1973, "leaning against the wind" policy has been adopted to solve short-term fluctuations in exchange rate. ( )
2. Governments are unwilling to use managed floating exchange rate system by the collapse of the Bretton Woods system. ( )
3. Under the managed floating exchange rate system, the SDRs were used as the unit of account in the IMF. ( )
4. The economic dominance of the USA has been robbed by Hong Kong, Singapore, Taiwan and Republic of Korea gradually. ( )

Part I EVOLUTION AND OPERATION OF THE INTERNATIONAL MONETARY SYSTEM

5. We can predict economic changes by studying the preferences of one country simply.   (   )
6. Lending business of the World Bank has been accused.   (   )
7. The author pointed out that there was no ideal international monetary system.   (   )
8. The ultimate goal of the EMS was to create a common currency and a central bank.   (   )
9. Inflation rate differentials contracted in Europe by the mid 1980s and most capital controls were strengthened by 1987.   (   )
10. The country which adopted the single currency can do nothing to reply to regional economic problems.   (   )

II. Translate the following expressions into Chinese.

1. with the responsibility to intervene in foreign exchange markets to smooth out short run fluctuations in exchange rates
2. to devise specific rules for managing the float to prevent competitive exchange rate depreciations
3. growing strength of an increasingly integrated Europe
4. be accused of assisting widespread global environmental destruction
5. defined as the weighted average of the currencies of member nations
6. when the fluctuation of a member nation's currency reaches 75 percent of its allowed range
7. eleven realignments occurred in the EMS between 1979 and 1987
8. bear the burden of economic adjustment after adoption of the single currency
9. examine the operation of the international monetary system from the gold standard period to the present
10. as postulated by the price-specie-flow mechanism
11. be featured by wildly fluctuating exchange rates
12. provide nations with borrowing facilities to correct their temporary balance of payments disequilibrium

III. Translate the following paragraphs into Chinese.

1. At the same time, there has been a movement away from a gold-based international monetary system. The role of gold has diminished as a result of the *Jamaica Accords*. The official price of gold was abolished. One-sixth of the gold paid into the IMF in quotas was to be returned to members, one-sixth to be auctioned by the IMF to private buyers with the proceeds being used to benefit the developing countries. The IMF was to retain the remaining two-thirds. Finally, gold was no longer to be the unit of account of the system. Since 1974, the IMF has measured all reserves and other official

transactions in terms of SDRs instead of U. S. dollars.

2. The European Monetary System (EMS) began in March 1979 with eight of the nine members of the European Community (all but Great Britain) participating in its Exchange Rate Mechanism (ERM) as part of its aim toward greater monetary integration among its members, including the ultimate goal of creating a common currency and a community-wide central bank.

3. It seems likely that with increasing financial and economic interdependence, the evolving international financial system will involve even closer cooperation. One of the consequences of the more even sharing of economic power is the potential emergence of three trading blocs of currencies, a dollar bloc based on the Americas, a yen bloc centered around Japanese trade, and a Euro bloc centered on the place of European trade.

4. In June 1989, a committee headed by Jacque Delors, the president of the European Commission, recommended a three-stage transition to the single currency. The first stage included widening the membership of the ERM. The second stage involved narrowing exchange rate bands as well as shifting control over some macroeconomic policies from national control to control by a central European Authority. The third stage would establish a European System of Central Banks to replace national central banks and replace national currencies with a single European currency.

Ⅳ. **Read the passage and decide whether the statements followed are true(T) or false (F).**

Economic and Monetary Union (EMU)

In June 1988 the European Council confirmed the objective of the progressive realization of Economic and Monetary Union (EMU). It mandated a committee chaired by Jacques Delors, the then President of the European Commission, to study and propose concrete stages leading to this union.

The committee was composed of the governors of the then European Community (EC) national central banks; Alexandre Lamfalussy, the then General Manager of the Bank for International Settlements (BIS); Niels Thygesen, professor of economics, Denmark; and Miguel Boyer, the then President **Banco Exterior de Espana**(西班牙对外银行).

The resulting Delors Report proposed that economic and monetary union should be achieved in three discrete but evolutionary steps.

Stage One of EMU

On the basis of the Delors Report, the European Council decided in June 1989 that the first stage of the realization of economic and monetary union should begin on 1 July 1990. On this date, in principle, all restrictions on the movement of capital between Member States were abolished.

Part I EVOLUTION AND OPERATION OF THE INTERNATIONAL MONETARY SYSTEM

Committee of Governors

The Committee of Governors of the central banks of the Member States of the European Economic Community, which had played an increasingly important role in monetary cooperation since its creation in May 1964, was given additional responsibilities. These were laid down in a Council Decision dated 12 March 1990. Their new tasks included holding consultations on, and promoting the coordination of the monetary policies of the Member States, with the aim of achieving price stability.

In view of the relatively short time available and the complexity of the tasks involved, the preparatory work for Stage Three of Economic and Monetary Union (EMU) was also initiated by the Committee of Governors. The first step was to identify all the issues which should be examined at an early stage, to establish a work program by the end of 1993 and to define accordingly the mandates of the existing sub-committees and working groups established for that purpose.

Legal preparations

For the realization of Stages Two and Three, it was necessary to revise the Treaty establishing the European Economic Community (the Treaty of Rome) in order to establish the required institutional structure. To this end, an Intergovernmental Conference on EMU was convened, which was held in 1991 in parallel with the Intergovernmental Conference on political union.

The negotiations resulted in the Treaty on European Union which was agreed in December 1991 and signed in Maastricht on 7 February 1992. However, owing to delays in the ratification process, the Treaty (which amended the Treaty establishing the European Economic Community—changing its name to the Treaty establishing the European Community—and introduced, inter alia, the Protocol on the Statute of the European System of Central Banks and of the European Central Bank and the Protocol on the Statute of the European Monetary Institute) did not come into force until 1 November 1993.

1. Jacque Delors, the chairman of the committee, was the then governor of the EMU.
(　)
2. The committee consisted of the leaders of the then EC national central banks, Alexandre L, Niels Thygesen and Miguel Boyer. (　)
3. From 1 July 1990, all restrictions on the movement of capital among European countries were repealed. (　)
4. One of the Committee of Governors' new tasks was stabilizing prices. (　)
5. Both the first and third step were prepared by the Committee of Governors. (　)
6. In 1991, intergovernment conferences on the EMU and political union were convened.
(　)
7. The Treaty establishing the European Economic Community was the former name of the Treaty on European Union. (　)

FURTHER READING

FIXED OR FLEXIBLE?
GETTING THE EXCHANGE RATE RIGHT IN THE 1990s

Analysts agree that "getting the exchange rate right" is essential for economic stability and growth in developing countries. Over the past two decades, many developing countries have shifted away from fixed exchange rates (that is, those that peg the domestic currency to one or more foreign currencies) and moved toward more flexible exchange rates (those that determine the external value of a currency more or less by the market supply and demand for it). During a period of rapid economic growth, driven by the twin forces of globalization and liberalization of markets and trade, this shift seems to have served a number of countries well. But as the currency market turmoil in Southeast Asia has dramatically demonstrated, globalization can amplify the costs of inappropriate policies. Moreover, the challenges facing countries may change over time, suggesting a need to adapt exchange rate policy to changing circumstances.

This paper examines the recent evolution of exchange rate policies in the developing world. It looks at why so many countries have made a transition from fixed or "pegged" exchange rates to "managed floating" or "independently floating" currencies. It discusses how economies perform under different exchange rate arrangements, issues in the choice of regime, and the challenges posed by a world of increasing capital mobility, especially when banking sectors are inadequately regulated or supervised. The analysis suggests that exchange rate regimes cannot be unambiguously rated in terms of economic performance. But it seems clear that, whatever exchange rate regime a country pursues, long-term success depends on a commitment to sound economic fundamentals—and a strong banking sector.

From Fixed to Flexible

A Brief History

The shift from fixed to more flexible exchange rates has been gradual, dating from the breakdown of the Bretton Woods system of fixed exchange rates in the early 1970s, when the world's major currencies began to float. At first, most developing countries continued to peg their exchange rates—either to a single key currency, usually the U.S. dollar or French franc, or to a basket of currencies. By the late 1970s, they began to shift from single currency pegs to basket pegs, such as to the IMF's special drawing right (SDR). Since the early 1980s, however, developing countries have shifted away from currency pegs—toward explicitly more flexible exchange rate arrangements. This shift has occurred in most of the world's major geographic regions.

Back in 1975, for example, 87 percent of developing countries had some type of pegged exchange rate. By 1996, this proportion had fallen to well below 50 percent. When the relative size of economies is taken into account, the shift is even more pronounced. In 1975, countries with pegged rates accounted for 70 percent of the developing world's total trade; by 1996, this figure had dropped to about 20 percent. The overall trend is clear, though it is probably less pronounced than these figures indicate because many countries that officially describe their exchange rate regimes as "managed floating" or even "independently floating" in practice often continue to set their rate unofficially or use it as a policy instrument.

Several important exceptions must be mentioned. A prime example is the **CFA franc**(非洲金融共同体法郎) zone in sub-Saharan Africa, where some 14 countries have pegged their rate to the French franc since 1948—with one substantial devaluation in 1994. In addition, some countries have reverted, against the trend, from flexible to fixed rate regimes. These include Argentina, which adopted a type of **currency-board**(货币局制度,阿根廷危机的根源) arrangement in 1991, and Hong Kong SAR, which has had a similar arrangement since 1983.

Nevertheless, the general shift from fixed to flexible has been broadly based worldwide. In 1976, pegged rate regimes were the norm in Africa, Asia, the Middle East, nonindustrial Europe, and the Western Hemisphere. By 1996, flexible exchange rate regimes predominated in all these regions.

Why the Shift?

The considerations that have led countries to shift toward more flexible exchange rate arrangements vary widely; also, the shift did not happen all at once. When the Bretton Woods fixed rate system broke down in 1973, many countries continued to peg to the same currency they had pegged to before, often on simple historical grounds. It was only later, when major currencies moved sharply in value, that countries started to abandon these single-currency pegs.

Many countries that traditionally pegged to the U.S. dollar, for instance, adopted a basket approach during the first half of the 1980s, in large part because the dollar was appreciating rapidly. Another key element was the rapid acceleration of inflation in many developing countries during the 1980s. Countries with inflation rates higher than their main trading partners often depreciated their currencies to prevent a severe loss of competitiveness. This led many countries in the Western Hemisphere, in particular, to adopt "**crawling pegs**"(浮动钉住, 小幅度调整汇率,小步调整的汇价钉住办法), whereby exchange rates could be adjusted according to such pre-set criteria as relative changes in the rate of inflation. Later, some countries that suffered very high rates of inflation shifted back to a pegged exchange rate as a central element of their stabilization efforts. (These exchange-rate-based stabilization programs have typically been short-lived, with the median duration of a peg about 10 months.)

Many developing countries have also experienced a series of external shocks. In the 1980s, these included a steep rise in international interest rates, a slowdown of growth in the industrial world, and the debt crisis. Often, adjustment to these disturbances required not only discrete currency depreciations but also the adoption of more flexible exchange rate arrangements. In recent years, increased capital mobility and, in particular, waves of capital inflows and outflows have heightened the potential for shocks and increased pressures for flexibility.

The trend toward greater exchange rate flexibility has been associated with more open, outward-looking policies on trade and investment generally and increased emphasis on market-determined exchange rates and interest rates. As a practical matter, however, most developing countries are still not well-placed to allow their exchange rates to float totally freely. Many have small and relatively thin financial markets, where a few large transactions can cause extreme volatility. Thus, active management is still widely needed to help guide the market. In these circumstances, a key issue for the authorities is where and when to make policy adjustments—including the use of official intervention to help avoid substantial volatility and serious misalignments.

Macroeconomic Performance under Different Regimes

Neither of the two main exchange regimes—fixed or flexible—ranks above the other in terms of its implications for macroeconomic performance. Although in previous years inflation appeared consistently lower and less volatile in countries with pegged exchange rates, in the 1990s the difference has narrowed substantially. Output growth also does not seem to differ across exchange rate regimes. While the median growth rate in countries with flexible exchange rates has recently appeared higher than in those with pegged rates, that result reflects the inclusion of the rapidly growing Asian countries in the "flexible" category; yet many of these countries in practice have operated a tightly managed policy. When these countries are excluded, growth performance does not differ significantly between the two sets of countries.

Evidence also suggests that, contrary to conventional wisdom, misalignments and currency "crashes" are equally likely under pegged and flexible exchange rate regimes. Indeed, in 116 separate cases between 1975 and 1996—where an exchange rate fell at least 25 percent within a year—nearly half were under flexible regimes. For both types, there was a large cluster of such crashes during the period immediately following the debt crisis of 1982. In part, this may reflect the fact that relatively few developing countries have truly floating exchange rates—and that, even if they had an officially declared flexible rate policy, they were often in practice pursuing an unofficial "target" rate that was then abandoned.

Choosing a Regime

The early literature on the choice of exchange rate regime took the view that the smaller and more "open" an economy (that is, the more dependent on exports and imports), the better it is served by a fixed exchange rate. A later approach to the choice of exchange rate regime looks at the effects of various **random disturbances**(随机干扰) on the domestic economy. In this framework the best regime is the one that stabilizes macroeconomic performance, that is, minimizes fluctuations in output, consumption, the domestic price level, or some other macroeconomic variable. The ranking of fixed and flexible exchange rate regimes depends on the nature and source of the shocks to the economy, policymakers' preferences (that is, the type of costs they wish to minimize), and the structural characteristics of the economy.

In an extension of this approach, economists have viewed the policymaker's decision not simply as a choice between a purely fixed and a purely floating exchange rate but as a range of choices with varying degrees of flexibility. In general, a fixed exchange rate (or a greater degree of fixity) is preferable if the disturbances impinging on the economy are predominantly monetary—such as changes in the demand for money—and thus affect the general level of prices. A flexible rate (or a greater degree of flexibility) is preferable if disturbances are predominantly real—such as changes in tastes or technology that affect the relative prices of domestic goods—or originate abroad.

Credibility Versus Flexibility

In the 1990s another strand of analysis has focused on the credibility that authorities can gain under a fixed regime. Some argue that adopting a pegged exchange rate—by providing an unambiguous objective "anchor" for economic policy—can help establish the credibility of a program to bring down inflation. The reasons for this seem intuitively obvious. In fixed regimes, monetary policy must be subordinated to the requirements of maintaining the peg. This in turn means that other key aspects of policy, including fiscal policy, must be kept consistent with the peg, effectively "tying the hands" of the authorities. A country trying to maintain a peg may not, for example, be able to increase its borrowing through the bond market because this may affect interest rates and, hence, put pressure on the exchange rate peg.

So long as the fixed rate is credible (that is, the market believes it can and will be maintained), expectations of inflation will be restrained—a major cause of **chronic inflation**(长期通货膨胀). The risk is, of course, that the peg becomes unsustainable if confidence in the authorities' willingness or ability to maintain it is lost.

A flexible exchange rate provides greater room for maneuver in a variety of ways. Not least, it leaves the authorities free to allow inflation to rise—which is also a way, indirectly, to increase tax revenue. The danger here is that it will probably be harder to establish that there is a credible policy to control inflation—and expectations of higher inflation often become self-fulfilling.

But the discipline of a pegged exchange rate need not necessarily be greater. Even with a peg, the authorities still retain some flexibility, such as an ability to shift the inflationary cost of running fiscal deficits into the future. Ways to do this include allowing international reserves to diminish, or allowing external debt to accumulate until the peg can no longer be sustained. In a more flexible regime, the costs of an unsustainable policy may be revealed more quickly—through widely observed movements in exchange rates and prices. If this is the case, then a flexible regime may exert an even stronger discipline on policy. In any event, a policymaker's commitment to a peg may not be credible for long if the economy is not functioning successfully. For example, maintaining interest rates at very high levels to defend the exchange rate may over time undermine the credibility of the peg—especially if it has damaging effects on real activity or the health of the banking system.

In many cases, the apparent trade-off between credibility and flexibility may depend not only on the economy but also on political considerations. For instance, it may be more costly in political terms to adjust a pegged exchange rate than to allow a flexible rate to move gradually by a corresponding amount. Authorities must shoulder the responsibility for adjusting a peg, whereas movements in an exchange rate that is allowed, to some degree at least, to fluctuate in response to changes in the demand and supply for the currency can be attributed to market forces. When the political costs of exchange rate adjustments are high, a more flexible regime will likely be adopted.

Pegging: A Single Currency or Basket?

For those that do adopt an exchange rate anchor, a further choice is whether to peg to a single currency or to a basket of currencies. The choice hinges on both the degree of concentration of a country's trade with particular trading partners and the currencies in which its external debt is denominated. When the peg is to a single currency, fluctuations in the anchor currency against other currencies imply fluctuations in the exchange rate of the economy in question against those currencies. By pegging to a currency basket instead, a country can reduce the vulnerability of its economy to fluctuations in the values of the individual currencies in the basket. Thus, in a world of floating exchange rates among the major currencies, the case for a single-currency peg is stronger if the peg is to the currency of the dominant trading partner. However, in some cases, a significant portion of the country's debt service may be denominated in other currencies. This may complicate the choice of a currency to which to peg.

Challenges Posed by Fast Growth and Capital Inflows

The successful development of an emerging market economy should, economists often conjecture, tend to result in an appreciation of the domestic currency in real (inflation-adjusted) terms. Such an appreciation over the long term has been evident in Korea, Taiwan Province of China, Singapore, Hong Kong SAR, and—to a lesser extent—Chile.

This relationship between economic growth and real appreciation is assumed to stem from a tendency for productivity growth in the manufacture of traded goods to outpace that of goods and services that are not traded internationally. In practice, that tendency has been apparent, so far at least, only in Korea and Taiwan Province of China. In other emerging market economies, the phenomenon appears muted or absent. This may be because those economies are at a (relatively) early stage of their development or perhaps because other influences—such as shifts in the international distribution of production of traded goods and changes in trade restrictions and transportation and other costs of market penetration—have obscured it.

In these circumstances, the choice between fixed and flexible exchange rate arrangements hinges largely on the preference of policymakers between nominal exchange rate appreciation and relatively more rapid inflation. The results in terms of real exchange rate changes may be nearly the same with either approach. For example, between 1980 and 1996, while Hong Kong SAR, which has had a type of currency board arrangement since 1983, experienced relatively higher inflation than Singapore, which had a managed floating regime, their real exchange rates appreciated at roughly similar rates.

Adjusting to Capital Inflows

In many fast-growing emerging market economies, upward pressure on the exchange rate in recent years has stemmed largely from vastly

Part I EVOLUTION AND OPERATION OF THE INTERNATIONAL MONETARY SYSTEM

increased private capital inflows. When capital inflows accelerate, if the exchange rate is prevented from rising, inflationary pressures build up and the real exchange rate will appreciate through higher domestic inflation. To avoid such consequences, central banks have usually attempted to "sterilize" the inflows—by using offsetting open market operations to try and "mop up" the inflowing liquidity.

Such operations tend to work at best only in the short term for several reasons. First, sterilization prevents domestic interest rates from falling in response to the inflows and, hence, typically results in the attraction of even greater capital inflows. Second, given the relatively small size of the domestic financial market compared with international capital flows, sterilization tends to become less effective over time. Finally, fiscal losses from intervention, arising from the differential between the interest earned on foreign reserves and that paid on debt denominated in domestic currency, will mount, so sterilization has a cost.

As capital inflows increase, tension will likely develop between the authorities' desire, on the one hand, to contain inflation and, on the other, to maintain a stable (and competitive) exchange rate. As signs of overheating appear, and investors become increasingly aware of the tension between the two policy goals, a turnaround in market sentiment may occur, triggering a sudden reversal in capital flows.

Since open market operations have only a limited impact in offsetting the monetary consequences of large capital inflows, many countries have adopted a variety of supplementary measures. In some countries the authorities have raised the amount of reserves that banks are required to maintain against deposits. In others, public sector deposits have been shifted from commercial banks into the central bank—to reduce banks' reserves. A number of countries have used prudential regulations, such as placing limits on the banking sector's foreign exchange currency exposure. Some central banks have used forward exchange swaps to create offsetting capital outflows—although there appear to be limits on how long such a policy can be used, given the likelihood, as with open market operations, that it can cause fiscal losses. In other cases the authorities have responded by widening the exchange rate bands for their currencies, thus allowing some appreciation. And a few have introduced selective capital controls.

While such instruments and policies can for a time relieve some upward pressure on a currency and ease inflationary pressure, none appears to have been able to prevent an appreciation of the real exchange rate completely.

Can exchange rate flexibility help manage the impact of volatile capital flows? As mentioned earlier, if interest rates and monetary policy are "locked in" by an exchange rate anchor, the burden of adjustment falls largely on fiscal policy—that is, government spending and tax policies. But often taxes cannot be raised or spending reduced in short order, nor can needed infrastructure investments be postponed indefinitely. (Clearly, policymakers who cannot adjust fiscal policy in the short run should not adopt a rigidly fixed exchange rate regime.) Allowing the exchange rate to appreciate gradually to accommodate upward pressures would appear to be a safer way of maintaining long-run economic stability. Furthermore, by allowing the exchange rate to adjust in response to capital inflows, policymakers can influence market expectations. In particular, policymakers can make market participants more aware that they face a "two-way" bet—exchange rate appreciations can be followed by depreciations. This heightened awareness of exchange rate risks should discourage some of the more speculative short-term capital flows, thereby reducing the need for sharp corrections.

Volatility and Banking Sector Weakness

How exchange rate changes affect an economy depends, among other things, on the health of the banking system. In many fast-growing emerging markets with large-scale capital inflows adding to liquidity, bank lending has increased markedly. In Mexico, for example, bank lending to the private sector surged to an average of 27 percent of GDP during 1989—94 from only 11 percent in the three preceding years. Such rapid credit expansion often occurs in an environment of booming optimism about the outlook for the economy more broadly, and the resulting rise in asset prices—and especially prices of real estate—often raises the value of loan collateral, stimulating yet more bank lending. If the banking sector lacks adequate prudential regulation and supervision, commercial banks may end up with **portfolios**(证券投资) excessively exposed to domestic assets with vulnerable values and to foreign currency liabilities. In the event of a sudden reversal of

Part I EVOLUTION AND OPERATION OF THE INTERNATIONAL MONETARY SYSTEM

sentiment and currency depreciation, the large losses banks face can become a macroeconomic problem—as in some Asian economies recently.

Various mechanisms, including improved banking regulation and the establishment of deposit insurance funds, have been put in place in developing countries in recent years to guard against such banking sector problems. More often than not, however, banking sector losses have continued to end up as a burden on taxpayers—as the authorities have been forced to bail out banks to prevent a systemic "chain reaction" of defaults. The establishment and observance of a set of core regulatory, supervisory, and accounting standards—such as those recommended by the Basle Committee on Banking Supervision—would go some way toward meeting the need for stronger standards and supervision in the banking sector.

Capital Account Convertibility

In recent years, many emerging economies have gradually relaxed or removed capital controls and are now proceeding toward full capital account convertibility. Remaining restrictions are nevertheless significant, and are mostly **asymmetric**(不均匀的,不对称的)—placing more restrictions on capital flowing out than on capital flowing in. More liberal rules in both directions would have the advantage of increasing economic efficiency (allowing more capital to flow to where it gets the best returns). Liberalization would also provide domestic investors with more opportunities to diversify their portfolios and reduce the concentration of exposure to domestic market risks.

A movement toward full capital account convertibility, however, can succeed only in the context of sound economic fundamentals, a sound banking sector, and an exchange rate policy that allows adequate flexibility. The increasing number of developing countries adopting more flexible exchange rate regimes probably reflects, at least in part, recognition that increased flexibility may be helpful in making the transition to full convertibility.

As developing countries become ever more integrated with global financial markets, they will likely experience more volatility in cross-border capital flows. How to manage such volatility has thus become an important issue for policymakers. One obvious way to contain volatility is to try to reduce reliance on short-term capital flows. It would be unrealistic, however, to try to distinguish between those flows that are destabilizing and those that perform important stabilizing functions in the foreign exchange and other markets. It would also be undesirable to eliminate short-term flows entirely—given that, among other things, they help provide liquidity to the currency market.

Greater exchange rate flexibility need not imply free floating. It may, for example, involve the adoption of wider bands around formal or informal central parities and active intervention within the band. The greater the role of fiscal policy—in helping to adjust the economy to changing conditions—the less the need for wider bands or large-scale intervention. Nevertheless, exchange rate adjustments may be needed at times. Under any regime, appropriate and transparent economic and financial policies are critical for safeguarding macroeconomic stability. They may not, however, always be sufficient to prevent exchange rate volatility.

Summary

Until recently, most evidence suggested that developing countries with pegged exchange rates enjoyed relatively lower and more stable rates of inflation. In recent years, however, many developing countries have moved toward flexible exchange rate arrangements—at the same time as inflation has come down generally across the developing world. Indeed, the average inflation rate for countries with flexible exchange rates has fallen steadily—to where it is no longer significantly different from that of countries with fixed rates. The perceived need for greater flexibility has probably resulted from the increasing globalization of financial markets—which has integrated developing economies more closely into the global financial system. This in turn imposes an often strict discipline on their macroeconomic policies.

Trade-offs exist between fixed and more flexible regimes. If economic policy is based on the "anchor" of a currency peg, monetary policy must be subordinated to the needs of maintaining the peg. As a result the burden of adjustment to shocks falls largely on fiscal policy (government spending and tax policies). For a peg to last, it must be credible. In practice, this often means that fiscal policy must be flexible enough to respond to shocks. Under a more flexible arrangement, monetary policy may be more independent but inflation can

Part I EVOLUTION AND OPERATION OF THE INTERNATIONAL MONETARY SYSTEM

be somewhat higher and more variable.

Considerations affecting the choice of regime may change over time. When inflation is very high, a pegged exchange rate may be the key to a successful short-run stabilization program. Later, perhaps in response to surging capital inflows and the risk of overheating, more flexibility is likely to be required to help relieve pressures and to signal the possible need for adjustments to contain an external imbalance. To move toward full capital account convertibility, especially in a world of volatile capital flows, flexibility may become inescapable.

(*FROM*: http://www.imf.org/external/pubs/ft/issues13/index.htm)

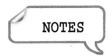

1 *The CFA franc*: new peg for a common currency 非洲共同体法郎,对于通用货币的新固定汇率

The CFA franc is the common currency of 14 countries in West and Central Africa, 12 of which are former French colonies. These 14 countries comprise the African Financial Community, which in turn is comprised of two regional economic and monetary groupings. Eight countries—Benin, Burkina Faso, Côte d'Ivoire, Guinea-Bissau, Mali, Niger, Senegal and Togo—form the West African Economic and Monetary Union (WAEMU) while six countries—Cameroon, Central African Republic, Chad, Republic of Congo, Equatorial Guinea and Gabon—are linked as members of the Central African Economic and Monetary Community (CEMAC).

Each regional grouping issues its own CFA franc. The common currency of WAEMU is the *franc de la Communauté financière de l'Afrique* (CFA franc), issued by the *Banque centrale des Etats de l'Afrique de l'Ouest* (BCEAO). CEMAC's common currency is the *franc de la Coopération financière africaine* (also known as CFA franc), issued by the *Banque des Etats de l'Afrique centrale* (BEAC). Although the two CFA francs are legal tender only in their respective regions, each region's central bank maintains the same parity of its CFA franc against the French franc and capital can move freely between the two regions.

The CFA franc has been pegged to the French franc since 1948[①]. Only one devaluation has occurred during the history of the currency peg—from CFA50 to CFA100 = FF1 in January 1994.

With the introduction of the euro on January 1, 1999, the French franc is fixed against the

---

① The Comoros also pegs its currency, the Comorian franc, to the French franc and, since January 1999, to the euro. The Comorian franc was also devalued against the French franc in January 1994, by 33 per cent.

currencies of the 10 other European countries participating in the euro. Nevertheless, the member countries of the CFA franc zone and France agreed to maintain the currency peg following the euro's introduction through an arrangement with the French Treasury.

The French Treasury has retained sole responsibility for guaranteeing convertibility of CFA francs into euros, without any monetary policy implication for the Bank of France (French central bank) or the European Central Bank. While the two CFA central banks maintain an overdraft facility with the French Treasury, the amount that can be withdrawn is limited by operating rules that have applied since 1973. Each CFA central bank must keep at least 65 per cent of its foreign assets in its operations account with the French Treasury; provide for foreign exchange cover of at least 20 per cent for sight liabilities; and impose a cap on credit extended to each member country equivalent to 20 per cent of that country's public revenue in the preceding year.

The fixed parity between the euro and the CFA franc is based on the official, fixed conversion rate for the French franc and the euro set on January 1, 1999 (FF6.55957 = EURO1). As a result, the value of the CFA franc is now fixed against all 11 euro-zone country currencies. Since the CFA100 = FF1 exchange rate has remained unchanged, the CFA franc-euro exchange rate is simply CFA665.957 = EURO1.

The CFA franc is actually pegged to the euro in de facto terms from January 1999. The peg will become official in 2002—when France and the other euro-zone countries must completely withdraw their national currencies from circulation.

(*FROM*: *http://www.un.org/ecosocdev/geninfo/afrec/subjindx/*124*euro*3.*htm*)

2 *crawling peg* 浮动钉住,小幅度调整汇率,只在小范围内上下浮动的稳定价格(或汇率)

Part II

ORGANIZATIONS

CHAPTER 4 THE INTERNATIONAL MONETARY FUND (IMF)

Learning Objectives

1. Foundation of the IMF;
2. Basic Functions;
3. Leadership and Membership.

The International Monetary Fund (IMF) is an international organization that was initiated in 1944 at the Bretton Woods Conference and formally created in 1945 by 29 member countries. The IMF's stated goal was to assist in the reconstruction of the world's international payment system post World War II.

With its near-global membership of 188 countries, the IMF is uniquely placed to help member governments take advantage of the opportunities—and manage the challenges—posed by globalization and economic development more generally. The IMF tracks global economic trends and performance, alerts its member countries when it sees problems on the horizon, provides a forum for policy dialogue, and passes on know-how to governments on how to tackle economic difficulties.

Marked by massive movements of capital and abrupt shifts in comparative advantage, globalization affects countries' policy choices in many areas, including labor, trade, and tax policies. Helping a country benefit from globalization while avoiding potential downsides is an important task for the IMF. The global economic crisis has highlighted just how interconnected countries have become in today's world economy.

BADGE OF THE IMF

Foundation of the IMF

The big question at the Bretton Woods conference with respect to the institution that would emerge as the IMF was the issue of future access to international liquidity and whether that source should be akin to a world central bank able to create new reserves at will or a more limited borrowing mechanism.

Although attended by 44 nations, discussions at the conference were dominated by two rival plans developed by the U. S. and Britain. As the chief international economist at the U. S. Treasury in 1942—44, Harry Dexter White drafted the U. S. blueprint for international access to liquidity, which competed with the plan drafted for the British Treasury by Keynes. Overall, White's scheme tended to favor incentives designed to create price stability within the world's economies, while Keynes' wanted a system that encouraged economic growth.

Harry Dexter White (left) and John Maynard Keynes (right) at the Bretton Woods Conference

At the time, gaps between the White and Keynes plans seemed enormous. Outlining the difficulty of creating a system that every nation could accept in his speech at the closing plenary session of the Bretton Woods conference on July 22, 1944, Keynes stated: "We, the delegates of this Conference, Mr. President, have been trying to accomplish something very difficult to accomplish. It has been our task to find a common measure, a common standard, a common rule acceptable to each and not irksome to any."

Keynes' proposals would have established a world reserve currency (which he thought might be called "bancor") administered by a central bank vested with the possibility of creating money and with the authority to take actions on a much larger scale (understandable considering deflationary problems in Britain at the time).

In case of balance of payments imbalances, Keynes recommended that both debtors and creditors should change their policies. As outlined by Keynes, countries with payment surpluses should increase their imports from the deficit countries and thereby create foreign trade equilibrium. Thus, Keynes was sensitive to the problem that placing too much of the burden on the deficit country would be deflationary.

But the U. S. , as a likely creditor nation, and eager to take on the role of the world's economic powerhouse, balked at Keynes' plan and did not pay serious attention to it. The U. S. contingent was too concerned about inflationary pressures in the postwar economy, and White saw an imbalance as a problem only of the deficit country.

Although compromise was reached on some points, because of the overwhelming economic and military power of the U. S. , the participants at Bretton Woods largely agreed on White's plan. As a result, the IMF was born with an economic approach and political ideology that stressed controlling inflation and introducing austerity plans over fighting poverty. This left the IMF severely detached from the realities of Third World countries struggling with underdevelopment from the onset.

Functions

The IMF works to foster global growth and economic stability. It provides policy advice and financing to members in economic difficulties and also works with developing nations to help them achieve macroeconomic stability and reduce poverty. The rationale for this is that private international capital markets function imperfectly and many countries have limited access to financial markets. Such market imperfections, together with balance of payments financing, provide the justification for official financing, without which many countries could only correct large external payment imbalances through measures with adverse effects on both national and international economic prosperity. The IMF can provide other sources of financing to countries in need that would not be available in the absence of an economic stabilization program supported by the Fund.

Upon initial IMF formation, its two primary functions were: to oversee the fixed exchange rate arrangements between countries, thus helping national governments manage their exchange rates and allowing these governments to prioritise economic growth, and to provide short-term capital to aid balance of payments. This assistance was meant to prevent the spread of international economic crises. The Fund was also intended to help mend the pieces of the international economy post the Great Depression and World War II.

The IMF's role was fundamentally altered after the floating exchange rates post 1971. It shifted to examining the economic policies of countries with IMF loan agreements to determine if a shortage of capital was due to economic fluctuations or economic policy. The IMF also researched what types of government policy would ensure economic recovery. The new challenge is to promote and implement policy that reduces the frequency of crises among the emerging market countries, especially the middle-income countries that are open to massive capital outflows. Rather than maintaining a position of oversight of only exchange rates, their function became one of "surveillance" of the overall macroeconomic performance of its member countries. Their role became a lot more active because the IMF now manages economic policy instead of just exchange rates.

In addition, the IMF negotiates conditions on lending and loans under their policy of conditionality, which was established in the 1950s. Low-income countries can borrow on concessional terms, which means there is a period of time with no interest rates, through the Extended Credit Facility (ECF), the Stand-By Credit Facility (SCF) and the Rapid Credit Facility (RCF). Nonconcessional loans, which include interest rates, are provided mainly through Stand-By Arrangements (SBA), the Flexible Credit Line (FCL), the Precautionary and Liquidity Line (PLL), and the Extended Fund Facility. The IMF provides emergency assistance via the newly introduced Rapid Financing Instrument (RFI) to all its members facing urgent balance of payments needs.

Leadership

The Board of Governors, the highest decision-making body of the IMF, consists of one governor and one alternate governor for each member country. The governor is appointed by the member country and is usually the minister of finance or the governor of the central bank. All powers of the IMF are vested in the Board of Governors. The Board of Governors may delegate to the Executive Board all except certain reserved powers. The Board of Governors normally meets once a year.

The Executive Board (the Board) is responsible for conducting the day-to-day business of the IMF. It is composed of 24 Directors, who are appointed or elected by member countries or by groups of countries, and the Managing Director, who serves as Chairman of the Executive Board. Historically the IMF's managing director has been European and the president of the World Bank has been from the United States. However, this standard is increasingly being questioned for these two posts may soon open up to include other qualified candidates from any part of the world. In July 2011, Christine Lagarde became the eleventh Managing Director of the IMF, and the first woman to hold that position.

Membership

The IMF currently has a near-global membership of 188 countries. To become a member, a country must apply and then be accepted by a majority of the existing members. In April 2012, Republic of South Sudan joined the IMF, becoming the institution's 188th member.

Upon joining, each member country of the IMF is assigned a quota, based broadly on its relative size in the world economy. The IMF's membership agreed in November 2010 on a major overhaul of its quota system to reflect the changing global economic realities, especially the increased weight of major emerging markets in the global economy.

A member country's quota defines its financial and organizational relationship with the IMF, including:

Subscriptions

A member country's quota subscription determines the maximum amount of financial resources the country is obliged to provide to the IMF. A country must pay its subscription in full upon joining the IMF: up to 25 percent must be paid in the IMF's own currency, called Special Drawing Rights (SDRs) or widely accepted currencies (such as the dollar, the euro, the yen, or pound sterling), while the rest is paid in the member's own currency.

Voting power

The quota largely determines a member's voting power in IMF decisions. Each IMF member's votes are comprised of basic votes plus one additional vote for each SDR 100,000 of quota. The number of basic votes attributed to each member is calculated as 5.502 percent of total votes. Accordingly, the United States has 421,965 votes (16.76 percent of the total), and Tuvalu has 759 votes (0.03 percent of the total).

Access to financing

The amount of financing a member country can obtain from the IMF is based on its quota. For instance, under Stand-By and Extended Arrangements, which are types of loans, a member country can borrow up to 200 percent of its quota annually and 600 percent cumulatively.

SDR allocations

SDRs are used as an international reserve asset. A member's share of general SDR allocations is established in proportion to its quota. The most recent general allocation of SDRs took place in 2009.

(*FROM*: http://www.imf.org/external/about/overview.htm)

WORDS AND EXPRESSIONS

- *on the horizon* likely to happen or exist soon 即将到来的
- *know-how* /ˈnəʊhaʊ/ *n.* knowledge of how to do something well 诀窍;实际知识;专门技能
- *tackle* /ˈtæk(ə)l/ *vt.* to set about dealing with 处理
- *comparative advantage* an advantage a country has over another country because it can produce a particular type of product more efficiently 比较优势,相对优势
- *downside* /ˈdaʊnsaɪd/ *n.* a downward trend 下降的趋势

- *liquidity* /lɪˈkwɪdɪtɪ/ *n.* (finance) state of having assets that can easily be changed into cash 资产折现力；资产流动性
- *akin* /əˈkɪn/ *adj.* having a similar quality or character; analogous 同类的；类/近/相似的
- *plenary session* meeting attended by all participants 全体大会
- *irksome* /ˈɜːks(ə)m/ *adj.* causing annoyance, weariness, or vexation; tedious 令人厌恶的，讨厌的，令人厌烦的
- *vest* /vest/ *vi.* to invest or endow (a person or group) with something, such as power or rights (used with "with") 授予，赋予（力量或者权利），与 with 连用

  to place (authority, property, or rights, for example) in the control of a person or group, especially to give someone an immediate right to present or future possession or enjoyment of (an estate, for example, used with "in") 授予（如房地产）权给某人或者群体，与 in 连用，如：vested his estate in his daughter 把他的地产授权于他的女儿
- *balk* /bɔːlk/ *vi., vt.* (usually used with "at") avoid, hesitate over, draw back from （常与 at 连用）回避；犹豫不决；畏缩不前
- *contingent* /kənˈtɪndʒ(ə)nt/ *n.* a representative group forming part of an assemblage 代表团
- *ideology* /ˌaɪdɪˈɒlədʒɪ/ *n.* the body of ideas reflecting the social needs and aspirations of an individual, a group, a class, or a culture; a set of doctrines or beliefs that form the basis of a political, economic, or other system. 思想体系/意识；意识形态
- *austerity* /ɒˈsterɪtɪ/ *n.* economic conditions created by government measures to reduce a budget deficit, especially by reducing public expenditure （经济的）紧缩；

  austerity program 经济紧缩方案
- *rationale* /ˌræʃəˈnɑːl/ *n.* the reason or explanation for something 基本原理
- *adverse effect* 不利影响，副作用
- *prioritise* /praɪˈɒrəˌtaɪz/ *v.* to make (something) the most important thing in a group; to organize (things) so that the most important thing is done or dealt with first 给予……优先权；按优先顺序处理
- *keep track of* to keep a record of 记录
- *Finance Ministry* 财政部
- *embark on* to start something new or important 从事，着手
- *performance measurement* a system for judging how well an employee, a company, an economy, etc. is doing 绩效测定
- *Board of Governors* 理事会
- *Executive Board* 执行委员会
- *quota* /ˈkwəʊtə/ *n.* an official limit on the number or amount of people or things that are allowed 配额；限额

- *emerging market* a country that has some characteristics of a developed market but is not yet a developed market 新兴市场
- *Managing Director* 常务董事
- *voting power* the right to give or register a vote 表决权,投票权
- *access to financing* the means or opportunity to provide funding to (a person or enterprise) 融资渠道
- *in proportion to* according to a particular relationship in size, amount or degree 与……成比例,与……相称

BACKGROUND KNOWLEDGE

1 *John Maynard Keynes* (1883—1946) and *Harry Dexter White* (1892—1948) 约翰·梅纳德·凯恩斯和哈利·德克斯特·怀特

They were the intellectual founding fathers of the IMF and the World Bank. White was the chief international economist at the U.S. Treasury. In 1944, he drafted the American plan for the IMF that competed with the British Treasury blueprint drafted by Keynes.

Most of White's plan was incorporated into the final acts adopted at Bretton Woods. The IMF was given the role of promoting global economic growth through international trade and financial stability.

One of Keynes' most significant roles was as chairman of the Bank Commission. Under his leadership, the Bank articles were drafted rapidly and successfully despite the lack of pre-conference groundwork regarding the organization of the World Bank.

Neither Keynes nor White lived to see their visions of the IMF and the World Bank become reality. Both men died of heart attacks, Keynes in April 1946, shortly after returning from the first meeting of IMF and World Bank Boards of Governors in Savannah, Georgia, and Harry Dexter White in August 1948.

2 *Bancor* 班科

A World Currency Unit of clearing that was proposed by John Maynard Keynes, but was never implemented. It was to be initially fixed in terms of 30 commodities, of which one would be gold. It would stabilize the average prices of commodities, and with them the international medium of exchange and a store of value. 1943 年,约·梅·凯恩斯建议,在国际权威机构管理之下,以 30 种有代表性的商品作为定值基础,建立国际货币单位。各国央行以 Bancor 为本位,发行国内流通的货币,而国际间的清算以 Bancor 进行。Bancor 的发行并不需要会员国缴纳黄金或者外汇储备,而根据经济和贸易占世界的比重进行分配,各国之间可以通过贸易结算自由借贷。

3 *IMF Lending Instruments*

Over the years, the IMF has developed various loan instruments that are tailored to address the specific circumstances of its diverse membership. Low-income countries may borrow on concessional terms through the Extended Credit Facility (ECF), the Stand-By Credit Facility (SCF) and the Rapid Credit Facility (RCF) (see IMF Support for Low-Income Countries). Concessional Loans carry zero interest rates until the end of 2014.

(1) Concessional Loans 优惠贷款

To make its financial support more flexible and tailored to the diversity of low-income countries, the IMF has established a Poverty Reduction and Growth Trust, which has three lending windows, all under highly concessional terms. These windows, which became effective in January 2010 and were further refined in April 2013 to improve the tailoring and flexibility of Fund support, are the following: The Extended Credit Facility (ECF), The Stand-By Credit Facility (SCF) and The Rapid Credit Facility (RCF).

All these facilities provide financing suitable to the diverse needs of LICs and on concessional terms. LICs are receiving exceptional forgiveness through end-2014 on all interest payments due to the IMF under its concessional lending instruments.

(2) Nonconcessional Loans 非优惠/非减让性贷款

Non-concessional loans are provided mainly through Stand-By Arrangements (SBA), the Flexible Credit Line (FCL), the Precautionary and Liquidity Line (PLL), and the Extended Fund Facility (which is useful primarily for medium- and longer-term needs).

(3) Rapid Financing Instrument (RFI)

The RFI was introduced to replace and broaden the scope of the earlier emergency assistance policies. The RFI provides rapid financial assistance with limited conditionality to all members facing an urgent balance of payments need. Access under the RFI is subject to an annual limit of 50 percent of quota and a cumulative limit of 100 percent of quota. Emergency loans are subject to the same terms as the FCL, PLL and SBA, with repayment within $3\frac{1}{4}$—5 years.

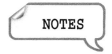

1 *international liquidity* 国际清偿能力

It used to mean the relative amount of resources available to a nation's monetary authorities that could be used to settle a balance of payments deficit. In the days of the gold standard, this term would mean access to gold that could be used to redeem a nation's currency held by foreigners. After Bretton Woods and the emergence of the dollar-gold exchange standard, liquidity meant access to dollars, either held as reserves or as credit lines, or the SDR system maintained by the International Monetary Fund. After 1971, with the abandonment of the dollar-gold exchange standard, as the world entered an era of "managed" exchange rates, "international liquidity" came to mean the resources available to national monetary authorities to maintain the value of their currencies as required by their exchange management programs to finance a balance of payments deficit. It may also be defined as the ratio of foreign reserves to foreign debt. 一国直接掌握或在必要时可以用于调节国际收支、清偿国际债务及支持本币汇率稳定的一切国际流通资金和资产。它实际上是一国的自有储备与借入储备的总和，包括黄金、外汇储备以及按规定限额可以从国际货币基金组织获得的储备资产和特别提款权。

2 *reserve currency* 储备货币

It is also called anchor currency, a currency which is held in significant quantities by many governments and institutions as part of their foreign exchange reserves. It also tends to be the international pricing currency for products traded on a global market, such as oil, gold, etc. This permits the issuing country to purchase the commodities at a marginally lower rate than other nations, which must exchange their currency with each purchase and pay a transaction cost. For major currencies, this transaction cost is negligible with respect to the price of the commodity. It also permits the government issuing the currency to borrow money at a better rate, as there will always be a larger market for that currency than others. 国际储备货币是指一国政府持有的可直接用于国际支付的国际通用的货币资金，是政府为维持本国货币汇率能随时动用的对外支付或干预外汇市场的一部分国际清偿能力。随着对外经济贸易发展和国际货币制度的变化，作为国际储备的货币资金也有所变化。各国实行金本位制时，黄金具有世界货币的职能，因此将黄金作为国际储备货币。金本位制崩溃后，除仍把黄金作为储备货币外，一些发达国家的货币逐渐成为各国储备对象。第二次世界大战后，建立了以美元为中心的国际货币体系，首先是美元，以后是西方其他可自由兑换的货币相继成为各国储备外汇资产的主要对象。

3 *policy of conditionality* 条件性/制约性政策

In political economy and international relations, conditionality is the use of conditions attached to the provision of benefits such as a loan, debt relief or bilateral aid. These conditions are typically imposed by international financial institutions, such as the International Monetary Fund, the World Bank or regional organizations, or a donor country with respect to loans, debt relief and financial aid.

Conditionalities may involve relatively uncontroversial requirements to enhance aid effectiveness, such as anti-corruption measures, but they may involve highly controversial ones, such as austerity or the privatization of key public services, which may provoke strong political opposition in the recipient country. These conditionalities are often grouped under the label structural adjustment as they were prominent in the structural adjustment programs following the debt crisis of the 1980s.

4 *quota subscription* 配额认缴

The IMF was provided with a fund, composed of contributions of member countries in gold and their own currencies. When joining the IMF, members were assigned "quotas" reflecting their relative economic power, and, as a sort of credit deposit, were obliged to pay a "subscription" of an amount commensurate to the quota. The subscription was to be paid 25% in gold or currency convertible into gold (effectively the dollar, which was the only currency then still directly gold convertible for central banks) and 75% in the member's own currency.

Quota subscriptions were to form the largest source of money at the IMF's disposal. The IMF set out to use this money to grant loans to member countries with financial difficulties. Each member was then entitled to withdraw 25% of its quota immediately in case of payment problems. If this sum was insufficient, each nation in the system was also able to request loans for foreign currency.

5 *Special Drawing Rights* (*SDRs*) 特别提款权

Special drawing rights (SDR) are supplementary foreign exchange reserve assets defined and maintained by the IMF. The SDR is not a currency per se. It instead represents a claim to currency held by IMF member countries for which they may be exchanged. As they can only be exchanged for Euro, Japanese yen, pounds sterling, or U.S. dollars, SDRs may actually represent a potential claim on IMF member countries' nongold foreign exchange reserves, which are usually held in those currencies. While they may appear to have a far more important part to play or, perhaps, an important future role, being the unit of account for the IMF has long been the main function of the SDR. SDRs are allocated to countries by the IMF. Private parties do not hold or use them. As of March 2011, the amount of SDRs in existence is around SDR 238.3 billion. 国际货币基金组织创设的一种储备资产和记账单位,亦称"纸黄金(Paper Gold)"。它是基金组织分配给会员国的一种使用资金的权利。会员国在发生国际收支逆差时,可用它向基金组织指定的其他会员国换取外汇,以偿付国际收支逆差或偿还基金组织的贷款,还可与黄金、自由兑换货币一样充当国际储备。但由于其只是一种记账单位,不是真正货币,使用时必须先换成其他货币,不能直接用于贸易或非贸易的支付。因为它是国际货币基金组织原有的普通提款权以外的一种补充,所以称为特别提款权。

EXERCISES

I. Decide whether the following statements are true(T) or false(F).

1. One of IMF's duties is to give advice to its member countries on how to take advantage of globalization while avoiding its side effects. ( )
2. Discussions at the Bretton Woods conference were dominated by two rival plans developed by the U.S. and Britain. ( )
3. Keynes's scheme tended to favor incentives designed to create price stability within the world's economies. ( )
4. In case of balance of payments imbalances, Keynes recommended that only debtors should change their policies. ( )

5. The U. S. contingent was too concerned about inflationary pressures in the postwar economy. ( )
6. With the help of the IMF, many countries could correct large external payment imbalances through measures with adverse effects on both national and international economic prosperity. ( )
7. The IMF's role has changed from overseeing the fixed exchange rate arrangements between countries to "surveillance" of the overall macroeconomic performance of its member countries. ( )
8. Low-income countries can borrow nonconcessional loans through the Extended Credit Facility (ECF), the Standby Credit Facility (SCF) and the Rapid Credit Facility (RCF). ( )
9. The Board of Governors is responsible for conducting the day-to-day business of the IMF. ( )
10. A member country's quota determines its subscriptions, voting powers as well as the amount of financing it can obtain from the IMF. ( )

II. Translate the following expressions into Chinese.

1. be akin to a world central bank able to create new reserves at will or a more limited borrowing mechanism
2. draft the U. S. blueprint for international access to liquidity
3. be our task to find a common measure, a common standard, a common rule acceptable to each and not irksome to any
4. both debtors and creditors should change their policies
5. to prioritise economic growth, and to provide short-term capital to aid balance of payments
6. to promote and implement policy that reduces the frequency of crises among the emerging market countries
7. this standard is increasingly being questioned for these two posts may soon open up to include other qualified candidates from any part of the world
8. is assigned a quota, based broadly on its relative size in the world economy
9. must pay its subscription in full upon joining the IMF
10. the number of basic votes attributed to each member

III. Translate the following passages into Chinese.

1. The IMF tracks global economic trends and performance, alerts its member countries when it sees problems on the horizon, provides a forum for policy dialogue, and passes on know-how to governments on how to tackle economic difficulties.
2. Keynes' proposals would have established a world reserve currency (which he thought might be called "bancor") administered by a central bank vested with the possibility of creating money and with the authority to take actions on a much larger scale

(understandable considering deflationary problems in Britain at the time).

3. Such market imperfections, together with balance of payments financing, provide the justification for official financing, without which many countries could only correct large external payment imbalances through measures with adverse effects on both national and international economic prosperity.

4. The Board of Governors, the highest decision-making body of the IMF, consists of one governor and one alternate governor for each member country. The governor is appointed by the member country and is usually the minister of finance or the governor of the central bank.

Ⅳ. **Read the passage and choose the correct answer.**

A year ago, Brazil, Russia, India and China were the darlings of the world economy. Today, Brazil is barely growing, Russia is struggling and India and China are on course for their lowest growth in a decade. Although they are as different as they are similar, all four of the original Bric countries(金砖国家) have contrived to stumble(蹒跚而行) simultaneously. The lessons are that microeconomics can matter as much as macroeconomics—and that belonging to a prestigious economic club is hazardous.

The Brics, and emerging economies generally, deserve enormous credit for their macroeconomic management. In the 1970s and 1980s, one in two emerging and developing economies had double-digit(两位数的) inflation. Today, fewer than one in five do. As recently as the 1990s, the median emerging economy had public debt to gross domestic product of more than 65 per cent. In the past two years, the median has been below 40 per cent. Add in bulging foreign exchange reserves, debt denominated in domestic currency(本国货币) rather than dollars and (with China the big exception) flexible exchange rates, and the hype surrounding emerging economies seems almost reasonable.

Since the emerging market crises of 1997-2002, these strong macro foundations have delivered extraordinary performance.

When the global financial crisis hit, emerging economies' budget deficits(预算赤字) were small so the fiscal counterattack could be forceful. Inflation was quiescent(静止的) so credit could be eased safely. In the 1990s, emerging economies that cut interest rates were punished with capital flight and currency collapse, triggering the bankruptcy of businesses with debts in dollars. This time, ample foreign exchange reserves offset capital flight and the shift away from dollar borrowing insured companies against depreciation.

That is the good news. But, as the rich world discovered in the wake of its own "Great Moderation"(大缓和), resilient growth encourages complacency. In the US, households borrowed too much and regulators grew indulgent. In Europe, this pattern was amplified by the "club effect" of euro membership. Countries that had tightened their belts to meet the criteria for accession went soft once they were admitted. With cheap foreign capital buoying living standards, there was no will to fix microeconomic problems such as sclerotic(僵化的) labor markets.

The Brics are following a version of this playbook. Macroeconomic management remains credible. China, in particular, has dramatically cut export dependence without suffering a hard landing(硬着陆). But macro success has bred micro complacency. Governments have permitted themselves to meddle(干预) destructively in markets. State companies have been allowed to stifle innovative competitors. The upshot is that the resilience of the Brics in the face of the 2008 financial shock has not been matched by resilience to an extended period of weak global demand.

Consider Brazil. It boasts moderate inflation, sober public finances and a partially flexible exchange rate. Its central bank has tried to revive growth by reducing its lending rate by 525 basis points(一个基点为万分之一,525个基点也就是5.25%) over the past 16 months. But growth this year will come in at barely more than 1 per cent because a blizzard of micro meddling has damaged business confidence. Petrobras(巴西石油公司), the state oil company that accounts for a 10th of the economy, epitomises(成为……的缩影) this malady. Despite the discovery in 2007 of lucrative(有利可图的,赚钱的) offshore oil, it is losing money because of local content rules and irrational fixed prices.

The story is similar in Russia. The current account is in surplus, inflation is modest and the budget is in balance. But microeconomic policy is lousy(差劲的,极坏的). Corruption deters investors. State companies elbow out private ones. Plans to diversify the economy have been a failure. Instead of building manufacturing exports, Russia is exporting skilled workers.

In some ways India is the odd one out(格格不入): it runs a chronic budget deficit but shares the microeconomic weaknesses of its brethren(兄弟,同胞). Corruption is pervasive and dysfunctional regulation inflicted blackouts on 600m consumers in the summer. Supply side rigidities handicap India's economy so thoroughly that stimulus quickly causes inflation, which is close to 10 per cent. Last year the IMF projected India could sustain growth of 8.1 per cent per year. This year that has been revised to 6.9 per cent.

The IMF's estimate of trend growth in China has come down from 9.5 per cent to 8.5 per cent. As elsewhere, corruption and distorted prices are the key challenges. State-owned companies account for more than half the capitalisation of the stock market. They hog subsidised credit, hire the best graduates and lobby fiercely against deregulation. Li Keqiang, the incoming premier, recently said that China had used up its "demographic dividend"(人口红利) of plentiful labor and would now have to rely on a "reform dividend". But China has yet to act accordingly.

For all their macroeconomic resilience, the business climate in the Brics is unreliable. In the World Bank's Doing Business rankings, China comes in a shameful 91st, Russia 112th, Brazil 130th and India 132nd. By contrast, Rwanda, Oman, Colombia and Kazakhstan are all in the top 60. The Rocks(石头国家) could teach the Brics how to regain momentum(动力).

(*December* 5, 2012 *Financial Times*)

Part II ORGANIZATIONS

( )1. "The Brics... deserve enormous credit for their macroeconomic management". This can be supported by?
   A. Inflation went down.
   B. Public debt to GDP ratio went down.
   C. Foreign exchange reserves grew.
   D. All of above.

( )2. For some European countries, the "club effect" is harmful in what way?
   A. Fosters economic growth and standard of living.
   B. Encourages foreign capital inflows.
   C. They are less willing to reform their labor market.
   D. Their once prudent fiscal policies became extravagant.

( )3. What are the similarities of the four BRIC countries?
   A. Government's meddling destructively in markets.
   B. Corruption deters investors.
   C. Skilled workers fleeing out of the country.
   D. Having used up "demographic dividend".

( )4. What is true about the state companies in BRIC?
   A. The state oil company accounts for 1/10 of the economy.
   B. Russian state companies elbow out private ones.
   C. Chinese state companies enjoy privileges of all kinds and lobby for maintaining them.
   D. All of above.

FURTHER READING

PROMOTING A MORE SECURE AND STABLE GLOBAL ECONOMY
—IMF ANNUAL REPORT 2013 (Overview)

The period from May 2012 through April 2013—the IMF's financial year 2013—saw the world dealing with the prolonged effects of a global crisis that had persisted well beyond initial expectations in an atmosphere of heightened global change. With economic activity remaining weak and the potential for renewed stresses still high, efforts to advance global stability and a secure future were as essential as ever.

In her Global Policy Agenda, the IMF's Managing Director charted a set of actions needed across the membership to secure the recovery and to lay the foundation for a more robust global financial architecture, and detailed the institution's role in assisting the membership with these formidable tasks.

Through assessments in its various multilateral and bilateral surveillance products and active engagement with its 188 member countries via policy and financial support and capacity development, the IMF continued to assist members in identifying systemic risks and designing strong policies to respond to threats to domestic and global stability.

THE GLOBAL ECONOMY

Although economic activity showed signs of stabilizing in advanced economies during the year and even accelerated somewhat in emerging market economies, it was clear that continued turbulence was likely, at least in the near term.

Serious threats to global recovery during the year—faltering market confidence in Europe, the looming fiscal cliff in the United States—were averted(避开,防止), and financial stability grew stronger, but growth prospects remained stubbornly low, and a multiple-speed recovery emerged that threatened global recovery in an increasingly interconnected world.

SURVEILLANCE

Following its comprehensive Triennial Surveillance Review in 2011, the IMF took steps during the year to reform its surveillance along the lines of the priorities identified in that review. It published a pilot report on the external sector, presenting a combination of multilateral and bilateral perspectives. Perhaps most significantly, the institution adopted a Decision on Bilateral and Multilateral Surveillance with the objective of better integrating IMF monitoring of the global economy with its oversight over individual countries. It also adopted a strategy for financial surveillance aimed at improving risk identification, developing better instruments to support integrated policy response to risks, and increasing engagement with stakeholders to improve impact.

FINANCING

With the ongoing crisis, financing remained an important mode of IMF support for its members. The Executive Board approved five arrangements under the IMF's nonconcessional financing facilities during the year, two fewer than in the previous year.

Successor arrangements under the Flexible Credit Line for Mexico and Poland accounted for the vast majority of the amount committed, and a sizable percentage of the amount disbursed went to three euro area countries with IMF programs.

The IMF continued its support to low-income member countries under the Poverty Reduction and Growth Trust (PRGT), with 9 new or augmented arrangements approved during the year, down from 20 the year before. The total number of countries supported under the PRGT changed little, however, with 62 countries (compared with the prior year's 64) having outstanding concessional financing as of the end of the year.

POLICY AGENDA

With endorsement from the International Monetary and Financial Committee (IMFC), the institution's policy work for the year reflected the priority areas identified in the Managing Director's Global Policy Agenda. In addition to short-term policy actions required to move the global economy from stabilization to growth, the focus of policy priorities needed over the medium term was on four areas. In the area of jobs and growth, analytical and operational considerations for the IMF, as well as fiscal policy and employment in advanced and emerging market economies, were examined. Work regarding debt sustainability spanned countries at all income levels. A review of the IMF's framework for assessing debt sustainability recommended changes to promote more uniform outcomes. A new Guidance Note on Public Debt Sustainability Analysis for Market Access Countries introduced a differentiated risk-based approach. Work toward strengthening financial systems included assessing work on the key attributes of effective resolution regimes and revising the IMF's Guidelines for Foreign Exchange Reserve Management. Finally, in the area of global analysis and spillovers, the IMF followed the previous year's pilot Spillover Reports for five systemic economies with a consolidated report on these same economies. It also approved an institutional view on liberalization and management of capital flows that will inform both its policy advice and its assessments of member policies.

CAPACITY DEVELOPMENT

As the year began, two existing IMF units were merged into the new Institute for Capacity Development, as part of a strategic approach to this core area of IMF activity. Significant accomplishments in the institute's first year included an agreement to establish a regional training center in Mauritius, key preparatory work for the opening of a new regional technical assistance center in West Africa, and a seminar celebrating the twentieth anniversary of the Joint Vienna Institute. The majority of technical assistance continued to be provided to the IMF's low-and middle-income members. Demand for IMF training programs, supported by external donors and training partners, remained robust, with the IMF's middle-income members the primary beneficiaries.

RESOURCES

Ensuring adequate resources to support members' financing needs has been a priority since the onset of the crisis. During the year, the Executive Board approved the modalities for bilateral borrowing from member countries to supplement quota resources and the institution's standing borrowing arrangements; as of the end of April 2013, 38 countries had made commitments to provide resources through this avenue, and 25 bilateral agreements had been approved by the Executive Board. Fourteen members had signed separate bilateral borrowing agreements specifically to support the IMF's concessional financing. To alleviate concerns that concessional financing needs might exceed capacity, the institution took steps to make that financing more sustainable over the long haul. The Board approved the use of the remaining portion of the windfall profits from the IMF's 2009—10 gold sales to bolster PRGT subsidy resources. It also endorsed a three-pillar strategy for PRGT sustainability that includes a base envelope of resources, contingent measures to cover needs that exceed that envelope, and a principle of self-sustainability for future modifications to the concessional financing architecture.

A CHANGING IMF

Efforts have been underway for some time to ensure that the IMF remains responsive to the changing needs of its members and reflects the rapid evolution of the global economy in the aftermath of the crisis. A change in the institution's quota and governance structure agreed to in December 2010 awaits completion by the membership of the necessary steps for implementation; it would double quotas and shift quota shares substantially in the direction of emerging market economies and developing countries, and institute an all-elected Executive Board. In addition, as part of these reforms, a comprehensive review of the formula for calculating members' quotas was undertaken during the year, and its outcome was reported to the Board of Governors.

(*FROM*: http://www.imf.org/external/pubs/ft/ar/2013/eng/index.htm)

Part II　ORGANIZATIONS

CHAPTER 5
THE WORLD BANK

Learning Objectives

1. History and leadership of the World Bank;
2. Voting Power;
3. Goals;
4. Criticism.

　　The World Bank is a United Nations international financial institution that provides loans to developing countries for capital programs. The World Bank is a component of the World Bank Group, and a member of the United Nations Development Group. The World Bank's official goal is the reduction of poverty.

　　The World Bank should not be confused with the World Bank Group, a family of five international organizations that make leveraged loans to poor countries:

The World Bank Group headquarters bldg. in Washington, D. C.

International Bank for Reconstruction and Development (IBRD)

International Development Association (IDA)

International Finance Corporation (IFC)

Multilateral Investment Guarantee Agency (MIGA)

International Centre for Settlement of Investment Disputes (ICSID)

History

The World Bank was created at the 1944 Bretton Woods Conference, along with three other institutions, including the International Monetary Fund (IMF). The World Bank and the IMF are both based in Washington, D. C. , and work closely with each other.

Although many countries were represented at the Bretton Woods Conference, the United States and United Kingdom were the most powerful in attendance and dominated the negotiations.

1944—1968

Before 1968, the reconstruction and development loans provided by the World Bank were relatively small. The Bank's staff was aware of the need to instill confidence in the bank. Fiscal conservatism ruled, and loan applications had to meet strict criteria. The first country to receive a World Bank loan was France. The Bank's president at the time, John McCloy, chose France over two other applicants, Poland and Chile. The loan was for US $250 million, half the amount requested, and it came with strict conditions.

When the Marshall Plan went into effect in 1947, many European countries began receiving aid from other sources. Faced with this competition, the World Bank shifted its focus to non-European countries. Until 1968, its loans were earmarked for the construction of income-producing infrastructure, such as seaports, highway systems, and power plants that would generate enough income to enable a borrower country to repay the loan.

1968—1980

From 1968 to 1980, the bank concentrated on meeting the basic needs of people in the developing world. The size and number of loans to borrowers was greatly increased as loan targets expanded from infrastructure into social services and other sectors.

These changes can be attributed to Robert McNamara who was appointed to the presidency in 1968 by Lyndon B. Johnson. McNamara imported a technocratic managerial style to the Bank that he had used as United States Secretary of Defense and President of the Ford Motor Company. McNamara shifted bank policy toward measures such as building schools and hospitals, improving literacy and agricultural reform. McNamara created a new system of gathering information from potential borrower nations that enabled the bank to process loan applications much faster. To finance more loans, McNamara told bank treasurer Eugene Rotberg to seek out new sources of capital outside of the northern banks that had been the primary sources of bank funding. Rotberg used the global bond market to increase the capital available to the bank. One consequence of the period of poverty alleviation lending was the rapid rise of third world debt. From 1976 to 1980 developing world debt rose at an average annual rate of 20%.

1980—1989

In 1980, McNamara was succeeded by US President Jimmy Carter's nominee, A. W. Clausen. Clausen replaced many members of McNamara's staff and instituted a new ideological focus. His 1982 decision to replace the bank's Chief Economist, Hollis B. Chenery, with Anne Krueger was an indication of this new focus. Krueger was known for her criticism of development funding and for describing Third World governments as "rent-seeking states."

During the 1980s, the bank emphasized lending to service Third-World debt, and structural adjustment policies designed to streamline the economies of developing nations. UNICEF reported in the late 1980s that the structural adjustment programs of the World Bank had been responsible for "reduced health, nutritional and educational levels for tens of millions of children in Asia, Latin America, and Africa".

1989—present

Beginning in 1989, in response to harsh criticism from many groups, the bank began including environmental groups and NGOs in its loans to mitigate the past effects of its development policies that had prompted the criticism. It also formed an implementing agency, in accordance with the Montreal Protocols, to stop ozone-depletion damage to the Earth's atmosphere by phasing out the use of 95% of ozone-depleting chemicals, with a target date of 2015. Since then, in accordance with its so-called "Six Strategic Themes," the bank has put various additional policies into effect to preserve the environment while promoting development. For example, in 1991, the bank announced that to protect against deforestation, especially in the Amazon, it would not finance any commercial logging or infrastructure projects that harm the environment.

In order to promote global public goods, the World Bank tries to control communicable disease such as malaria, delivering vaccines to several parts of the world and joining combat forces. In 2000, the bank announced a "war on AIDS", and in 2011, the Bank joined the Stop Tuberculosis Partnership.

Leadership

The World Bank is like a cooperative, made up of 188 member countries. These member countries, or shareholders, are represented by a Board of Governors, who are the ultimate policymakers at the World Bank. Generally, the governors are member countries' ministers of finance or ministers of development. They meet once a year at the Annual Meetings of the Boards of Governors of the World Bank Group and the International Monetary Fund.

The governors delegate specific duties to 25 Executive Directors, who work on-site at the Bank. The five largest shareholders appoint an executive director, while other member countries are represented by elected executive directors.

Traditionally, based on a tacit understanding between the United States and Europe, the president of the World Bank has always been selected from candidates nominated by the United States. In 2012, for the first time, two non-US citizens were nominated. The current president Jim Yong Kim chairs meetings of the Boards of Directors and is responsible for overall management of the Bank. The President is selected by the Board of Executive Directors for a five-year, renewable term.

The Executive Directors make up the Boards of Directors of the World Bank. They normally meet at least twice a week to oversee the Bank's business, including approval of loans and guarantees, new policies, the administrative budget, country assistance strategies and borrowing and financial decisions.

The World Bank operates day-to-day under the leadership and direction of the president, management and senior staff, and the vice presidents in charge of regions, sectors, networks and functions.

Voting power

In 2010, voting powers at the World Bank were revised to increase the voice of developing countries, notably China. The countries with most voting power are now the United States (15.85%), Japan (6.84%), China (4.42%), Germany (4.00%), the United Kingdom (3.75%), France (3.75%), India (2.91%), Russia (2.77%), Saudi Arabia (2.77%) and Italy (2.64%). Under the changes, known as "Voice Reform—Phase 2", countries other than China that saw significant gains included South Korea, Turkey, Mexico, Singapore, Greece, Brazil, India, and Spain. Most developed countries' voting power was reduced, along with a few poor countries such as Nigeria. The voting powers of the United States, Russia and Saudi Arabia were unchanged.

The changes were brought about with the goal of making voting more universal in regards to standards, rule-based with objective indicators, and transparent among other things. Now, developing countries have an increased voice in the "Pool Model," backed especially by Europe. Additionally, voting power is based on economic size in addition to International Development Association contributions.

Goals

Although poverty has declined rapidly over the past three decades, humanity still faces urgent and complex challenges. More than 1 billion people worldwide still live in destitution, a state of affairs that is morally unacceptable given the resources and the technology available today. Moreover, rising inequality and social exclusion seem to accompany the rising prosperity in many countries. Under these circumstances, the World Bank Group's overarching mission of a world free of poverty is as relevant today as it has ever been.

The World Bank Group has established ambitious but achievable goals to anchor its overarching mission and to galvanize international and national efforts in this endeavor. Accordingly, the institution will strive to (ⅰ) end extreme poverty at the global level within a generation and (ⅱ) promote what may be called "shared prosperity": a sustainable increase in the well-being of the poorer segments of society. This second goal reflects the fact that all countries aspire to rapid and sustained increases in living standards for all of their citizens, not just the already privileged. These two goals and their respective indicators can be summarized as:

(ⅰ) End extreme poverty: the percentage of people living with less than $1.25 a day to fall to no more than 3 percent globally by 2030;

(ⅱ) Promote shared prosperity: foster income growth of the bottom 40 percent of the population in every country.

Ending extreme poverty within a generation and promoting shared prosperity must be achieved in such a way as to be sustainable over time and across generations. This requires promoting environmental, social, and fiscal sustainability. Efforts are needed to secure the long-term future of our planet and its resources so future generations do not find themselves in a wasteland. The Bank also must aim for sustained social inclusion and limit the size of economic debt inherited by future generations.

Ending poverty and promoting shared prosperity are unequivocally also about progress in non-monetary dimensions of welfare including education, health, nutrition, and access to essential infrastructure, as well as about enhancing voice and participation of all segments of society in economic, social, and political spheres.

Ending extreme poverty

Ending extreme poverty is a moral imperative and arguably one of the most compelling challenges facing the development community. A target date is set for reaching an extreme poverty rate of no more than 3 percent in 2030, using the internationally established measure of the proportion of people living on less than $1.25 a day.

While representing a very frugal threshold, the $1.25 standard is well-accepted in the development community as one of the Millennium Development Goals, and it would allow the World Bank Group to focus its central mission in measurable, intuitive, and transparent terms.

Reaching the target, which would effectively end extreme poverty globally in less than a generation, is an ambitious endeavor. It will require sustaining high rates of economic growth across the developing world, as well as translating growth more effectively into poverty reduction in each developing country. Reaching the target also requires governance, institutional, and social policy changes not seen yet in many poor countries, and hence enormous efforts from national governments and the international community.

Increasing the welfare of the poor in low-income countries will require complex institutional and governance reforms that enhance the accountability of the state, raise the quality of service delivery, and improve the overall economic and social environment.

Promoting shared prosperity

The World Bank Group's mission of a world free of poverty involves a continuing commitment to increasing the welfare of the poor and vulnerable in every country. Ending extreme poverty wherever it exists is a priority. However, its mission is not just about the poorest developing countries, but about poor people everywhere. Judged by the standards of each society, significant levels of poverty remain in most developing countries and must be addressed if societies are to achieve the stability and well-being to which they aspire.

Raising the incomes of the poor in every country means ensuring that rising prosperity benefits the less well-off. The World Bank Group and the development community as a whole have a responsibility toward them. While shared prosperity requires the pursuit of rapid and sustained expansion of the economy, any type of growth will not suffice. What is needed is sustainable growth that achieves the maximum possible increase in living standards of the less well-off.

Two elements are central to the notion of shared prosperity: a growing economy and a fundamental concern for equity. Sustained growth is necessary; without it, the less well-off are unlikely to increase their living standards to long run. But improvement in the indicator requires growth to be inclusive, which in turn calls for a social contract within each country demanding that the poor be a priority in the policy environment that supports the growth process.

Shared prosperity, understood in this way, is not an agenda of redistributing an economic pie of a fixed size. Rather, it means expanding the size of the pie continuously and sharing it in such a way that the welfare of those at the lower end of the income distribution rises as quickly as possible. It also requires that progress is sustainable over time and across generations, in terms of the environment, social inclusion, and fiscal prudence.

Sustainability

Sustainability is an overarching theme that frames both goals of the World Bank Group. These goals must be achieved in an environmentally, socially, and fiscally sustainable manner. A sustainable path of development and poverty reduction would be one that: (i) manages the resources of our planet for future generations, (ii) ensures social inclusion, and (iii) adopts fiscally responsible policies that limit future debt burden.

Economic growth, which is critical to continuing the process of poverty reduction, has to be compatible with the limits imposed by the resources of the planet. The past two decades have seen a significant toll on the environment. For example, an estimated 5.2 million hectares of forest were lost annually between 2000 and 2010. More than 550 billion tons of CO_2 have been emitted globally between 2000 and 2010—leading to increased global temperatures and more frequent and intense floods, droughts, and storm surges. Air pollution is a major problem in almost all megacities of the developing world, and 87 percent of the world's ocean fisheries are over-exploited or depleted.

Continuing along such a path will threaten the long-term future of the planet and its resources, and, of course, the process of economic growth and poverty reduction itself. There are signs of this happening already. Unsustainable management of ecosystems has disproportionate impact on the poor, since the poor are often more dependent on ecosystems and the goods and services they provide. Poor people are always the least able to protect their children from the harmful impacts of pollution on health and educational outcomes, the accumulated impacts of which reduce earnings and quality of life across generations. Water and land constraints are already affecting poverty. Some 28 percent of the world's population today lives in areas of high water stress, and a full quarter of the world's agricultural land is degraded, thus compromising the ability of those who farm these lands to aspire to prosperity.

The adverse impacts of climate change are also likely to fall disproportionally on the poorest countries that have the least economic, institutional, and technical capacity to cope and adapt, and on the poorest people within countries. For example, recent projections suggest that the poor are especially sensitive to increased drought intensity in a warming world, especially in Sub-Saharan Africa and South Asia.

The World Bank Group recognizes that green growth offers the only way of reconciling the rapid economic development required to reduce poverty and boost shared prosperity with the imperative of a better-managed environment. The recent report Inclusive Green Growth: The Pathway to Sustainable Development articulates the bank's commitment to supporting sustainable growth that is efficient and takes into account the social costs of resource depletion.

Criticism

The World Bank has long been criticized by non-governmental organizations, including its former Chief Economist Joseph Stiglitz, Henry Hazlitt and Ludwig Von Mises. Henry Hazlitt argued that the World Bank along with the monetary system it was designed within would promote world inflation and "a world in which international trade is State-dominated" when they were being advocated. Stiglitz argued that the so-called free market reform policies which the Bank advocates are often harmful to economic development if implemented badly, too quickly ("shock therapy"), in the wrong sequence or in weak, uncompetitive economies.

One of the strongest criticisms of the World Bank has been the way in which it is governed. While the World Bank represents 188 countries, it is run by a small number of economically powerful countries. These countries (which also provide most of the institution's funding) choose the leadership and senior management of the World Bank, and so their interests dominate the bank.

In the 1990s, the World Bank and the IMF forged the Washington Consensus, policies which included deregulation and liberalization of markets, privatization and the downscaling of government. Though the Washington Consensus was conceived as a policy that would best promote development, it was criticized for ignoring equity, employment and how reforms like privatization were carried out. Joseph Stiglitz argued that the Washington Consensus placed too much emphasis on the growth of GDP, and not enough on the permanence of growth or on whether growth contributed to better living standards.

United States Senate Committee on Foreign Relations report criticized the World Bank and other international financial institutions for focusing too much "on issuing loans rather than on achieving concrete development results within a finite period of time" and called on the institution to "strengthen anti-corruption efforts".

Criticism of the World Bank often takes the form of protesting as seen in recent events such as the World Bank Oslo 2002 Protests, the October Rebellion, and the Battle of Seattle. Such demonstrations have occurred all over the world, even amongst the Brazilian Kayapo people.

Another source of criticism has been the tradition of having an American head the bank, implemented because the United States provides the majority of World Bank funding. "When economists from the World Bank visit poor countries to dispense cash and advice," observed The Economist in 2012, "they routinely tell governments to reject cronyism and fill each important job with the best candidate available. It is good advice. The World Bank should take it."

Structural adjustment

The effect of structural adjustment policies on poor countries has been one of the most significant criticisms of the World Bank. The 1979 energy crisis plunged many countries into economic crisis. The World Bank responded with structural adjustment loans which distributed aid to struggling countries while enforcing policy changes in order to reduce inflation and fiscal imbalance. Some of these policies included encouraging production, investment and labour-intensive manufacturing, changing real exchange rates and altering the distribution of government resources. Structural adjustment policies were most effective in countries with an institutional framework that allowed these policies to be implemented easily. For some countries, particularly in Sub-Saharan Africa, economic growth regressed and inflation worsened. The alleviation of poverty was not a goal of structural adjustment loans, and the circumstances of the poor often worsened, due to a reduction in social spending and an increase in the price of food, as subsidies were lifted.

By the late 1980s, international organizations began to admit that structural adjustment policies were worsening life for the world's poor. The World Bank changed structural adjustment loans, allowing for social spending to be maintained, and encouraging a slower change to policies such as transfer of subsidies and price rises. In 1999, the World Bank and the IMF introduced the Poverty Reduction Strategy Paper approach to replace structural adjustment loans. The Poverty Reduction Strategy Paper approach has been interpreted as an extension of structural

Part II ORGANIZATIONS

adjustment policies as it continues to reinforce and legitimize global inequities. Neither approach has addressed the inherent flaws within the global economy that contribute to economic and social inequities within developing countries. By reinforcing the relationship between lending and client states, many believe that the World Bank has usurped indebted countries' power to determine their own economic policy.

Fairness of assistance conditions

Some critics are of the opinion that the World Bank Group's loans and aid have unfair conditions attached to them that reflect the interests, financial power and political doctrines (notably the Washington Consensus) of the Bank and, by extension, the countries that are most influential within it. Amongst other allegations, Klein says the Group's credibility was damaged "when it forced school fees on students in Ghana in exchange for a loan; when it demanded that Tanzania privatise its water system; when it made telecom privatisation a condition of aid for Hurricane Mitch; when it demanded labour 'flexibility' in Sri Lanka in the aftermath of the Asian tsunami; when it pushed for eliminating food subsidies in post-invasion Iraq."

WORDS AND EXPRESSIONS

- *instill* /ɪnˈstɪl/ v. to put a feeling, idea, or principle gradually into someone's mind, so that it has a strong influence on the way that person thinks or behaves 灌输
- *earmark* /ˈɪəmɑːk/ v. to designate (as funds) for a specific use or owner 指定用途，专款专用，如 money earmarked for education
- *technocratic* /ˌteknəʊˈkrætɪk/ a. of, relating to, or suggestive of a technocrat or a technocracy 技术专家治国论的；技术专家政治论的
- *alleviation* /əˌliːvɪˈeɪʃən/ n. the action of lightening weight, gravity, severity, or pain 缓解，减轻
- *streamline* /ˈstriːmlaɪn/ v. to make something such as a business, organization etc. work more simply and effectively 组织；使合理化；使简单化；重组
- *mitigate* /ˈmɪtɪɡeɪt/ v. to make a situation or the effects of something less unpleasant, harmful, or serious [=alleviate] 缓和，减轻
- *communicable* /kəˈmjuːnɪkəb(ə)l/ a. able to be given from one person to another 传染的
- *tacit* /ˈtæsɪt/ a. understood without being expressed directly 不言而喻的；心照不宣的 tacit understanding 默契
- *destitution* /ˌdestɪˈtjuːʃn/ n. a state of extreme poverty 贫困
- *overarching* /ˌəʊvərˈɑːtʃɪŋ/ a. most important, because of including or affecting all

other areas 首要的；支配一切的
- *anchor* /ˈæŋkə/ *v.* provide with a firm basis or foundation 使固定
- *galvanize* /ˈgælvənaɪz/ *v.* shock or excite (someone) into taking action 刺激
- *foster* /ˈfɒstə/ *v.* encourage the development of (something, especially something desirable) 培养
- *unequivocal* /ʊnɪˈkwɪvəkəl/ *ad.* leaving no doubt; unambiguous 明确的，不含糊的
- *imperative* /ɪmˈperətɪv/ *n.* an essential or urgent thing 需要；命令
- *frugal* /ˈfruːg(ə)l/ *a.* sparing or economical as regards money 节俭的；朴素的；花钱少的
- *well-off* /ˌwelˈɒf/ *a.* wealthy; in a favourable situation or circumstances 手头宽裕的，富有的；走运的，幸运的
- *suffice* /səˈfaɪs/ *v.* be enough or adequate 足够
- *prudence* /ˈpruːd(ə)ns/ *n.* the quality of being careful; cautiousness 谨慎
- *compatible* /kəmˈpætɪb(ə)l/ (of two things) able to exist or occur together without problems or conflict; (of two things) able to have a harmonious relationship; well suited 兼容的；能共处的；可并立的
- *megacity* /ˈmegəsɪtɪ/ *n.* a very large city, typically one with a population of over ten million people 大城市（人口超过1000万的）
- *disproportionate* /dɪsprəˈpɔːʃ(ə)nət/ *a.* too large or too small in comparison with something else 不成比例的
- *degrade* /dɪˈgreɪd/ *v.* lower the character or quality of 贬低；使……降级
- *projection* /prəˈdʒekʃ(ə)n/ *n.* an estimate or forecast of a future situation based on a study of present trends 规划；推测
- *reconcile* /ˈrek(ə)nsaɪl/ *v.* to find a way in which two situations or beliefs that are opposed to each other can agree and exist together 使一致；使和解；调停，调解
- *depletion* /dɪˈpliːʃn/ *n.* reduction in the number or quantity of something 消耗；损耗
- *downscale* /ˈdaʊnskeɪl/ *v.* reduce in size, scale, or extent 缩减规模
- *cronyism* /ˈkrəʊnɪɪz(ə)m/ *n.* the practice of favoring one's close friends, especially in political appointments. 任人唯亲；任用亲信
- *subsidy* /ˈsʌbsɪdɪ/ *n.* a financial aid supplied by a government, as to industry, for reasons of public welfare, the balance of payments, etc; any monetary contribution 补贴；津贴；补贴
- *legitimize* /lɪˈdʒɪtɪmaɪz/ *v.* to make something legal or acceptable 使合法；合理化
- *usurp* /jʊˈzɜːp/ *v.* to take or assume (power, a position, property, rights, etc.) and hold in possession by force or without right 篡夺；夺取；侵占
- *allegation* /æliˈgeɪʃ(ə)n/ *n.* an assertion made with little or no proof 主张，断言

Part II ORGANIZATIONS

BACKGROUND KNOWLEDGE

1 The World Bank Group 世界银行集团

The World Bank Group (WBG) is a family of five international organizations that make leveraged loans to developing countries. The WBG came into formal existence on 27 December, 1945 following international ratification of the Bretton woods Agreements, which emerged from the United Nations Monetary and Financial conference (1—22 July 1944). It is the largest and most famous development bank in the world and is an observer at the United Nations Development Group. The bank is based in Washington, D. C. and provided around $30 billion in loans and assistance to "developing" and transition countries in 2012. The bank's stated mission is to achieve the twin goals of ending extreme poverty and building shared prosperity.

The World Bank's (the IBRD and IDA's) activities are focused on developing countries, in fields such as human development (e. g. education, health), agriculture and rural development (e. g. irrigation and rural services), environmental protection (e. g. pollution reduction, establishing and enforcing regulations), infrastructure (e. g. roads, urban regeneration, and electricity), large industrial construction projects, and governance (e. g. anti-corruption, legal institutions development). The IBRD and IDA provide loans at preferential rates to member countries, as well as grants to the poorest countries. Loans or grants for specific projects are often linked to wider policy changes in the sector or the country's economy as a whole. For example, a loan to improve coastal environmental management may be linked to development of new environmental institutions at national and local levels and the implementation of new regulations to limit pollution, or not, such as in the World Bank financed constructions of paper mills along the Rio Uruguay in 2006.

2 structural adjustment 结构调整

Structural adjustment programs (SAPs) consist of loans provided by the International Monetary Fund (IMF) and the World Bank (WB) to countries that experienced economic crises. The two Bretton Woods Institutions require borrowing countries to implement certain policies in order to obtain new loans (or lower interest rates on existing ones).

SAPs are created with the goal of reducing the borrowing country's fiscal imbalances in the short and medium term or in order to adjust the economy to long-term growth. The bank from which a borrowing country receives its loan depends upon the type of necessity. The IMF usually implements stabilization policies and the WB is in charge of adjustment measures. SAPs are supposed to allow the economies of the developing countries to become more market oriented. This then forces them to concentrate more on trade and production so it can boost their economy.

Since the late 1990s, some proponents of structural adjustment, such as the World Bank, have spoken of "poverty reduction" as a goal. SAPs were often criticized for implementing generic free-market policy and for their lack of involvement from the borrowing country. To increase the borrowing country's involvement, developing countries are now encouraged to draw up Poverty Reduction Strategy Papers (PRSPs), which essentially take the place of SAPs.

3 Millennium Development Goals 新千年发展目标

The Millennium Development Goals (MDGs) are eight international development goals that were established following the Millennium Summit of the United Nations in 2000, following the adoption of the United Nations Millennium Declaration. All 189 United Nations member states at the time (there are 193 currently), and at least 23 international organizations, committed to help achieve the following Millennium Development Goals by 2015:

(1) To eradicate extreme poverty and hunger
(2) To achieve universal primary education
(3) To promote gender equality and empower women
(4) To reduce child mortality
(5) To improve maternal health
(6) To combat HIV/AIDS, malaria, and other diseases
(7) To ensure environmental sustainability
(8) To develop a global partnership for development.

Each goal has specific targets, and dates for achieving those targets. To accelerate progress, the G8 finance ministers agreed in June 2005 to provide enough funds to the World Bank, the International Monetary Fund (IMF) and the African Development Bank (AfDB) to cancel $40 to $55 billion in debt owed by members of the heavily indebted poor countries (HIPC) to allow them to redirect resources to programs for improving health and education and for alleviating poverty.

Critics of the MDGs complained of a lack of analysis and justification behind the chosen objectives, and the difficulty or lack of measurements for some goals and uneven progress, among others. Although developed countries' aid for achieving the MDGs rose during the challenge period, more than half went for debt relief, with much of the remainder going towards natural disaster relief and military aid, neither of which further development.

As of 2013, progress towards the goals was uneven. Some countries achieved many goals, while others were not on track to realize any. A UN conference in September 2010 reviewed progress to date and concluded with the adoption of a global plan to achieve the eight goals by their target date. New commitments targeted women's and children's health, and new initiatives in the worldwide battle against poverty, hunger and disease.

Among the non-governmental organizations assisting were the United Nations Millennium

Campaign, the Millennium Promise Alliance, Inc., the Global Poverty Project, the Micah Challenge, The Youth in Action EU Programme, "Cartoons in Action" video project and the 8 Visions of Hope global art project.

4 Washington Consensus 华盛顿共识

The term Washington Consensus was coined in 1989 by English economist John Williamson to refer to a set of 10 relatively specific economic policy prescriptions that he considered the "standard" reform package promoted for crisis-wracked developing countries by Washington, D.C.-based institutions such as the International Monetary Fund (IMF), World Bank, and the US Treasury Department.

The prescriptions encompassed policies in such areas as macroeconomic stabilization, economic opening with respect to both trade and investment, and the expansion of market forces within the domestic economy.

The framework included:

- Fiscal discipline—strict criteria for limiting budget deficits
- Public expenditure priorities—moving them away from subsidies and administration towards previously neglected fields with high economic returns
- Tax reform—broadening the tax base and cutting marginal tax rates
- Financial liberalization—interest rates should ideally be market-determined
- Exchange rates—should be managed to induce rapid growth in non-traditional exports
- Trade liberalization
- Increasing foreign direct investment (FDI)—by reducing barriers
- Privatization—state enterprises should be privatized
- Deregulation—abolition of regulations that impede the entry of new firms or restrict competition (except in the areas of safety, environment and finance)
- Secure intellectual property rights (IPR)—without excessive costs and available to the informal sector
- Reduced role for the state.

These ideas proved very controversial, both inside and outside the Bretton Woods Institutions. However, they were implemented through conditionality under International Monetary Fund (IMF) and World Bank guidance. They are now being replaced by a post-Washington consensus.

1 *leveraged loans* 杠杆贷款

In finance, leverage (also known as gearing or levering) refers to the use of borrowed capital for (an investment), expecting the profits made to be greater than the interest payable. Companies usually leverage to increase returns to stock, as this practice can maximize gains (and losses). Financial leverage (FL) takes the form of a loan or other borrowings (debt), the proceeds of which are (re)invested with the intent to earn a greater rate of return than the cost of interest.

"杠杆"在金融界有多重含义,其英文单词的最基本意思是"杠杆作用",通常情况下它指的是利用信贷手段使自己的资本基础扩大,以期获得比所付利息更高的利润。

2 *fiscal conservatism* 财政保守主义

It is a political term used in North America to describe a fiscal policy that advocates a reduction in overall government spending. Fiscal conservatives often consider deficit and national debt reduction as well as balancing the federal budget of paramount importance. Free trade, deregulation of the economy, lower taxes, and other neoliberal policies are also often affiliated with fiscal conservatism.

用来形容主张避免赤字开支(deficit spending)的财政政策。财政保守主义者往往考虑减少整体政府开支和国债,以及最重要的预算平衡(balanced budget)。自由贸易、解除经济管制、低税和其他保守政策也是财政保守主义十分常见的主张。

3 *rent-seeking* 寻租

In economics, rent-seeking is spending wealth on political lobbying to increase one's share of existing wealth without creating wealth. The effects of rent-seeking are reduced economic efficiency through poor allocation of resources, reduced wealth creation, lost government revenue, increased income inequality, and, potentially, national decline. Current studies of rent-seeking focus on the manipulation of regulatory agencies to gain monopolistic advantages in the market while imposing disadvantages on competitors. The term itself derives, however, from the far older practice of gaining a portion of production through ownership or control of land.

经济学中,寻租是指人们把财富花费在政治游说,通过不创造财富而增加某人现有财富的份额。寻租活动的影响将是通过低劣的资源配置,减少经济效益,降低财富创造,失去政府的收入,加大收入不均,而且会有潜在的国家衰落。目前对寻租活动的研究集中于监管机构的操纵,即强令对手处于劣势地位而获得市场中垄断利益。但是,该词本身源自久已存在的通过所有权或者控制土地而获得生产份额的行为。

寻租往往使政府的决策或运作受利益集团或个人的摆布。这些行为有的是非法的,有的合法不合理,往往成为腐败、社会不公和社会动乱之源。

4 *free market* 自由市场

Part Ⅱ　ORGANIZATIONS

It's a market economy based on supply and demand with little or no government control. A completely free market is an idealized form of a market economy where buyers and sellers are allowed to transact freely (i. e. buy/sell/trade) based on a mutual agreement on price without state intervention in the form of taxes, subsidies or regulation.

不受到政府干预和调控的市场,政府对其只行使最低限度的职能,如维护法律制度和保护财产权。在自由市场中,财产权在一个买卖双方都满意的价格进行自由交换。

5　*fiscal imbalance* 财政不平衡

Fiscal imbalance is a mismatch in the revenue powers and expenditure responsibilities of a government. In the literature on fiscal federalism, two types of fiscal imbalances are measured: Vertical Fiscal Imbalance and Horizontal Fiscal Imbalance. When the fiscal imbalance is measured between the two levels of government (Center and States or Provinces) it is called Vertical Fiscal Imbalance. When the fiscal imbalance is measured between the governments at the same level it is called Horizontal Fiscal Imbalance. This imbalance is also known as regional disparity.

财政不平衡是指一个国家在一定时期(通常为一年)财政收支不相等。相关文献把财政不平衡分为两种:纵向财政不平衡与横向财政不平衡。纵向财政不平衡是指上级政府与下级政府(中央政府与州政府或者省政府)的财政收支之间的不平衡;而横向财政不平衡是指同级地方政府之间在收入能力、支出水平以及最终在公共服务能力上所存在的差异,亦叫做地方性不平衡。

EXERCISES

Ⅰ. Decide whether the following statements are true(T) or false(F).

1. The World Bank is an international financial institution that provides leveraged loans to developed countries for capital programs. (　　)
2. World Bank Group comprises IBRD, IDA, IFC, MIGA and ICSID. (　　)
3. The United States and United Kingdom, mainly shaped negotiations at the Bretton Woods Conference. (　　)
4. Bank president John McCloy selected Germany to be the first recipient of World Bank aid. (　　)
5. McNamara imported a technocratic managerial style to the Bank. (　　)
6. Krueger was known for her approval of development funding as well as third world governments as rent-seeking states. (　　)
7. Environmental groups and NGOs are often now integrated into the lending practices of the World Bank. (　　)
8. Voting powers at the World Bank were revised to increase the voice of developing countries, and all developed countries' voting power was reduced. (　　)

9. Ending extreme poverty within a generation and promoting shared prosperity must be achieved in an environmentally, socially, and fiscally sustainable way. ( )
10. Washington Consensus was agreed to be a policy that could best promote world economic development. ( )

Ⅱ. **Translate the following expressions into Chinese.**
1. loan targets expanded from infrastructure into social services and other sectors.
2. gathering information from potential borrower nations that enabled the bank to process loan applications much faster
3. to stop ozone-depletion damage to the Earth's atmosphere by phasing out the use of 95% of ozone-depleting chemicals
4. including approval of loans and guarantees, new policies, the administrative budget, country assistance strategies and borrowing and financial decisions
5. a state of affairs that is morally unacceptable given the resources and the technology available today
6. focus its central mission in measurable, intuitive, and transparent terms
7. a continuing commitment to increasing the welfare of the poor and vulnerable in every country
8. the adverse impacts of climate change are also likely to fall disproportionally on the poorest countries
9. reconciling the rapid economic development required to reduce poverty and boost shared prosperity with the imperative of a better-managed environment
10. distributed aid to struggling countries while enforcing policy changes in order to reduce inflation and fiscal imbalance

Ⅲ. **Translate the following paragraphs into Chinese.**
1. When the Marshall Plan went into effect in 1947, many European countries began receiving aid from other sources. Faced with this competition, the World Bank shifted its focus to non-European countries. Until 1968, its loans were earmarked for the construction of income-producing infrastructure, such as seaports, highway systems, and power plants that would generate enough income to enable a borrower country to repay the loan.
2. During the 1980s, the bank emphasized lending to service Third-World debt, and structural adjustment policies designed to streamline the economies of developing nations. UNICEF reported in the late 1980s that the structural adjustment programs of the World Bank had been responsible for "reduced health, nutritional and educational levels for tens of millions of children in Asia, Latin America, and Africa".
3. Ending poverty and promoting shared prosperity are unequivocally also about progress in non-monetary dimensions of welfare including education, health, nutrition, and access to essential infrastructure, as well as about enhancing voice and participation of all

segments of society in economic, social, and political spheres.
4. Reaching the target, which would effectively end extreme poverty globally in less than a generation, is an ambitious endeavor. It will require sustaining high rates of economic growth across the developing world, as well as translating growth more effectively into poverty reduction in each developing country.

Ⅳ. **Read the passage and answer the questions.**

The 25 resident Executive Directors, representing the 188 World Bank Group member countries, are responsible for the conduct of the World Bank's general operations under delegated powers from the Board of Governors. As provided in the Articles of Agreement, 5 Executive Directors are appointed by each of the five members having the largest number of shares; 20 Executive Directors are elected by other member countries to form constituencies in an election process every two years. The Executive Directors select a President, who serves as Chairman of the Board. The current Board was elected or appointed on November 1, 2012.

Executive Directors fulfill an important role in deciding on the policies that guide the general operations of the Bank and its strategic direction, and they represent member countries' viewpoints on the Bank's role. They consider and decide on proposals made by the President for loans, credits, and guarantees from IBRD and IDA; new policies; and the administrative budget. They also discuss Country Partnership Strategies—the central tool with which management and the Board review and guide the World Bank Group's support for a country's development programs. They are responsible for presenting to the Board of Governors an audit of accounts, an administrative budget, and the annual report on fiscal year results.

Executive Directors serve on one or more standing committees: the Audit Committee, the Budget Committee, the Committee on Development Effectiveness, the Committee on Governance and Administrative Matters, and the Human Resources Committee. These committees help the Board discharge its oversight responsibilities through in-depth examinations of policies and practices. The Executive Directors' Steering Committee plays an important role in preparing the Board's work program.

Directors periodically travel to member countries to gain firsthand knowledge of a country's economic and social challenges, visit project activities financed by the World Bank Group, and discuss with government officials their assessment of the collaboration with the World Bank Group. The stakeholders they meet include government officials, beneficiaries, representatives of nongovernmental organizations, other development partners (including those in the business community), and Bank staff. In 2013, Directors visited countries in southeast Africa and East Asia.

The Board, through its committees, attends to the effectiveness of the World Bank Group's activities by regularly engaging with the independent Inspection Panel and the Independent Evaluation Group—which report directly to the Board—as well as with the Internal Audit Department and the external auditor.

Board Achievements of 2013

Although development challenges persist and the global economy remains fragile, the Bank continues its drive toward ending extreme poverty and pursuing shared prosperity in an environmentally, socially, and economically sustainable manner, which are goals the Executive Directors and Governors recently endorsed. The Executive Directors also engaged with senior management on the upcoming World Bank Group Strategy, which will guide the institution in carrying out these goals. Relatedly, the Board discussed the paper "A Common Vision for the World Bank Group," which the Governors considered at the Spring 2013 Development Committee meeting.

Central to the Board's discussions on achieving the Bank's goals were the themes of jobs, disaster risk, and gender. The jobs theme was covered extensively in the World Bank's flagship report World Development Report 2013: Jobs and its subsequent policy directions. "Managing Disaster Risks for a Resilient Future: The Sendai Report" informed Board conversations on disaster risk issues. Other discussions on the topic of disaster risk included food security concerns; strategies and support for specific natural disasters, such as those in Haiti and Samoa; and the issues raised by the United Nations (UN) Conference on Sustainable Development (Rio +20) and the UN Climate Change Conference in Doha. And the Update on the Implementation of the Gender Equality Agenda at the World Bank Group reported on gender challenges. The Directors also discussed the flagship report Global Monitoring Report 2013: Rural-Urban Dynamics and the Millennium Development Goals. Fragility and conflict-affected economies were at the forefront during discussions of strategies and operations. The Executive Directors look forward to the World Development Report 2014: Risk and Opportunity—Managing Risk for Development, which will be published in time for the Annual Meetings in Washington, DC, in October of this year.

To streamline the Bank Group's operational effectiveness, the Board discussed and approved changes to investment lending policies with the aim of focusing lending on performance and results. It also considered reforms to the procurement framework and greater disclosure of Board records. The Executive Directors endorsed a series of measures to enhance the effectiveness of corporate governance by setting criteria for identifying IBRD/IDA operations for Board discussion and aligning them more closely with corporate priorities. The Board also welcomed the Bank's reengagement with Myanmar after a 25-year absence and with Suriname after a 30-year absence.

The Board approved $31.5 billion in World Bank financial assistance in fiscal 2013, comprising $15.2 billion in IBRD lending and $16.3 billion in IDA support. The Executive Directors also reviewed 22 Country Partnership Strategy products, 21 of which were prepared jointly with the International Finance Corporation (IFC). The Board approved an administrative budget for the World Bank of $1.9 billion for fiscal 2014.

(*FROM*: See worldbank.org/boards.)

1. How were the present Executive Directors as well as the president of the World Bank elected?
2. What are the main duties of the 25 Executive Directors?
3. What achievements has the Board made in 2013?

FURTHER READING

THE WORLD BANK: THE ROLES OF IBRD AND IDA

The World Bank Group comprises the International Bank for Reconstruction and Development (IBRD) and the International Development Association (IDA), which together form the World Bank; the International Finance Corporation (IFC); the Multilateral Investment Guarantee Agency (MIGA); and the International Centre for Settlement of Investment Disputes (ICSID). These institutions work together and complement one another's activities to achieve their shared goals of reducing poverty and improving lives. Collaboration by the affiliates is increasing as the World Bank Group works more closely with the private sector. Each institution discloses its fiscal year highlights in a separate annual report.

The Role of IBRD

This global development cooperative is owned by 188 member countries. IBRD works with its members to achieve equitable and sustainable economic growth in their national economies and to find solutions to pressing regional and global problems in economic development and other important areas, such as environmental sustainability. It pursues its overriding goals—to overcome poverty and improve standards of living—primarily by providing loans, risk management products, and expertise on development-related disciplines and by coordinating responses to regional and global challenges. (See worldbank.org/ibrd.)

IBRD Financial Commitments and Services

New lending commitments by IBRD were $15.2 billion in fiscal 2013 for 92 operations. This volume was higher than the precrisis historical average ($13.5 billion in fiscal 2005—08) but lower than the $20.6 billion in fiscal 2012. Latin America and the Caribbean ($4.8 billion) and Europe and Central Asia ($4.6 billion) received the largest shares of new lending, followed by East Asia and Pacific ($3.7 billion). Commitments to the Middle East and North Africa ($1.8 billion), South Asia ($378 million), and Africa ($42 million) followed. Public Administration, Law, and Justice received the largest commitment ($4.4 billion), followed by Transportation ($2.6 billion), Health and Other Social Services ($1.8 billion), and Finance ($1.6 billion). The theme receiving the highest share of commitments was Financial and Private Sector Development (18 percent), followed by Public Sector Governance (14 percent) and Social Protection and Risk Management (13 percent).

In addition to its lending activities, IBRD offers financial products that allow clients to efficiently fund their development programs and manage risks related to currency and interest rates, commodity prices, and natural disasters. In fiscal 2013, the Bank's Treasury executed U.S. dollar equivalent (USDeq) 4.8 billion in hedging transactions on behalf of member countries, including USDeq 3.7 billion in interest rate hedges, USDeq 82 million in currency hedges (all local currency conversions), and USDeq 1 billion of currency hedges against non-IBRD obligations. It also executed swaps to provide catastrophe risk insurance to five Pacific Island countries and 16 Caribbean nations, and USDeq 878 million in funding and swaps for the International Finance Facility for Immunisation. The Bank's Treasury also served as arranger for the government of Mexico's second MultiCat bond, a three-year, $315 million, multitranche catastrophe bond providing parametric risk insurance coverage against earthquakes and hurricanes.

IBRD Resources

IBRD issues bonds in international capital markets and provides long-term loans to middle-income countries. In fiscal 2013, IBRD raised USDeq 22.1 billion by issuing bonds in 21 currencies. Its standing in the capital markets and its financial strength allowed IBRD to borrow these large volumes on very favorable terms despite volatile market conditions.

The Bank's strength is based on IBRD's robust capital position and shareholder support, as well as on prudent financial policies and practices, which help maintain its AAA credit rating. IBRD's equity comprises primarily paid-in capital and reserves. Under the terms of the general and selective capital increase resolutions approved by the Board of Governors on March 16, 2011, subscribed capital is expected to increase by $86.2 billion, of which $5.1 billion will be paid in over a five-year period. As of June 30, 2013, the cumulative increase in subscribed capital totaled $32.2 billion. Related paid-in amounts in connection with these capital increase resolutions were $1.9 billion.

As a cooperative institution, IBRD seeks not to maximize profit but to earn enough income to ensure its financial strength and sustain its development activities. Of fiscal 2012 allocable net income, the Executive Directors approved the addition of $147 million to the general reserve and recommended to the Board of Governors the transfer of $621 million to IDA and the allocation of $200 million to surplus.

Consistent with IBRD's development mandate, the principal risk it takes is the country credit risk inherent in its portfolio of loans and guarantees. One summary measure of the Bank's risk profile is the ratio of equity to loans, which is closely managed in line with the Bank's financial and risk outlook. This ratio stood at 26.8 percent as of June 30, 2013.

The Role of IDA

The International Development Association (IDA) is the largest multilateral source of concessional financing for the world's poorest countries. Its funding supports countries' efforts to boost economic growth, reduce poverty, and improve the living conditions of the poor. In fiscal 2013, a total of 82 countries were eligible to receive IDA assistance. (See http://www.worldbank.org/ida.)

IDA Financial Commitments

IDA commitments amounted to $16.3 billion in fiscal 2013, including $13.8 billion in credits, $2.5 billion in grants, and $60 million in guarantees. The largest share of resources ($8.2 billion) was committed to Africa. South Asia ($4.1 billion) and East Asia and Pacific ($2.6 billion) also received large shares of committed funding, followed by Europe and Central Asia ($729 million), Latin America and the Caribbean ($435 million), and Middle East and North Africa ($249 million). Vietnam ($2.0 billion) and Bangladesh ($1.6 billion) received the largest shares of committed financing.

Commitments for infrastructure—including the Energy and Mining sector; Transportation; Water, Sanitation, and Flood Protection; and Information and Communications—reached $6.1 billion. Significant support was also committed to the Education sector and Health and Other Social Services (combined $4.2 billion); Public Administration, Law, and Justice ($3.6 billion); and Agriculture ($1.3 billion). The themes receiving the highest share of commitments were Rural Development ($2.9 billion), Human Development ($2.8 billion), and Social Protection and Risk Management ($1.9 billion).

IDA Resources

IDA is financed largely by contributions from partner governments. Additional financing comes from transfers from IBRD's net income, grants from IFC, and borrowers' repayments of earlier IDA credits. Every three years, partner governments and representatives of borrower countries meet to agree on IDA's strategic direction, priorities, and financing for the subsequent three-year implementation period.

IDA Replenishment

Under the 16th replenishment (IDA16), which covers fiscal years 2012—14, total resources (revised to reflect IDA's currency hedging and updated subsequent to the replenishment discussions) amounted to Special Drawing Rights (SDR) 33.9 billion (equivalent to $50.9 billion). This figure includes partner resources of SDR 17.6 billion (equivalent to $26.4 billion) from 51 countries, 7 of which are new contributing partners; partner compensation for debt forgiveness of SDR 3.5 billion (equivalent to $5.3 billion); credit reflows of SDR 8.9 billion (equivalent to $13.4 billion), including reflows from contractual and voluntary acceleration of credit repayments and hardening of the lending terms for IDA's blend and gap borrowers; transfers from within the World Bank Group, including associated investment income of SDR 1.9 billion (equivalent to $2.8 billion); and balances carried forward from prior replenishments of SDR 2.0 billion (equivalent to $2.9 billion). As of June 30, 2013, SDR 19.9 billion (equivalent to $29.9 billion) of the IDA16 envelope had been committed to credits, grants, and guarantees. The U.S. dollar equivalents are based on the reference exchange rate for IDA16, and the amounts are provided for illustrative purposes only because IDA cash flows are hedged to SDRs, the currency in which IDA's commitment authority is recorded.

The overarching theme and main focus of IDA16 is the delivery of development results. Special themes include crisis response, gender, climate change, and fragile and conflict affected situations. IDA16 includes funding for a dedicated Crisis Response Window to help low-income countries deal with the impact of natural disasters and severe economic shocks.

Part Ⅱ ORGANIZATIONS

ASIAN DEVELOPMENT BANK

Learning Objectives

1. Organization of the Asian Development Bank;
2. History of ADB;
3. Lending and Effectiveness.

The Asian Development Bank (ADB) is a regional development bank established on 22 August 1966 to facilitate economic development of countries in Asia. ADB's vision is a region free of poverty. Its mission is to help its developing member countries reduce poverty and improve the quality of life of their citizens. The work of the Asian Development Bank is aimed at improving the welfare of the people in Asia and the Pacific, particularly the 1.7 billion who live on less than $2 a day. Despite many success stories, Asia and the Pacific remains home to two thirds of the world's poor.

From 31 members at its establishment, ADB now has 67 members—of which 48 are from within Asia and the Pacific and 19 outside. ADB was modeled closely on the World Bank, and has a similar weighted voting system where votes are distributed in proportion with member's capital subscriptions.

By the end of 2013, Japan holds the largest proportions of shares at 15.67%. The United States holds 15.56%, China holds 6.47%, India holds 6.36%, and Australia holds 5.81%.

Organization

The highest policy-making body of the bank is the Board of Governors composed of one representative from each member state. The Board of Governors, in turn, elect among themselves the 12 members of the Board of Directors and their deputy. Eight of the 12 members come from regional (Asia-Pacific) members while the others come from non-regional members.

The Board of Governors also elects the bank's President who is the chairperson of the Board of Directors and manages ADB. The president has a term of office lasting five years, and may be reelected. Traditionally, and because Japan is one of the largest shareholders of the bank, the president has always been Japanese.

The most recent president was Takehiko Nakao, who succeeded Haruhiko Kuroda in 2013.

The headquarters of the bank is at 6 ADB Avenue, Mandaluyong City, Metro Manila, Philippines, and it has representative offices around the world. The bank employs 3,051 people, of which 1,463 (48%) are from the Philippines.

History

Origins

ADB was conceived amid the postwar rehabilitation and reconstruction efforts of the early 1960s. The vision was of a financial institution that would be Asian in character and foster economic growth and cooperation in the region—then one of the poorest in the world.

A resolution passed at the first Ministerial Conference on Asian Economic Cooperation held by the United Nations Economic Commission for Asia and the Far East in 1963 set that vision on the way to becoming reality.

The Philippines capital of Manila was chosen to host the new institution—the Asian Development Bank—which opened on 19 December 1966, with 31 members that came together to serve a predominantly agricultural region. Takeshi Watanabe was ADB's first President.

For the rest of the 1960s, ADB focused much of its assistance on food production and rural development. Its operations included ADB's first technical assistance, loans, including a first on concessional terms in 1969, and bond issue in Germany.

1970s

ADB's assistance expanded in the 1970s into education and health, and then to infrastructure and industry. The gradual emergence of Asian economies in the latter part of the decade spurred demand for better infrastructure to support economic growth. ADB focused on improving roads and providing electricity.

When the world suffered its first oil price shock, ADB shifted more of its assistance to support energy projects, especially those promoting the development of domestic energy sources in member countries.

Cofinancing operations began to provide additional resources for ADB projects and programs. ADB first bond issue in Asia—worth $16.7 million and issued in Japan—took place in 1970.

A major landmark was the establishment in 1974 of the Asian Development Fund to provide concessional lending to ADB's poorest members.

At the close of the decade, some Asian economies had improved considerably and graduated from ADB's regular assistance.

1980s

As the region's economy evolved, it became clear that the private sector was an important ally in driving growth. ADB thus in the 1980s made its first direct equity investment and began to use its track record to mobilize additional resources for development from the private sector.

In the wake of the second oil crisis, ADB continued its support to infrastructure development, particularly energy projects. ADB also increased its support to social infrastructure, including gender, microfinance, environmental, education, urban planning, and health issues.

In 1982, ADB opened its first field office—a Resident Mission in Bangladesh—to bring operations closer to their intended beneficiaries. Later in the decade, ADB approved a policy supporting collaboration with nongovernment organizations to address the basic needs of disadvantaged groups in its developing member countries.

1990s

The start of the 1990s saw ADB begin promoting regional cooperation, forging close ties among neighboring countries in the Greater Mekong Subregion.

In 1995, ADB became the first multilateral organization to have a Board-approved governance policy to ensure that development assistance fully benefits the poor. Policies on the inspection function, involuntary resettlement, and indigenous peoples—designed to protect the rights of people affected by a project—were also approved.

ADB's membership, meanwhile, continued to expand with the addition of several Central Asian countries following the end of the Cold War.

In mid-1997, a severe financial crisis hit the region, setting back Asia's spectacular economic gains. ADB responded with projects and programs to strengthen financial sectors and create social safety nets for the poor. ADB approved its largest single loan—a $4 billion emergency loan to the Republic of Korea—and established the Asian Currency Crisis Support Facility to accelerate assistance.

In 1999, recognizing that development was still bypassing so many in the region, ADB adopted poverty reduction as its overarching goal.

Into the 21st century

With the new century, a new focus on helping its developing members achieve the Millennium Development Goals and making development more effective was adopted within ADB.

In 2003, a severe acute respiratory syndrome (SARS) epidemic hit the region, making it clear that fighting infectious diseases requires regional cooperation. ADB began providing support at national and regional levels to help countries more effectively respond to avian influenza and the growing threat of HIV/AIDS.

ADB also had to respond to unprecedented natural disasters, committing more than $850 million for recovery in areas of India, Indonesia, Maldives, and Sri Lanka hit by the December 2004 Asian tsunami. In addition, a $1 billion line of assistance to help victims of the October 2005 earthquake in Pakistan was set up.

In 2008, ADB's Board of Directors approved Strategy 2020: The Long-Term Strategic Framework of the Asian Development Bank 2008-2020, a policy document guiding its operations to 2020.

In 2009, ADB's Board of Governors agreed to triple ADB's capital base from $55 billion to $165 billion, giving it much-needed resources to respond to the global economic crisis. The 200% increase is the largest in ADB's history, and the first since the 1994 100% capital increase.

Lending

The ADB offers "hard" loans from ordinary capital resources (OCR) on commercial terms, and the Asian Development Fund (ADF) affiliated with the ADB extends "soft" loans from special fund resources with concessional conditions. For OCR, members subscribe capital, including paid-in and callable elements, a 50 percent paid-in ratio for the initial subscription, 5 percent for the Third General Capital Increase (GCI) in 1983 and 2 percent for the Fourth General Capital Increase in 1994. The ADB borrows from international capital markets with its capital as guarantee.

In 2009, ADB obtained member-contributions for its Fifth General Capital Increase of 200%, in response to a call by G20 leaders to increase resources of multilateral development banks so as to support growth in developing countries amid the global financial crisis. For 2010 and 2011, a 200% GCI allows lending of $12.5-13.0 billion in 2010 and about $11.0 billion in 2011. With this increase, the bank's capital base has tripled from $55 billion to $165 billion.

Effectiveness

Given ADB's annual lending volume, the return on investment in lesson-learning for operational and developmental impact is likely to be high; maximizing it is a legitimate concern. All projects funded by ADB are evaluated to find out what results are being achieved, what improvements should be considered, and what is being learned.

There are two types of evaluation: independent and self-evaluation. Self-evaluation is conducted by the units responsible for designing and implementing country strategies, programs, projects, or technical assistance activities. It comprises several instruments, including project/program performance reports, midterm review reports, technical assistance or project/program completion reports, and country portfolio reviews. All projects are self-evaluated by the relevant units in a project completion report. ADB's project completion reports are publicly disclosed on ADB's Internet site. Client governments are required to prepare their own project completion reports.

Independent evaluation is a foundation block of organizational learning. It is essential to transfer increased amounts of relevant and high-quality knowledge from experience into the hands of policy makers, designers, and implementers. ADB's Independent Evaluation Department (IED) conducts systematic and impartial assessment of policies, strategies, country programs, and projects, including their design, implementation, results, and associated business processes to determine their relevance, effectiveness, efficiency, and sustainability following prescribed methods and guidelines. It also validates self-evaluations. By this process of evaluation, ADB demonstrates three elements of good governance: accountability, by assessing the effectiveness of ADB's operations; transparency, by independently reviewing operations and publicly reporting findings and recommendations; and improved performance, by helping ADB and its clients learn from experience to enhance ongoing and future operations.

Operations evaluation has changed from the beginnings of evaluation in ADB in 1978. Initially, the focus was on assessing after completion the extent to which projects had achieved their expected economic and social benefits. Operations evaluation now shapes decision making throughout the project cycle and in ADB as a whole. Since the establishment of its independence in 2004, IED reports directly to ADB's Board of Directors through the Board's Development Effectiveness Committee. Behavioral autonomy, avoidance of conflicts of interest, insulation from external influence, and organizational independence have made evaluation a dedicated tool—governed by the principles of usefulness, credibility, transparency, and independence—for greater accountability and making development assistance work better. Independent Evaluation at the Asian Development Bank presents a perspective of evaluation in ADB from the beginnings and looks to a future in which knowledge management plays an increasingly important role.

In recent years, there has been a major shift in the nature of IED's work program from a dominance of evaluations of individual projects to one focusing on broader and more strategic studies. To select priority topics for evaluation studies, IED seeks input from the Development Effectiveness Committee, ADB Management, and the heads of ADB departments and offices. The current thrusts are to improve the quality of evaluations by using more robust methodologies; give priority to country/sector assistance program evaluations; increase the number of joint evaluations; validate self-evaluations to shorten the learning cycle; conduct more rigorous impact evaluations; develop evaluation capacity, both in ADB and in DMCs; promote portfolio performance; evaluate business processes; and disseminate findings and recommendations and ensure their use. IED's work program has also been reinterpreted to emphasize organizational learning in more clearly defined results architecture and results framework. It entails conducting and disseminating strategic evaluations (in consultation with stakeholders), harmonizing performance indicators and evaluation methodologies, and developing capacity in evaluation and evaluative thinking. All evaluation studies are publicly disclosed on IED's website (some evaluations of private sector operations are redacted to protect commercially confidential information). IED's evaluation resources are displayed by resource type, topic, region and country, and date. Learnings are also gathered in an online Evaluation Information System offering a database of lessons, recommendations, and ADB Management responses to these. Details of ongoing evaluations and updates on their progress are made public too.

Of the 1,106 ADB-funded projects evaluated and rated so far (as of December 2007), 65% were assessed as being successful, 27% partly successful and 8% as unsuccessful.

WORDS AND EXPRESSIONS

- *policy-making body* 决策机构
- *term of office* 任期
- *rehabilitation* /ˌriːhəˌbɪlɪˈteɪʃən/ *n.* the action or status of restoring to good condition, operation, or management 复原
- *spur* /spɜː/ *v.* to encourage an activity or development or make it happen faster 激励, 鞭策, 刺激
- *private sector* 私营部门
- *track record* a record of achievements or performance 历史记录
- *in the wake of* as a result of; succeeding; following 作为……的结果;紧紧跟随;随着……而来
- *field office* [管理]外地办事处
- *involuntary resettlement* 非自愿移民
- *indigenous peoples* 土著民族
- *social safety net* 社会保障系统
- *epidemic* /epɪˈdemɪk/ *n.* a temporary prevalence of a disease 传染病
- *avian influenza* 禽流感
- *unprecedented* /ʌnˈpresɪdentɪd/ *a.* without previous instance; never known or experienced before; unexampled or unparalleled 空前的;无前例的
- *affiliate* /əˈfɪlɪeɪt/ *v.* to bring into close association or connection 使附属;使紧密联系
- *paid-in* /pedˈɪn/ *a.* having paid the dues, initiation fees, etc., required by an organization or association 已缴会费的
- *callable* /ˈkɔːləb(ə)l/ *a.* subject to redemption prior to maturity, as a corporate bond;

subject to payment on demand, as money loaned 请求即付的;随时可偿还的
- *General Capital Increase* 总增资
- *legitimate concern* 合法/理关注
- *impartial* /ɪmˈpɑːʃ(ə)l/ *a.* not partial or biased; fair; just 公平的,公正的;不偏不倚的
- *validate* /ˈvælɪdeɪt/ *v.* to make valid, substantiate, confirm; to give legal force to, legalize 证实,验证;确认;使生效
- *good governance* 善治;良好治理
- *insulation* /ɪnsjʊˈleɪʃ(ə)n/ *n.* the state of being insulated 隔离,孤立
- *thrust* /θrʌst/ *n.* a forcible push or shove; the main point, purpose, or essence 推力;要旨
- *disseminate* /dɪˈsemɪneɪt/ *vt.* to spread or disperse (something, especially information) widely 散布,传播(尤指信息)
- *entail* /ɪnˈteɪl/ *v.* to make something necessary, or to involve something 使需要,必需;蕴含
- *redact* /rɪˈdækt/ *v.* to revise, edit; to draw up or frame 编辑;编写

BACKGROUND KNOWLEDGE

1 *Takehiko Nakao* 中尾武彦

Takehiko Nakao is the President of the Asian Development Bank (ADB) and the Chairperson of ADB's Board of Directors. He was elected President by ADB's Board of Governors and assumed office in April 2013.

Before joining ADB, Mr. Nakao was the Vice Minister of Finance for International Affairs at the Ministry of Finance of Japan. In a career spanning more than three decades, Mr. Nakao has gained extensive experience in international finance and development. He has held senior positions in the Ministry of Finance in Japan, which he joined in 1978, including Director-General of the International Bureau, where he fostered close ties with leading figures in the Asia-Pacific region, and G20 nations.

He was assigned as Minister at the Embassy of Japan in Washington D. C., between 2005 and 2007, and from 1994 to 1997 served as economist and advisor at the International Monetary Fund.

Born in 1956, Mr. Nakao holds a Bachelor's degree in Economics from the University of Tokyo and a Master of Business Administration from the University of California, Berkeley.

2 *Mandaluyong City* 曼达卢永市

The City of Mandaluyong (Filipino: Lungsod ng Mandaluyong) is one of the cities and municipalities that comprise Metro Manila in the Philippines. It is bordered on the west by the country's capital, Manila, to the north by San Juan City, to the east by Quezon City and Pasig City, and by Makati City to the south. At present, its nicknames are "Tiger City of the Philippines", "Metro Manila's Heart", and the "Shopping Mall Capital of the Philippines".

Mandaluyong City is located right at the center of Metro Manila. Among the many attractions in the city is the western half of the Ortigas Center, one of the major centers of business and commerce in the metropolis (the eastern half is in Pasig City). Found within the Mandaluyong portion of the Ortigas Center is the main headquarters of the Asian Development Bank, Banco De Oro and the headquarters of San Miguel Corporation, Southeast Asia's largest food and beverage company. One of the most prominent pharmaceutical laboratories and factories, the UniLab, is located here.

3 Metro Manila, also: Metropolitan Manila 马尼拉大都会区

Metro Manila (Filipino: Kalakhang Maynila, Kamaynilaan) or the National Capital Region (NCR) (Filipino: Pambansang Punong Rehiyon) is the greater metropolitan area of the city of Manila, the national capital of the Philippines.

The National Capital Region has a population of 11,855,975 (by the end of the year of 2012), making it the most populous region in the Philippines, as well as the 7th most populous metropolitan area in Asia. Its total urban area, referring to its continuous urban expansion into the provinces of Bulacan, Cavite, Laguna and Batangas has a population of 24,123,000, making it the 11th most populous metropolitan area in the world and the 6th most populous urban area in the world.

The region is the center of culture, economy, education, and government of the Philippines. A global power city, NCR exerts a significant impact upon commerce, finance, media, art, fashion, research, technology, education, and entertainment. It is the home to all the consulates and embassies in the Philippines, thereby making it an important center for international diplomacy in the country.

Its economical power makes the region the country's premier center for finance and commerce. NCR accounts for 37.2% of the gross domestic product of the Philippines.

4 Greater Mekong Subregion 大湄公河次区域

The Greater Mekong Subregion (GMS) comprises Cambodia, the People's Republic of China, Lao People's Democratic Republic, Myanmar, Thailand, and Viet Nam.

In 1992, with ADB's assistance, the six countries entered into a program of subregional economic cooperation, designed to enhance economic relations among the countries.

The program has contributed to the development of infrastructure to enable the development and sharing of the resource base, and promote the freer flow of goods and people in the subregion. It has also led to the international recognition of the subregion as a growth area.

5 *Strategy 2020* 2020 战略

Strategy 2020 is a new long-term strategy for its vision of an Asia and Pacific region free of poverty. To fight poverty in a region of more than 600 million poor people surviving on $1 a day, Strategy 2020 will refocus ADB operations on three development agendas—inclusive economic growth, environmentally sustainable growth, and regional integration.

Strategy 2020 sets ADB's new strategic course, emphasizing that poverty reduction can only be sustained if more people are economically productive, economic growth takes place in a well-managed natural environment, and neighboring economies work within larger and freer markets to achieve shared interests through cooperation.

By 2012, 80% of ADB's lending will be in five core operational areas identified as ADB's comparative strengths—infrastructure, environment, regional cooperation and integration, finance sector development, and education. By 2020, about 50% of operations will be in private sector development and private sector operations, and 30% in regional cooperation and integration. ADB will continue to operate on a more selective basis in health, agriculture, and disaster and emergency assistance.

6 *G20* 20 国集团

The Group of Twenty (also known as the G-20 or G20) is an international forum for the governments and central bank governors from 20 major economies. The members, shown highlighted on the map at right, include 19 individual countries—Argentina, Australia, Brazil, Canada, China, France, Germany, India, Indonesia, Italy, Japan, Mexico, Russia, Saudi Arabia, South Africa, South Korea, Turkey, the United Kingdom and the United States—along with the European Union (EU). The EU is represented by the European Commission and by the European Central Bank.

The G-20 was founded in 1999 with the aim of studying, reviewing, and promoting high-level discussion of policy issues pertaining to the promotion of international financial stability. It seeks to address issues that go beyond the responsibilities of any one organization. Collectively, the G-20 economies account for around 85% of the gross world product (GWP), 80% of world trade (or, if excluding EU intra-trade, 75%), and two-thirds of the world population. The G-20 heads of government or heads of state have periodically conferred at summits since their initial meeting in 2008.

With the G-20 growing in stature after the 2008 Washington summit, its leaders announced on 25 September 2009, that the group would replace the G8 as the main economic council of wealthy nations. Since its inception, the G-20's membership policies have been criticized by numerous intellectuals, and its summits have been a focus for major protests by anti-globalists, nationalists and others.

The heads of the G-20 nations met semi-annually at G-20 summits between 2008 and 2011. Since the November 2011 Cannes summit, all G-20 summits have been held annually. In

December 2014, Turkey took over the presidency of the G-20 from Australia, and will host the group's 2015 summit in Antalya.

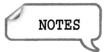

1 *infrastructure* 基础设施

The basic facilities, services, and installations needed for the functioning of a community or society, such as transportation and communications systems, water and power lines, and public institutions including schools, post offices, and prisons. 社会或社区正常运作所需要的基本设施、服务和安装设备等,如交通与通信系统,水与电力供给线,以及学校、邮局和监狱等公共机构。

2 *capital base* 资本基数,资本金基础

The capital acquired during an IPO, or the additional offerings of a company, plus any retained earnings; an initial investment plus subsequent investments made by an investor into their portfolio. 公司通过原始发行和追加发行筹集的资本金以及所有未分配利润;投资者对投资组合的原始投资及后续投资。

3 *hard loan* 硬贷款,条件苛刻的贷款

A foreign loan that must be paid in the currency of a nation that has stability and a reputation abroad for economic strength (a hard currency). 硬贷款是指贷款条件较严,偿还款必须是硬货币的国外贷款,这里硬货币主要指稳定及经济实力强大的国家的货币。

4 *soft loan* 软贷款

A soft loan is a loan with a below-market rate of interest. Sometimes soft loans provide other concessions to borrowers, such as long repayment periods. 软贷款是指利息低于市场利率的贷款,有时软贷款向借款人提供其他优惠,如较长还款期。

5 *return on investment* 投资回报率;投资利润率

The amount of profit, before tax and after depreciation, from an investment made, usually expressed as a percentage of the original total cost invested. 投资利润率是指在税前和折旧后项目的利润总额与总投资的比率,通常以原始投资总成本的百分比表示。

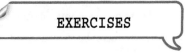

Ⅰ. Decide whether the following statements are true(T) or false(F).

1. Despite many success stories, Africa and the Pacific remains home to two thirds of the world's poor.　　　　　　　　　　　　　　　　　　　　　　　　　　　　(　　)

Part II ORGANIZATIONS

2. The highest policy-making body of ADP is the Board of Directors. (　)
3. ADB was conceived amid the postwar rehabilitation and reconstruction efforts of the early 1970s. (　)
4. In the 1980s, ADB's focus was on improving roads and providing electricity. (　)
5. Strategy 2020 refers to a Long-Term Strategic Framework of the Asian Development Bank, a policy document guiding its operations from 2008 to 2020. (　)
6. The ADB offers soft loans from ordinary capital resources (OCR) on commercial terms. (　)
7. In 2011, the bank's capital base has tripled from $55 billion to $165 billion. (　)
8. Two types of evaluation: independent and self-evaluation are conducted in ADB to find out what results are being achieved and what improvements should be considered. (　)
9. Self-evaluation is essential to transfer increased amounts of relevant and high-quality knowledge from experience into the hands of policy makers, designers, and implementers. (　)
10. There has been a major shift in the nature of IED's work program from a dominance of evaluations of individual projects to one focusing on broader and more strategic studies. (　)

II. **Translate the following expressions into Chinese.**
1. a regional development bank established on 22 August 1966 to facilitate economic development of countries in Asia
2. a financial institution that would be Asian in character and foster economic growth and cooperation in the region
3. to use its track record to mobilize additional resources for development from the private sector
4. a severe financial crisis hit the region, setting back Asia's spectacular economic gains
5. in response to a call by G20 leaders to increase resources of multilateral development banks so as to support growth in developing countries amid the global financial crisis
6. to transfer increased amounts of relevant and high-quality knowledge from experience into the hands of policy makers, designers, and implementers
7. behavioral autonomy, avoidance of conflicts of interest, insulation from external influence, and organizational independence
8. validate self-evaluations to shorten the learning cycle

III. **Translate the following paragraphs into Chinese.**
1. From 31 members at its establishment, ADB now has 67 members—of which 48 are from within Asia and the Pacific and 19 outside. ADB was modeled closely on the World Bank, and has a similar weighted voting system where votes are distributed in

proportion with member's capital subscriptions.

2. ADB's assistance expanded in the 1970s into education and health, and then to infrastructure and industry. The gradual emergence of Asian economies in the latter part of the decade spurred demand for better infrastructure to support economic growth. ADB focused on improving roads and providing electricity.

3. In the wake of the second oil crisis, ADB continued its support to infrastructure development, particularly energy projects. ADB also increased its support to social infrastructure, including gender, microfinance, environmental, education, urban planning, and health issues.

4. For OCR, members subscribe capital, including paid-in and callable elements, a 50 percent paid-in ratio for the initial subscription, 5 percent for the Third General Capital Increase (GCI) in 1983 and 2 percent for the Fourth General Capital Increase in 1994.

5. Self-evaluation is conducted by the units responsible for designing and implementing country strategies, programs, projects, or technical assistance activities. It comprises several instruments, including project/program performance reports, midterm review reports, technical assistance or project/program completion reports, and country portfolio reviews.

6. Operations evaluation has changed from the beginnings of evaluation in ADB in 1978. Initially, the focus was on assessing after completion the extent to which projects had achieved their expected economic and social benefits. Operations evaluation now shapes decision making throughout the project cycle and in ADB as a whole.

IV. Read the passage and choose the correct answer.

The Asian Development Bank says education and health care in South Asia are the worst in the world, except for Sub-Saharan Africa.

The bank says high economic growth in recent years in countries like India, Pakistan and Bangladesh has excluded too many people, and has failed to reduce poverty significantly. A director in ADB's South Asia Department in Manila, Frederick Roche, says the quality of education needs to be improved at all levels, particularly in rural areas.

He says the region is not producing the number of educated people demanded by its growing economies. India, for example has only 12,000 training and vocational institutes, compared to half a million in China.

"The region now stands poised to take advantage for tremendous opportunities for growth," said Roche. "But the educational institutions of secondary and tertiary level in India are not able to produce the number of graduates which the market is presently demanding, and there are deficiencies in vocational and skills training throughout the region."

The report also underlines new health challenges faced by the region. It says the incidence of non-communicable diseases such as diabetes is increasing due to changing lifestyles and urbanization.

Health specialists at the bank say diseases like diabetes are affecting people at a younger age in countries like India than they do in Western countries. They say this could have a serious impact on labor productivity.

The ADB is calling on governments to devote more resources to both education and healthcare.

Frederick Roche says the region has a "window of opportunity" to make sure its working-age population has the skills required by its growing economies.

"If that working-age population has the appropriate human capital, by that I mean not only skills as a result of education, but also physical health and vitality, then you have an opportunity there for an even greater acceleration of growth," he added.

The ADB's concerns about a lack of education have been echoed by India's thriving private sector(私营部门/公司). Businessmen here say they are rapidly running out of people with the right skills and training that are needed if their companies are to grow.

( )1. Which of the following statements is in accordance with the passage?
    A. Education and health care in Sub-Saharan Africa are the worst in the world.
    B. High economic growth in recent years in Pakistan has failed to reduce poverty significantly.
    C. The quality of education in India needs to be improved only in rural areas.
    D. Economic growth in recent years in Bangladesh has included the majority of people.

( )2. India is not producing the number of educated people demanded by _____.
    A. the government   B. the public
    C. its growing economies   D. the ADB

( )3. There are deficiencies in _____ in India.
    A. secondary education   B. colleges and universities
    C. kindergartens   D. vocational and skills training

( )4. The incidence of diabetes in India is increasing due to _____.
    A. infrastructural construction   B. changing lifestyles and urbanization
    C. modernization   D. special lifestyles

( )5. Which of the following statements is incorrect according to the passage?
    A. The ADB is calling on governments to devote more resources to both education and healthcare.
    B. Appropriate human capital of the working-age population in India may bring an opportunity for an even greater acceleration of growth.
    C. Diseases like diabetes are affecting people at a younger age in countries like India than they do in other Asian countries.

D. India's thriving private sector has echoed the ADB's concerns about a lack of education

FURTHER READING

PEOPLE'S REPUBLIC OF CHINA, ASIAN DEVELOPMENT OUTLOOK 2014

Last year saw high and stable economic growth, subdued inflation, and a smaller current account surplus. Slightly lower growth, higher inflation, and a still smaller current account surplus are forecast for 2014 and 2015. Containing credit growth while maintaining growth momentum is one policy challenge, and another to improve income distribution.

Economic performance

After decelerating to 7.6% year on year in the first half of 2013 as domestic demand weakened, GDP growth in the People's Republic of China (PRC) rose to 7.8% in the third quarter following a limited fiscal and monetary stimulus, then moderated slightly to 7.7% in the fourth quarter. Over the full year, GDP grew by 7.7%, the same rate as in 2012 and above the government target of 7.5%.

On the supply side, the service sector expanded by 8.3%, contributing 3.6 percentage points to GDP growth. Providing the impetus to growth in the sector were urbanization, rising household incomes, and the rollout since August 2013 of reforms to taxes on services, which effectively lowered them. Industry (including manufacturing, mining, and construction) grew by 7.8%, driven mainly by infrastructure projects and real estate development. The share of services in GDP rose to 46.1% in 2013 current prices, while that of industry fell to 43.9%. Domestic rebalancing from industry to services has thus continued to gain traction, as planned by the government. As in previous years, the private sector registered higher growth than the public sector. Similarly, growth in the western and central regions, the main beneficiaries of development programs, was higher than in eastern provinces. Monthly data indicate that the growth momentum has weakened in both industry and services since December 2013, most likely owing to monetary tightening and stronger controls on local governments' off-budget spending.

A good harvest brought agricultural growth up to 4.0% in 2013, after a weaker performance in the first 9 months. The grain harvest reached a new peak above 600 million tons, or 442 kilograms of raw grain per capita. This is well above the 400-kilogram benchmark considered sufficient to meet the aspirations of an increasingly affluent population for a more protein-rich diet. However, agricultural growth remained below its 5-year average of 4.5%, and the share of agriculture in GDP slipped to 10.0%.

On the demand side, investment contributed 4.2 percentage points to GDP growth in 2013, up from 3.8 in 2012, and consumption contributed 3.8 percentage points, down from 4.1. Thus no further progress was made toward replacing investment-driven growth with growth driven by consumption. Investment growth was strongest in agriculture, underlining the government's perception of agriculture as the "foundation" of the economy, followed by services and industry. Within industry, investment growth was strongest in infrastructure, followed by manufacturing, utilities, and mining. Real estate investment continued to grow at a very high rate on the back of strong demand. The floor space sold in residential buildings increased by 17.5% year on year, and in commercial buildings by 17.3%. Weaker net exports dragged GDP growth down by 0.3 percentage points.

Monthly figures suggest that investment growth has decelerated sharply since October 2013 while that of retail sales, a proxy for consumption, has been robust. This is good news for domestic rebalancing. Within investment, the picture was mixed, with infrastructure plummeting while manufacturing and real estate performed better. Housing starts posted a rebound in November 2013, as did housing sales.

Consumption was supported by strong income growth in 2013. For the sixth successive year, real per capita income growth for rural households, at 9.3%, exceeded that for urban households, at 7.0%. The income of migrant workers increased even more quickly as demand for their services rose in labor-intensive services and construction. Income distribution improved marginally as the official Gini-coefficient edged down to 0.473 from 0.474 in 2012.

Annual consumer price inflation averaged 2.6% in 2013, the same as in 2012, with fluctuations over the year caused mainly by food price volatility. Nonfood inflation and core inflation (which omits energy as well as food) remained relatively low and stable within a range of 1.6%—1.7%. Average producer price deflation accelerated to 1.9% in 2013 from 1.7% in 2012, reflecting lower commodity prices and overcapacity in domestic industries. This suggests that inflationary pressures within the economy remain modest. Although producer price deflation moderated to 1.4% year on year in December 2013, it reverted to 2.0% in February 2014, casting doubt on the possibility that demand is strengthening or capacity utilization improving.

The official budget deficit for 2013 stood at 1.9% of GDP, slightly higher than in 2012 but within the government target of 2.0%. Revenue growth slowed to 10.1% in 2013, the lowest annual rate since 1991 and only marginally above nominal GDP growth, while expenditure growth moderated to 10.9% in 2013 from 15.3% in 2012. The decline in revenue reflected mainly overdependence on indirect taxes. Value-added, business, and consumption taxes currently bring in over 60% of total tax revenues. Reflecting the higher sensitivity of these taxes to economic up- and down-swings compared with direct taxes, falling import growth suppressed import-related duties and taxes.

A recent audit suggests that the augmented budget deficit, which includes off-budget spending, was higher than officially reported, and the fiscal stance more expansionary. The audit showed local government debt increasing from 26.7% of GDP in 2010 to about 36.0% at the end of June 2013. Most of this debt was borrowed off budget through special financing vehicles because local governments are prohibited from borrowing on budget, despite their expenditure needs substantially exceeding their revenues. The augmented local government debt was partly invested in nonearning infrastructure assets, making it difficult for these governments to meet their debt service burden, which is high for some, particularly in light of maturity mismatches. Deeply indebted governments are now allowed to borrow only to refinance existing liabilities with longer-term loans. As central government debt is still low at 13.6% of GDP, however, consolidated central and local government debt does not appear excessive from an international perspective.

The M2 money supply was growing at 13.6% year on year at the end of 2013. This exceeded the 13.0% target set by the People's Bank of China

(PBOC), the central bank, for 2013, as in the previous years. The ratio of M2 to GDP rose to nearly 200%, which is high for a developing country. Despite efforts to pursue a firmer monetary stance to rein in credit growth and financial risks, which have driven up interbank interest rates since May 2013, credit growth outpaced nominal GDP growth. The root cause of high credit growth in 2013 was an increase in the PBOC's net foreign assets resulting from strong capital inflows, which put upward pressure on the currency. The PBOC had to purchase foreign currency to stem renminbi appreciation, thereby inflating the monetary base and the money supply. The government and banks increased their deposits at the central bank, but this sterilized only about a third of the expansion.

Another factor behind strong money supply growth in 2013 was the difficulty of controlling lending, particularly lending associated with shadow banking. However, some progress was made in the second half of 2013, when tighter interbank market conditions and stricter regulations forced a sharp decline in the issuance of trust loans and bankers' acceptances. This trend continued into 2014, helping to further reduce broad money growth to 13.2% year on year in January 2014.

The trend appreciation of the renminbi vis-à-vis the US dollar continued as capital inflows remained strong except for short interruptions in mid-2013 and early 2014. By December 2013, the renminbi had appreciated by 3.1% year on year against the US dollar. In nominal effective terms, the appreciation was higher at 7.2% because the Japanese yen depreciated early in 2013. In real effective terms, the renminbi appreciated by 7.9% year on year. Real effective appreciation peaked in September 2013 at 9.3% year on year—a magnitude that, if sustained, might be difficult to compensate for through productivity gains. The downward trend since then, resulting mainly from yen stabilization and higher inflation in Japan, is thus good news for the PRC's external competitiveness.

As its foreign trade continued to grow, the PRC replaced the US in 2013 as the largest goods-trading nation. Merchandise export growth was volatile throughout the year but reached 7.8% year on year based on customs statistics, only marginally below the export growth rate in 2012. Export figures since late 2013 do not yet clearly support the view that stronger growth in developed economies translates into higher export demand for the PRC, as export growth was strong in November 2013 and January 2014 but weak in October and December 2013, and even negative in February 2014. Import growth was lower than export growth but more stable. It reached 7.3% for the year as a whole. Therefore, the trade surplus rose to $261 billion, 12.3% higher than in 2012, but remained unchanged as a percentage of GDP at 2.8%.

The improved trade balance and lower deficit in the income account were offset by an expanding deficit in the service account and a small deficit in net transfers. The current account surplus thus narrowed to $188.7 billion or 2.1% of GDP from $193.1 billion or 2.3% of GDP in 2012. In contrast, the financial and capital accounts closed with a large surplus of $262.7 billion in 2013, following a deficit of $16.8 billion in 2012. This impressive turnaround came mainly from strong net inflows of portfolio investment in 2013, particularly in the first and fourth quarters, following strong net outflows in 2012. Gross inflows of foreign direct investment also increased in 2013, by 5.3% to $117.6 billion according to the Ministry of Commerce, but the PRC's direct investment abroad rose more quickly, recording 17.3% expansion to reach $87.8 billion. This means that net foreign direct investment inflows may well have declined, but the balance of payment figures to confirm this have yet to be disclosed. The overall balance of payments surplus increased fourfold over 2012, boosting official reserves by $510 billion to nearly $4 trillion.

Economic prospects

GDP growth is projected to decelerate somewhat to 7.5% in 2014, which is the official target, and 7.4% in 2015. Slightly weaker growth momentum from the fourth quarter of 2013 is carrying over into 2014. Support for growth over the forecast period should come from more equitable income growth and higher social spending in line with government objectives, which will sustain growth in consumption. GDP growth should also benefit from the upturn in developed countries, which should sooner or later generate stronger demand for PRC exports despite continuing real renminbi appreciation and higher unit labor costs.

Investment growth, on the other hand, will likely decelerate as the government tries to rein in high credit growth, reduce industrial overcapacity, and bring local government debt under control. These efforts are already forcing many local governments to adjust their investment targets for 2014. Other structural reforms outlined at the Third Plenary Session of the 18th Central Committee of the Communist Party of the PRC in November 2013 may also weigh on headline growth: state-owned enterprise reform, higher prices and/or taxes for primary resources, and a change in how senior local government officials are evaluated that depends less on economic growth. However, such reforms have the potential to improve the quality of growth and ensure its long-term sustainability. The government has announced that it will try to prevent a sharp downturn to avoid social problems, implying that reforms will be rolled out over longer periods. Therefore, GDP growth is forecast to decelerate slowly over several years before it stabilizes or rises again.

Inflation is forecast to remain subdued at 2.6% on average in 2014, below the government target of 3.5%, as moderating GDP and credit growth keeps price pressure in check. Low capacity utilization in manufacturing should help contain domestic price pressures for some time to come. However, increases in administered prices, in line with the government's plans to reform the pricing of energy, water, and other commodities, may push annual average inflation to around 3.0% in 2015. Volatile food prices harbor risks to this inflation forecast.

As the government has announced that fiscal policies will stay broadly unchanged, the consolidated budget deficit is forecast to remain at about 2.1% of GDP in 2014 and 2015. The government will likely try to broaden its fiscal space and options by gradually increasing budget revenues through tax system reforms. Efforts to reduce local governments' off-budget spending may, however, have the effect of fiscal tightening. Government current expenditure should rise more than in 2013 as fiscal spending related to social security, public housing, education, and health care will continue to increase in line with announced government policies. In contrast, administrative spending will be cut further.

Monetary policy needs to strike a balance between mitigating risks in the financial and property sectors that stem from high past credit growth and supporting sustainable economic growth. As current growth momentum seems sufficiently high to provide enough jobs, monetary policy is expected to lean further toward tightening over the forecast period. This should bring the growth rate of money supply closer to that of nominal GDP and possibly even below the official target of 13%. As global commodity prices are forecast to fall, the PRC's foreign trade will likely benefit from improved terms of trade. The merchandise trade surplus should thus widen further in 2014 and 2015. As the deficit in the service account will also likely widen, the current account surplus is forecast to narrow marginally to 2.0% of GDP in 2014 and 1.9% in 2015.

If strong net capital inflows continue, which seems likely, the PBOC will find it difficult to widen the exchange rate band for the renminbi, which was already extended from ±1% to ±2% in mid-March this year as an intermediate step toward the declared policy objective of full exchange rate liberalization. It will also be more difficult to rein in money supply growth. The authorities are therefore likely to facilitate capital outflows to ease upward pressure on the renminbi, followed in later years by steps toward further exchange rate liberalization. A more balanced capital and financial account would help slow the accumulation of reserves, which boosted money supply in 2013, given the limited scope for sterilization owing to the shallow financial market. Unexpectedly high trade surpluses and net capital inflows harbor risks for these exchange rate and monetary forecasts.

Among the international risks to the forecast is unexpectedly severe financial volatility in developing economies as the US Federal Reserve gradually tapers quantitative easing. If some countries suffer excessive capital outflows, the PRC may be affected indirectly through weaker demand for its exports. Another global risk is recovery in developed economies remaining sluggish. While there seems to be evidence of improved performance in these markets, a setback to recovery in the PRC's main trading partners would translate into lackluster demand for its exports, which would slow growth during the forecast period. On the other hand, an unexpectedly strong external environment would improve the upside potential for the PRC economy and create room for bolder structural reforms.

The principal domestic risks to the forecast stem from uncertainties regarding the effectiveness of monetary management and the concern over credit quality. A number of trust funds are already facing difficulties, and a few have reportedly defaulted on bonds in recent months for lack of repayment from their own borrowers. Many of these borrowers, which include real estate developers and companies in industries with excess capacity, are subprime and struggle in an environment of decelerating economic growth. The factors mitigating these risks are that debts are mainly domestic and, at least in the case of local government debt, largely backed by long-term assets. Further, given relatively low central government debt and a well-capitalized banking system, the PRC is in a strong position to forestall domestic risks.

Policy challenge—maintaining GDP growth while taming credit expansion

The key challenge for policy makers during the forecast period is to implement policies that help to decelerate investment growth in a controlled manner, thereby ensuring orderly debt accumulation by local governments and state-owned enterprises and the safety and soundness of the banking system, without derailing the growth momentum of the economy. After launching the key structural reforms outlined at the November 2013 party plenum, the government will pursue, as in the past, a gradual reform strategy and regularly fine-tune the speed of reform and the selection of specific measures to apply.

While this strategy will help to contain instability, achieving results will take time. In the short term, the PBOC needs to find the right balance between subduing credit growth and supporting economic growth. Attempts to slow credit growth too rapidly may impose additional stress on enterprises and financial institutions, eroding investor confidence. However, if continued, the current pace of credit growth and the associated increase in debt, including the debt of local governments and state-owned enterprises, may aggravate existing asset quality problems, which also risks undermining investor confidence. Responding to this bind requires strengthening monetary, fiscal, and exchange rate policies in a coordinated way. To this end, the PBOC can be expected to target a monetary growth rate in 2014 that exceeds nominal GDP growth but by less than in 2013, invigorate competition in the financial sector to help allocate credit more efficiently, and strengthen sector oversight to prevent excessive risk taking. Other needs are further interest rate liberalization, financial market deepening, and more flexibility in exchange rate policy to reduce the need to sterilize eventual large capital inflows.

In the fiscal area, the government intends to further improve tax collection and cut preferential tax treatments, introduce property taxes, and start adjusting the distribution of fiscal responsibilities and resources between the central and local governments by recentralizing social expenditure responsibilities and enlarging the block transfers that the central government pays to local governments. Both measures will, over time, ease the need for local governments to accumulate more debt.

Reform of personal income tax may also be launched during the forecast period, as a broader income tax base would go a long way toward mobilizing the resources needed to better provision social and infrastructure services without accumulating more debt. Equally important, progressive income taxes would help to shift the tax burden from low-income to high-income households. This would improve income distribution and equity, which are declared policy objectives.

Part III

CURRENCIES

CHAPTER 7

THE FEDERAL RESERVE SYSTEM

Learning Objectives

1. Purpose of the federal reserve system;
2. Structure of the federal reserve system;
3. Monetary policy and the economy.

The Eccles Building in Washington, D. C., which serves as the Federal Reserve System's headquarters.

Headquarters: Eccles Building, Washington, D. C., U. S.
Established: December 23, 1913
Chair: Janet Yellen

Central Bank of: United States of America

Currency: United States dollar USD (ISO 4217)

Reserve requirements: 0 to 10%

Bank rate: 0.15% to 1.25%

Interest rate target: 0 to 0.25%

Interest paid on excess reserves yes

Website: federalreserve. gov

1 Purpose

The primary motivation for creating the Federal Reserve System was to address banking panics. Other purposes are stated in the Federal Reserve Act, such as "to furnish an elastic currency, to afford means of rediscounting commercial paper, to establish a more effective supervision of banking in the United States, and for other purposes". Before the founding of the Federal Reserve System, the United States underwent several financial crises. A particularly severe crisis in 1907 led Congress to enact the Federal Reserve Act in 1913. Today the Federal Reserve System has responsibilities in addition to ensuring the stability of the financial system.

This is the latest accepted revision, reviewed on 21 July 2015.

Current functions of the Federal Reserve System include:

- To address the problem of banking panics
- To serve as the central bank for the United States
- To strike a balance between private interests of banks and the centralized responsibility of government

    ◎ To supervise and regulate banking institutions

    ◎ To protect the credit rights of consumers

Seal of the Federal Reserve System

- To manage the nation's money supply through monetary policy to achieve the sometimes-conflicting goals of

    ◎ maximum employment

    ◎ stable prices, including prevention of either inflation or deflation

    ◎ moderate long-term interest rates

- To maintain the stability of the financial system and contain systemic risk in financial markets

- To provide financial services to depository institutions, the U. S. government, and foreign official institutions, including playing a major role in operating the nation's payments system

    ◎ To facilitate the exchange of payments among regions

    ◎ To respond to local liquidity needs

- To strengthen U. S. standing in the world economy

1.1 Addressing the problem of bank panics

Banking institutions in the United States are required to hold reserves—amounts of currency and deposits in other banks—equal to only a fraction of the amount of the banks' deposit liabilities owed to customers. This practice is called fractional-reserve banking. As a result, banks usually invest the majority of the funds received from depositors. On rare occasions, too many of the bank's customers will withdraw their savings and the bank will need help from another institution to continue operating; this is called a bank run. Bank runs can lead to a multitude of social and economic problems. The Federal Reserve System was designed as an attempt to prevent or minimize the occurrence of bank runs, and possibly act as a lender of last resort when a bank run does occur. Many economists, following Milton Friedman, believe that the Federal Reserve inappropriately refused to lend money to small banks during the bank runs of 1929.

1.1.1 Check clearing system

Because some banks refused to clear checks from certain others during times of economic uncertainty, a check-clearing system was created in the Federal Reserve System. It is briefly described in the Federal Reserve System—Purposes and Functions as follows:

By creating the Federal Reserve System, Congress intended to eliminate the severe financial crises that had periodically swept the nation, especially the sort of financial panic that occurred in 1907. During that episode, payments were disrupted throughout the country because many banks and clearinghouses refused to clear checks drawn on certain other banks, a practice that contributed to the failure of otherwise solvent banks. To address these problems, Congress gave the Federal Reserve System the authority to establish a nationwide check-clearing system. The System, then, was to provide not only an elastic currency—that is, a currency that would expand or shrink in amount as economic conditions warranted—but also an efficient and equitable check-collection system.

1.1.2 Lender of last resort

In the United States, the Federal Reserve serves as the lender of last resort to those institutions that cannot obtain credit elsewhere and the collapse of which would have serious implications for the economy. It took over this role from the private sector "clearing houses" which operated during the Free Banking Era; whether public or private, the availability of liquidity was intended to prevent bank runs.

1.1.3 Fluctuations

Through its discount window and credit operations, Reserve Banks provide liquidity to banks to meet short-term needs stemming from seasonal fluctuations in deposits or unexpected withdrawals. Longer term liquidity may also be provided in exceptional circumstances. The rate the Fed charges banks for these loans is called the discount rate (officially the primary credit rate).

By making these loans, the Fed serves as a buffer against unexpected day-to-day fluctuations in reserve demand and supply. This contributes to the effective functioning of the banking system, alleviates pressure in the reserves market and reduces the extent of unexpected movements in the interest rates. For example, on September 16, 2008, the Federal Reserve Board authorized an $85 billion loan to stave off the bankruptcy of international insurance giant American International Group (AIG).

1.2 Central bank

In its role as the central bank of the United States, the Fed serves as a banker's bank and as the government's bank. As the banker's bank, it helps to assure the safety and efficiency of the payments system. As the government's bank, or fiscal agent, the Fed processes a variety of financial transactions involving trillions of dollars. Just as an individual might keep an account at a bank, the U.S. Treasury keeps a checking account with the Federal Reserve, through which incoming federal tax deposits and outgoing government payments are handled. As part of this service relationship, the Fed sells and redeems U.S. government securities such as savings bonds and Treasury bills, notes and bonds. It also issues the nation's coin and paper currency. The U.S. Treasury, through its Bureau of the Mint and Bureau of Engraving and Printing, actually produces the nation's cash supply and, in effect, sells the paper currency to the Federal Reserve Banks at manufacturing cost, and the coins at face value. The Federal Reserve Banks then distribute it to other financial institutions in various ways. During the Fiscal Year 2008, the Bureau of Engraving and Printing delivered 7.7 billion notes at an average cost of 6.4 cents per note.

1.3 National payments system

The Federal Reserve plays an important role in the U.S. payments system. The twelve Federal Reserve Banks provide banking services to depository institutions and to the federal government. For depository institutions, they maintain accounts and provide various payment services, including collecting checks, electronically transferring funds, and distributing and receiving currency and coin. For the federal government, the Reserve Banks act as fiscal agents, paying Treasury checks; processing electronic payments; and issuing, transferring, and redeeming U.S. government securities.

In the Depository Institutions Deregulation and Monetary Control Act of 1980, Congress reaffirmed that the Federal Reserve should promote an efficient nationwide payments system. The act subjects all depository institutions, not just member commercial banks, to reserve requirements and grants them equal access to Reserve Bank payment services. It also encourages competition between the Reserve Banks and private-sector providers of payment services by requiring the Reserve Banks to charge fees for certain payments services listed in the act and to recover the costs of providing these services over the long run.

The Federal Reserve plays a role in the nation's retail and wholesale payments systems by providing financial services to depository institutions. Retail payments are generally for relatively small-dollar amounts and often involve a depository institution's retail clients—individuals and smaller businesses. The Reserve Banks' retail services include distributing currency and coin, collecting checks, and electronically transferring funds through the automated clearinghouse system. By contrast, wholesale payments are generally for large-dollar amounts and often involve a depository institution's large corporate customers or counterparties, including other financial institutions. The Reserve Banks' wholesale services include electronically transferring funds through the Fedwire Funds Service and transferring securities issued by the U. S. government, its agencies, and certain other entities through the Fedwire Securities Service. Because of the large amounts of funds that move through the Reserve Banks every day, the System has policies and procedures to limit the risk to the Reserve Banks from a depository institution's failure to make or settle its payments.

In 2003, the Federal Reserve Banks began a multi-year restructuring of their check operations to respond to the declining use of checks by consumers and businesses and the greater use of electronics in check processing. It planned to reduce the number of full-service check processing locations from 45 in 2003 to 4 by early 2011.

The Federal Reserve has been researching Bitcoin. In 2013 it believed that collaboration and engagement with the industry was the way forward. In 2015, a white paper called "Strategies for Improving the U. S. Payment System" called it an "emergent payment infrastructure".

2　Structure

The Federal Reserve System has a "unique structure that is both public and private" and is described as "independent within the government" rather than "independent of government". The System does not require public funding, and derives its authority and purpose from the Federal Reserve Act, which was passed by Congress in 1913 and is subject to Congressional modification or repeal. The four main components of the Federal Reserve System are (1) the Board of Governors, (2) the Federal Open Market Committee, (3) the twelve regional Federal Reserve Banks, and (4) the member banks throughout the country.

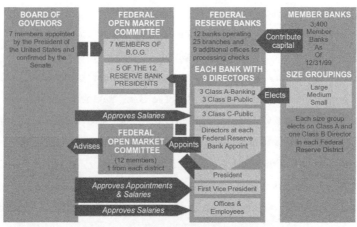

Organization of the Federal Reserve System

2.1 Board of Governors

The seven-member Board of Governors is a federal agency. It is charged with the overseeing of the 12 District Reserve Banks and setting national monetary policy. It also supervises and regulates the U.S. banking system in general. Governors are appointed by the President of the United States and confirmed by the Senate for staggered 14-year terms. One term begins every two years, on February 1 of even-numbered years, and members serving a full term cannot be renominated for a second term. "Upon the expiration of their terms of office, members of the Board shall continue to serve until their successors are appointed and have qualified." The law provides for the removal of a member of the Board by the President "for cause". The Board is required to make an annual report of operations to the Speaker of the U.S. House of Representatives.

The Chair and Vice Chair of the Board of Governors are appointed by the President from among the sitting Governors. They both serve a four-year term and they can be renominated as many times as the President chooses, until their terms on the Board of Governors expire.

2.1.1 List of members of the Board of Governors

The current members of the Board of Governors are as follows:

Governor	Entered office	Term expires
Janet Yellen (Chair)	February 3, 2014 (as Chair) October 4, 2010 (as Governor)	February 3, 2018 (as Chair) January 31, 2024 (as Governor)
Stanley Fischer (Vice-Chair)	May 28, 2014 June 16, 2014 (as Vice Chair)	January 31, 2020 (as Governor) June 12, 2018 (as Vice Chair)
Daniel Tarullo	January 28, 2009	January 31, 2022
Jerome H. Powell	May 25, 2012 June 16, 2014 (new term)	January 31, 2028
Lael Brainard	confirmed June 12, 2014	January 31, 2026
Vacant		
Vacant		

2.1.2 Nominations, confirmations and resignations

In late December 2011, President Barack Obama nominated Stein, a Harvard University finance professor and a Democrat, and Powell, formerly of Dillon Read, Bankers Trust and The Carlyle Group and a Republican. Both candidates also have Treasury Department experience in the Obama and George H. W. Bush administrations respectively.

"Obama administration officials had regrouped to identify Fed candidates after Peter Diamond, a Nobel Prize-winning economist, withdrew his nomination to the board in June 2011 in the face of Republican opposition. Richard Clarida, a potential nominee who was a Treasury official under George W. Bush, pulled out of consideration in August 2011", one account of the December nominations noted. The two other Obama nominees in 2011, Yellen and Raskin, were confirmed in September. One of the vacancies was created in 2011 with the resignation of Kevin Warsh, who took office in 2006 to fill the unexpired term ending January 31, 2018, and resigned his position effective March 31, 2011. In March 2012, U. S. Senator David Vitter (R, LA) said he would oppose Obama's Stein and Powell nominations, dampening near-term hopes for approval. However Senate leaders reached a deal, paving the way for affirmative votes on the two nominees in May 2012 and bringing the board to full strength for the first time since 2006 with Duke's service after term end. Later, on January 6, 2014, the United States Senate confirmed Yellen's nomination to be Chair of the Federal Reserve Board of Governors; she is slated to be the first woman to hold the position and will become Chair on February 1, 2014. Subsequently, President Obama nominated Stanley Fischer to replace Yellen as the Vice Chair.

In April 2014, Stein announced he was leaving to return to Harvard May 28 with four years remaining on his term. At the time of the announcement, the FOMC "already is down three members as it awaits the Senate confirmation of Fischer and Lael Brainard, and as President Obama has yet to name a replacement for Duke. Powell is still serving as he awaits his confirmation for a second term."

Allan R. Landon, 65, former president and CEO of the Bank of Hawaii, was nominated in early 2015 by President Barack Obama to the Board.

In July 2015, President Obama nominated University of Michigan economist Kathryn M. Dominguez to fill the second vacancy on the Board. The Senate had not yet acted on Landon's confirmation by the time of the second nomination.

2.2 Federal Open Market Committee

The Federal Open Market Committee (FOMC) consists of 12 members, seven from the Board of Governors and 5 of the regional Federal Reserve Bank presidents. The FOMC oversees open market operations, the principal tool of national monetary policy. These operations affect the amount of Federal Reserve balances available to depository institutions, thereby influencing overall monetary and credit conditions. The FOMC also directs operations undertaken by the Federal Reserve in foreign exchange markets. The president of the Federal Reserve Bank of New York is a permanent member of the FOMC; the presidents of the other banks rotate membership at two- and three-year intervals. All Regional Reserve Bank presidents contribute to the committee's assessment of the economy and of policy options, but only the five presidents who are then members of the FOMC vote on policy decisions. The FOMC determines its own internal organization and, by tradition, elects the Chair of the Board of Governors as its chair and the president of the Federal Reserve Bank of New York as its vice chair. It is informal policy within the FOMC for the Board of Governors and the New York Federal Reserve Bank president to vote with the Chair of the FOMC; anyone who is not an expert on monetary policy traditionally votes with the chair as well; and in any vote no more than two FOMC members can dissent. Formal meetings typically are held eight times each year in Washington, D. C. Nonvoting Reserve

Bank presidents also participate in Committee deliberations and discussion. The FOMC generally meets eight times a year in telephone consultations and other meetings are held when needed.

2.3 Federal Advisory Council

The Federal Advisory Council, composed of twelve representatives of the banking industry, advises the Board on all matters within its jurisdiction.

2.4 Federal Reserve Banks

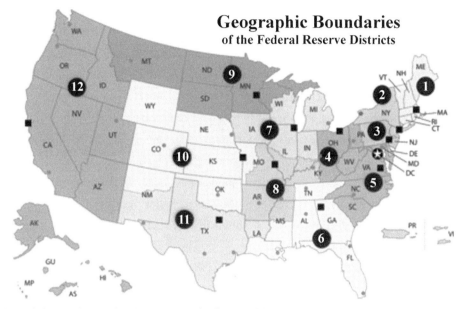

Map of the twelve Federal Reserve Districts, with the twelve Federal Reserve Banks marked as black squares, and all Branches within each district (24 total) marked as red circles. The Washington DC Headquarters is marked with a star. (Also, a 25th branch in Buffalo, NY had been closed in 2008.)

There are 12 Federal Reserve Banks located in Boston, New York, Philadelphia, Cleveland, Richmond, Atlanta, Chicago, St. Louis, Minneapolis, Kansas City, Dallas, and San Francisco. Each reserve Bank is responsible for member banks located in its district. The size of each district was set based upon the population distribution of the United States when the Federal Reserve Act was passed. Each regional Bank has a president, who is the chief executive officer of their Bank. Each regional Reserve Bank's president is nominated by their Bank's board of directors, but the nomination is contingent upon approval by the Board of Governors. Presidents serve five-year terms and may be reappointed.

Each regional Bank's board consists of nine members. Members are broken down into three classes: A, B, and C. There are three board members in each class. Class A members are chosen by the regional Bank's shareholders, and are intended to represent member banks' interests. Member banks are divided into three categories: large, medium, and small. Each category elects one of the three class A board members. Class B board members are also nominated by the region's member banks, but class B board members are supposed to represent the interests of the public. Lastly, class C board members are nominated by the Board of Governors, and are also intended to represent the interests of the public.

A member bank is a private institution and owns stock in its regional Federal Reserve Bank. All nationally chartered banks hold stock in one of the Federal Reserve Banks. State chartered banks may choose to be members (and hold stock in their regional Federal Reserve bank), upon meeting certain standards. About 38% of U. S. banks are members of their regional Federal Reserve Bank. The amount of stock a member bank must own is equal to 3% of its combined capital and surplus. However, holding stock in a Federal Reserve bank is not like owning stock in a publicly traded company. These stocks cannot be sold or traded, and member banks do not control the Federal Reserve Bank as a result of owning this stock. The charter and organization of each Federal Reserve Bank is established by law and cannot be altered by the member banks. Member banks, do however, elect six of the nine members of the Federal Reserve Banks' boards of directors. From the profits of the Regional Bank of which it is a member, a member bank receives a dividend equal to 6% of their purchased stock. The remainder of the regional Federal Reserve Banks' profits is given over to the United States Treasury Department. In 2009, the Federal Reserve Banks distributed $1.4 billion in dividends to member banks and returned $47 billion to the U. S. Treasury.

2.5 Member banks

Plaque marking a bank is a member

According to the website for the Federal Reserve Bank of Richmond, "more than one-third of U. S. commercial banks are members of the Federal Reserve System. National banks must be members; state chartered banks may join by meeting certain requirements."

3 Monetary policy

The term "monetary policy" refers to the actions undertaken by a central bank, such as the Federal Reserve, to influence the availability and cost of money and credit to help promote national economic goals. What happens to money and credit affects interest rates (the cost of credit) and the performance of an economy. The Federal Reserve Act of 1913 gave the Federal Reserve authority to set monetary policy in the United States.

3.1 Interbank lending

The Federal Reserve sets monetary policy by influencing the Federal funds rate, which is the rate of interbank lending of excess reserves. The rate that banks charge each other for these loans is determined in the interbank market and the Federal Reserve influences this rate through the three "tools" of monetary policy described in the Tools section below. The Federal funds rate is a short-term interest rate that the FOMC focuses on, which affects the longer-term interest rates throughout the economy. The Federal Reserve summarized its monetary policy in 2005:

The Federal Reserve implements U. S. monetary policy by affecting conditions in the market for balances that depository institutions hold at the Federal Reserve Banks... By conducting open market operations, imposing reserve requirements, permitting depository institutions to hold contractual clearing balances, and extending credit through its discount window facility, the Federal Reserve exercises considerable control over the demand for and supply of Federal Reserve balances and the federal funds rate. Through its control of the federal funds rate, the Federal Reserve is able to foster financial and monetary conditions consistent with its monetary policy objectives.

Effects on the quantity of reserves that banks used to make loans influence the economy. Policy actions that add reserves to the banking system encourage lending at lower interest rates thus stimulating growth in money, credit, and the economy. Policy actions that absorb reserves work in the opposite direction. The Fed's task is to supply enough reserves to support an adequate amount of money and credit, avoiding the excesses that result in inflation and the shortages that stifle economic growth.

3.2 Tools

There are three main tools of monetary policy that the Federal Reserve uses to influence the amount of reserves in private banks:

Tool	Description
Open marked operations	Purchases and sales of U. S. Treasury and federal agency securities—the Federal Reserve's principal tool for implementing monetary policy. The Federal Reserve's objective for open market operations has varied over the years. During the 1980s, the focus gradually shifted toward attaining a specified level of the federal funds rate (the rate that banks charge each other for overnight loans of federal funds, which are the reserves held by banks at the Fed), a process that was largely complete by the end of the decade.
Discount rate	The interest rate charged to commercial banks and other depository institutions on loans they receive from their regional Federal Reserve Bank's lending facility—the discount window.
Reserve requirements	The amount of funds that a depository institution must hold in reserve against specified deposit liabilities.

3.2.1 Federal funds rate and open market operations

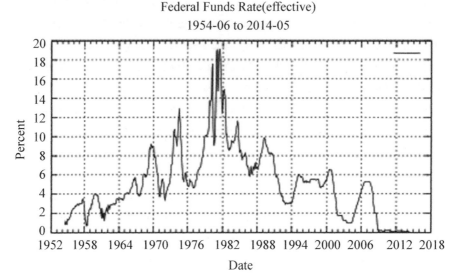

The effective federal funds rate charted over more than fifty years

The Federal Reserve System implements monetary policy largely by targeting the federal funds rate. This is the interest rate that banks charge each other for overnight loans of federal funds, which are the reserves held by banks at the Fed. This rate is actually determined by the market and is not explicitly mandated by the Fed. The Fed therefore tries to align the effective federal funds rate with the targeted rate by adding or subtracting from the money supply through open market operations. The Federal Reserve System usually adjusts the federal funds rate target by 0.25% or 0.50% at a time.

Open market operations allow the Federal Reserve to increase or decrease the amount of money in the banking system as necessary to balance the Federal Reserve's dual mandates. Open market operations are done through the sale and purchase of United States Treasury security, sometimes called "Treasury bills" or more informally "T-bills" or "Treasuries". The Federal Reserve buys Treasury bills from its primary dealers. The purchase of these securities affects the federal funds rate, because primary dealers have accounts at depository institutions.

The Federal Reserve education website describes open market operations as follows:

Open market operations involve the buying and selling of U. S. government securities (federal agency and mortgage-backed). The term "open market" means that the Fed doesn't decide on its own which securities dealers it will do business with on a particular day. Rather, the choice emerges from an "open market" in which the various securities dealers that the Fed does business with—the primary dealers—compete on the basis of price. Open market operations are flexible and thus, the most frequently used tool of monetary policy.

Open market operations are the primary tool used to regulate the supply of bank reserves. This tool consists of Federal Reserve purchases and sales of financial instruments, usually securities issued by the U.S. Treasury, Federal agencies and government-sponsored enterprises. Open market operations are carried out by the Domestic Trading Desk of the Federal Reserve Bank of New York under direction from the FOMC. The transactions are undertaken with primary dealers.

The Fed's goal in trading the securities is to affect the federal funds rate, the rate at which banks borrow reserves from each other. When the Fed wants to increase reserves, it buys securities and pays for them by making a deposit to the account maintained at the Fed by the primary dealer's bank. When the Fed wants to reduce reserves, it sells securities and collects from those accounts. Most days, the Fed does not want to increase or decrease reserves permanently so it usually engages in transactions reversed within a day or two. That means that a reserve injection today could be withdrawn tomorrow morning, only to be renewed at some level several hours later. These short-term transactions are called repurchase agreements (repos)—the dealer sells the Fed a security and agrees to buy it back at a later date.

3.2.2 Discount rate

The Federal Reserve System also directly sets the "discount rate", which is the interest rate for "discount window lending", overnight loans that member banks borrow directly from the Fed. This rate is generally set at a rate close to 100 basis points above the target federal funds rate. The idea is to encourage banks to seek alternative funding before using the "discount rate" option. The equivalent operation by the European Central Bank is referred to as the "marginal lending facility".

Both the discount rate and the federal funds rate influence the prime rate, which is usually about 3 percent higher than the federal funds rate.

3.2.3 Reserve requirements

Another instrument of monetary policy adjustment employed by the Federal Reserve System is the fractional reserve requirement, also known as the required reserve ratio. The required reserve ratio sets the balance that the Federal Reserve System requires a depository institution to hold in the Federal Reserve Banks, which depository institutions trade in the federal funds market discussed above. The required reserve ratio is set by the Board of Governors of the Federal Reserve System. The reserve requirements have changed over time and some history of these changes is published by the Federal Reserve.

Reserve Requirements in the U.S. Federal Reserve System

Liability Type	Requirements	
	Percentage of liabilities	Effective date
Net transaction accounts		
$0 to $11.5 million	0	December 29, 2011
More than $11.5 million to $71 million	3	December 29, 2011

续表

More than $71 million	10	December 29, 2011
Nonpersonal time deposits	0	December 27, 1990
Eurocurrency liabilities	0	December 27, 1990

As a response to the financial crisis of 2008, the Federal Reserve now makes interest payments on depository institutions' required and excess reserve balances. The payment of interest on excess reserves gives the central bank greater opportunity to address credit market conditions while maintaining the federal funds rate close to the target rate set by the FOMC.

(FROM: https://en.wikipedia.org/wiki/Federal_Reserve_System)

WORDS AND EXPRESSIONS

- *address* /əˈdres/ vt. If you address a problem or task or if you address yourself to it, you try to understand it or deal with it. 对付;处理;设法了解并解决
- *bank panics* 银行恐慌,指多家银行同时倒闭的现象。
- *Fedwire Funds Service* Formally known as the Federal Reserve Wire Network, Fedwire is a real-time gross settlement funds transfer system operated by the United States Federal Reserve Banks that enables financial institutions to electronically transfer funds between its more than 9,289 participants (as of March 19, 2009). 联邦电子资金转账系统
- *Bitcoin* Bitcoin uses peer-to-peer (点对点) technology to operate with no central authority or banks; managing transactions and the issuing of bitcoins is carried out collectively by the network. Bitcoin is open-source; its design is public, nobody owns or controls Bitcoin and everyone can take part in. Through many of its unique properties, Bitcoin allows exciting uses that could not be covered by any previous payment system. 比特币
- *bank runs* A bank run occurs when a large number of bank customers withdraw their deposits because they believe the bank might fail. As more people withdraw their deposits, the likelihood of default increases, and this encourages further withdrawals. This can destabilize the bank to the point where it faces bankruptcy. 银行挤兑
- *check clearing system* Movement of a check from the bank in which it was deposited to the bank on which it was drawn, and the movement of its face amount in the opposite direction. This process (called "clearing cycle") normally results in a credit to the account at the bank of deposit, and an equivalent debit to the account at the bank on which it was drawn. It is also called clearing. 支票交换制

- *check collection* 支票托收
- *lender of last resort* The discretionary provision of liquidity to a financial institution (or the market as a whole) by the central bank in reaction to an adverse shock which causes an abnormal increase in demand for liquidity which cannot be met from an alternative source. This means that the central bank is the lender (provider of liquidity) of last resort (if there is no other way to increase the supply of liquidity when there is a lack thereof). The function has been performed by many central banks since the beginning of the 20th century. The goal is to prevent financial panics and bank runs spreading from one bank to the next due to a lack of liquidity. 最后贷款者
- *Federal Reserve District* (Reserve District, or District) one of the twelve geographic regions served by a Federal Reserve Bank 联邦储备区
- *excess reserves* In banking, excess reserves are bank reserves in excess of a reserve requirement set by a central bank. They are reserves of cash more than the required amounts. 超额准备金
- *reserve requirements* requirements set by the Board of Governors for the amounts of certain liabilities that depository institutions must set aside in the form of reserves 法定存款准备标准；准备金规定
- *stifle* /ˈstaɪfl/ *vt.* to make (something) difficult or impossible 阻止；扼杀
- *align* /əˈlaɪn/ to adjust 调整
- *repurchase agreements* (Repo) It is a form of short-term borrowing for dealers in government securities. The dealer sells the government securities to investors, usually on an overnight basis, and buys them back the following day. 回购协议

注：For the party selling the security (and agreeing to repurchase it in the future) it is a repo. 回购协议；For the party on the other end of the transaction, (buying the security and agreeing to sell in the future) it is a reverse repurchase agreement. 逆回购协议

- *marginal lending facility* A standing facility of the Eurosystem which counterparties may use to receive overnight credit from a national central bank at a pre-specified interest rate against eligible assets. 边际贷款工具
- *reserve requirements* requirements set by the Board of Governors for the amounts of certain liabilities that depository institutions must set aside in the form of reserves. 法定存款准备标准；准备金规定

BACKGROUND KNOWLEDGE

1 *Federal Advisory Council* 联邦咨询委员会

Advisory group made up of one representative (in most cases a banker) from each of the twelve Federal Reserve Districts. Established by the Federal Reserve Act, the council meets periodically with the Board of Governors to discuss business and financial conditions and to make recommendations.

2 *The Depository Institutions Deregulation and Monetary Control Act of 1980* 储蓄机构解除管制和货币控制法(1980)

- A United States federal financial statute law passed in 1980, gave the Federal Reserve greater control over non-member banks.
- It forced all banks to abide by the Fed's rules.
- It allowed banks to merge.
- It removed the power of the Federal Reserve Board of Governors under the Glass-Steagall Act and Regulation Q to set the interest rates of savings accounts.
- It raised the deposit insurance of US banks and credit unions from $40,000 to $100,000.
- It allowed credit unions and savings and loans to offer checkable deposits.
- It allowed institutions to charge any interest rates they chose.

3 *Janet Louise Yellen* (born August 13, 1946) is an American economist. She is the Chair of the Board of Governors of the Federal Reserve System, previously serving as Vice Chair from 2010 to 2014.

Previously, she was President and Chief Executive Officer of the Federal Reserve Bank of San Francisco; Chair of the White House Council of Economic Advisers under President Bill Clinton; and Professor Emerita at the University of California, Berkeley, Haas School of Business. On January 6, 2014, the United States Senate confirmed Yellen's nomination to be Chair of the Federal Reserve Board of Governors. Yellen was sworn in on February 3, 2014, making her the first woman to hold the position.

Janet L. Yellen 珍妮特·耶伦

珍妮特·耶伦(Janet L. Yellen),女,1946年8月3日出生于美国纽约州布鲁克林,美国布朗大学经济学学士,耶鲁大学经济学博士,美国犹太裔经济学家及经济学教授,柏克莱加州大学哈斯商学院的名誉教授,第十八任美国总统经济顾问委员会主席,由前美国总统比尔·克林顿提名。曾两次荣获加州大学伯克利分校哈斯商学院的杰出教学奖。曾任美国联邦储备委员会副主席(任期2010年10月4日—2013年10月4日)。耶伦是美联储历史上第二位"女副总",现任(2014年2月1日起至今)美国联邦储备委员会主席,成为了美联储百年历史上第一位女性掌门人,也成为上世纪八十年代以来保罗·沃尔克之后的首位民主党主席。

4 *Federal Open Market Committee* (*FOMC, or the Committee*) 联邦公开市场政策委员会

Twelve-voting-member committee made up of the seven members of the Board of Governors; the president of the Federal Reserve Bank of New York; and, on a rotating basis, the presidents of four other Reserve Banks. Nonvoting Reserve Bank presidents also participate in Committee deliberations and discussion. The FOMC generally meets eight times a year in Washington, D. C., to set the nation's monetary policy. It also establishes policy relating to system operations in the foreign exchange markets.

5 *Open Market Operation* 公开市场操作,又称"公开市场业务",是指中央银行在国内货币市场通过买卖有价证券和进行外汇交易,来调节市场流动性,影响货币和信贷量的主要货币政策工具。

An open market operation (OMO) is an activity by a central bank to buy or sell government bonds on the open market. A central bank uses them as the primary means of implementing monetary policy. The usual aim of open market operations is to manipulate the short-term interest rate and the supply of base money in an economy, and thus indirectly control the total money supply, in effect expanding money or contracting the money supply. This involves meeting the demand of base money at the target interest rate by buying and selling government securities, or other financial instruments. Monetary targets, such as inflation, interest rates, or exchange rates, are used to guide this implementation.

6 *discount window* 贴现窗口

It is an instrument of monetary policy (usually controlled by central banks) that allows eligible institutions to borrow money from the central bank, usually on a short-term basis, to meet temporary shortages of liquidity caused by internal or external disruptions. The term originated with the practice of sending a bank representative to a reserve bank teller window when a bank needed to borrow money.

The interest rate charged on such loans by a central bank is called the discount rate, base rate, repo rate, or primary rate. It is distinct from the federal funds rate or its equivalents in other currencies, which determine the rate at which banks lend money to each other. In recent years, the discount rate has been approximately a percentage point above the federal funds rate (see Lombard credit). Because of this, it is a relatively unimportant factor in the control of the money supply and is only taken advantage of at large volume during emergencies.

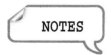

1 *fractional-reserve banking* 部分准备金银行制度

It is the practice whereby a bank accepts deposits, and holds reserves that are a fraction of the amount of its deposit liabilities. Reserves are held at the bank as currency, or as deposits in the bank's accounts at the central bank. Fractional-reserve banking is the current form of banking practiced in most countries worldwide.

Fractional-reserve banking allows banks to act as financial intermediaries between borrowers and savers, and to provide longer-term loans to borrowers while providing immediate liquidity to depositors (providing the function of maturity transformation). However, a bank can experience a bank run if depositors wish to withdraw more funds than the reserves held by the bank. To mitigate the risks of bank runs and systemic crises (when problems are extreme and widespread), governments of most countries regulate and oversee commercial banks, provide deposit insurance and act as lender of last resort to commercial banks.

Because bank deposits are usually considered money in their own right, and because banks hold reserves that are less than their deposit liabilities, fractional-reserve banking permits the money supply to grow beyond the amount of the underlying reserves of base money originally created by the central bank. In most countries, the central bank (or other monetary authority) regulates bank credit creation, imposing reserve requirements and capital adequacy ratios. This can limit the amount of money creation that occurs in the commercial banking system, and helps to ensure that banks are solvent and have enough funds to meet demand for withdrawals. However, rather than directly controlling the money supply, central banks usually pursue an interest rate target to control inflation and bank issuance of credit.

2 *a clearing house* 清算所,票据所

It is a financial institution that provides clearing and settlement services for financial and commodities derivatives and securities transactions. These transactions may be executed on a futures exchange or securities exchange, as well as off-exchange in the over-the-counter (OTC) market.

3 *The discount window* 贴现窗口

It is an instrument of monetary policy (usually controlled by central banks) that allows eligible institutions to borrow money from the central bank, usually on a short-term basis, to meet temporary shortages of liquidity caused by internal or external disruptions. The term originated with the practice of sending a bank representative to a reserve bank teller window when a bank needed to borrow money.

The interest rate charged on such loans by a central bank is called the discount rate, base rate, repo rate, or primary rate. It is distinct from the federal funds rate or its equivalents in other currencies, which determine the rate at which banks lend money to each other. In recent years, the discount rate has been approximately a percentage point above the federal funds rate (see Lombard credit). Because of this, it is a relatively unimportant factor in the control of the money supply and is only taken advantage of at large volume during emergencies.

Part III CURRENCIES

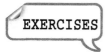
EXERCISES

I. Decide whether the following statements are true(T) or false(F).

1. The initiative motivation for creating the Federal Reserve System was to smooth out economic uncertainty. ( )
2. The U.S. Treasury, through its Bureau of the Mint and Bureau of Engraving and Printing, actually produces the nation's cash supply and, in effect, sells the paper currency to the Federal Reserve Banks at manufacturing cost, and the coins at face value. The Federal Reserve Banks then distribute it to other financial institutions in various ways. ( )
3. During the Fiscal Year 2008, the Bureau of Engraving and Printing delivered 7.7 billion notes at an average cost of 8.4 cents per note. ( )
4. The Federal Reserve plays a role in the nation's retail and wholesale payments systems by providing financial settlements to depository institutions. ( )
5. The Federal Reserve has been researching Bitcoin and gives approval to it. ( )
6. The Federal Open Market Committee (FOMC) consists of 12 members, 5 from the Board of Governors and 7 of the regional Federal Reserve Bank presidents. ( )
7. There are 12 Federal Reserve Banks located in Boston, New York, Philadelphia, Cleveland, Richmond, Atlanta, Chicago, St. Louis, Minneapolis, Kansas City, Dallas, and San Francisco. ( )
8. Each regional Bank's board consists of 8 members. Members are broken down into three classes: A, B, and C. ( )
9. The federal funds rate is the interest rate that banks charge each other for overnight loans of federal funds, which are the reserves held by banks at the Fed. ( )
10. "Discount rate" is generally set at a rate close to 100 basis points above the target federal funds rate. ( )

II. Translate the following expressions into Chinese.

1. whether public or private, the availability of liquidity was intended to prevent bank runs
2. provide liquidity to banks to meet short-term needs stemming from seasonal fluctuations in deposits or unexpected withdrawals
3. described as "independent within the government" rather than "independent of government"
4. be subject to congressional modification or repeal
5. provide various payment services, including collecting checks, electronically transferring funds, and distributing and receiving currency and coin
6. to supervise and regulate the U.S. banking system in general
7. upon the expiration of their terms of office

8. rotate membership at two- and three-year intervals

9. to advise the Board on all matters within its jurisdiction

10. be also intended to represent the interests of the public

III. Translate the following paragraphs into Chinese.

1. On rare occasions, too many of the bank's customers will withdraw their savings and the bank will need help from another institution to continue operating; this is called a bank run. Bank runs can lead to a multitude of social and economic problems. The Federal Reserve System was designed as an attempt to prevent or minimize the occurrence of bank runs, and possibly act as a lender of last resort when a bank run does occur.

2. In its role as the central bank of the United States, the Fed serves as a banker's bank and as the government's bank. As the banker's bank, it helps to assure the safety and efficiency of the payments system. As the government's bank, or fiscal agent, the Fed processes a variety of financial transactions involving trillions of dollars.

3. The Federal Reserve implements U.S. monetary policy by affecting conditions in the market for balances that depository institutions hold at the Federal Reserve Banks... By conducting open market operations, imposing reserve requirements, permitting depository institutions to hold contractual clearing balances, and extending credit through its discount window facility, the Federal Reserve exercises considerable control over the demand for and supply of Federal Reserve balances and the federal funds rate. Through its control of the federal funds rate, the Federal Reserve is able to foster financial and monetary conditions consistent with its monetary policy objectives.

IV. Read the passage and choose the correct answer.

THE HISTORY OF THE UNITED STATES DOLLAR

The history of the United States dollar covers more than 200 years.

Early history

The history of the dollar in North America pre-dates US independence. Even before the Declaration of Independence, the Continental Congress had authorized the issuance of dollar denominated coins and currency, since the term "dollar" was in common usage referring to Spanish colonial 8 real coins or "Spanish Milled Dollars". Though several monetary systems were proposed for the early republic, the dollar was approved by Congress in a largely symbolic resolution on August 8, 1786. After passage of the Constitution was secured, the government turned its attention to monetary issues again in the early 1790s under the leadership of Alexander Hamilton, the secretary of the treasury at the time. Congress acted on Hamilton's recommendations in the Coinage Act of 1792, which established the Dollar as the basic unit of account for the United States. The word "dollar" is derived from Low Saxon "*daler*", an abbreviation of "*Joachimsdaler*"—(coin) from Joachimsthal (St. Joachim's Valley, now Jáchymov, Bohemia, then part of the Holy Roman Empire, now part of the Czech Republic;

for further history of the name, see dollar.)—so called because it was minted from 1519 onwards using silver extracted from a mine which had opened in 1516 near Joachimstal, a town in the Ore Mountains of northwestern Bohemia. The term "dollar" was widely used in reference to a Spanish coin at the time it was adopted by the United States.

Because prices of gold and silver in the open marketplace vary independently, the production of coins of full intrinsic worth(内在价值) under any ratio will nearly always result in the melting of either all silver coins or all gold coins. In the early 1800s, gold rose in relation to silver, resulting in the removal from commerce of nearly all gold coins, and their subsequent melting. Therefore, in 1834, the 15:1 ratio was changed to a 16:1 ratio by reducing the weight of the nation's gold coinage. This created a new U.S. dollar that was backed by 1.50 g (23.22 grains) of gold. However, the previous dollar had been represented by 1.60 g (24.75 grains) of gold. The result of this revaluation, which was the first-ever devaluation of the U.S. dollar, was that the value in gold of the dollar was reduced by 6%. Moreover, for a time, both gold and silver coins were useful in commerce.

In 1853, the weights of US silver coins (except, interestingly, the dollar itself, which was rarely used) were reduced. This had the effect of placing the nation effectively (although not officially) on the gold standard. The retained weight in the dollar coin was a nod to bimetallism (复本位制), although it had the effect of further driving the silver dollar coin from commerce.

With the enactment (1863) of the National Banking Act during the American Civil War and its later versions that taxed states' bonds and currency out of existence, the dollar became the sole currency of the United States and remains so today.

In 1878, the Bland-Allison Act was enacted to provide for freer coinage of silver. This act required the government to purchase between $2 million and $4 million worth of silver bullion each month at market prices and to coin it into silver dollars. This was, in effect, a subsidy for politically influential silver producers.

The discovery of large silver deposits in the Western United States in the late 19th century created a political controversy. Due to the large influx of silver, the value of silver in the nation's coinage dropped precipitously(急剧地). On one side were agrarian interests such as the United States Greenback Party that wanted to retain the bimetallic standard in order to inflate the dollar, which would allow farmers to more easily repay their debts. On the other side were Eastern banking and commercial interests, who advocated sound money and a switch to the gold standard. This issue split the Democratic Party in 1896. It led to the famous "cross of gold" speech given by William Jennings Bryan, and may have inspired many of the themes in *The Wizard of Oz*. Despite the controversy, the status of silver was slowly diminished through a series of legislative changes from 1873 to 1900, when a gold standard was formally adopted. The gold standard survived, with several modifications, until 1971.

Gold standard

Bimetallism persisted until March 14, 1900, with the passage of the Gold Standard Act, which provided that:

"…the dollar consisting of twenty-five and eight-tenths grains (1.67 g) of gold nine-tenths fine, as established by section thirty-five hundred and eleven of the Revised Statutes of the United States, shall be the standard unit of value, and all forms of money issued or coined by the United States shall be maintained at a parity of value with this standard…"

Thus the United States moved to a gold standard, made gold the sole legal-tender coinage of the United States, and set the value of the dollar at $20.67 per ounce (66.46 ¢/g) of gold. This made the dollar convertible to 1.5 g (23.22 grains)—the same convertibility into gold that was possible on the bimetallic standard.

Date of first series: 1963; date of last series: (current) 2006; Obverse: George Washington

Reverse: Great Seal of the United States

Date of first series: 1976; date of last series: (current) 2003; obverse: Thomas Jefferson

Reverse: Trumbull's Declaration of Independence

Date of first series: 1928; date of last series: 1995; obverse: Abraham Lincoln

Reverse: Lincoln Memorial

Part III CURRENCIES

Date of first series: 1928; date of last series: 1995; obverse: Alexander Hamilton

Reverse: United States Department of Treasury Building

Date of first series: 1928; date of last series: 1995; obverse: Andrew Jackson; reverse: White House

Reverse: White House

Date of first series: 1928; date of last series: 1993; obverse: Ulysses S. Grant

Reverse: United States Capitol

Date of first series: 1928; date of last series: 1993; obverse: Benjamin Franklin

Reverse: Independence Hall

Date of first series: 1928; date of last series: 1934; obverse: William McKinley

Reverse: value

Date of first series: 1928; date of last series: 1934; obverse: Grover Cleveland

Reverse: value

Date of first series: 1928; date of last series: 1934; obverse: James Madison

Reverse: value

Date of first series: 1928; date of last series: 1934; obverse: Salmon P. Chase

Reverse: value

The gold standard was suspended twice during World War Ⅰ, once fully and then for foreign exchange. At the onset of the war, US corporations had large debts payable to European entities, whom began liquidating their debts in gold. With debts looming to Europe, the dollar to British pound exchange rate reached as high as $6.75, far above the (gold) parity of $4.8665. This caused large gold outflows until July 31, 1914 when the New York Stock Exchange closed and the gold standard was temporarily suspended. In order to defend the exchange value of the dollar, the US Treasury Department authorized state and nationally-chartered banks to issue emergency currency under the Aldrich-Vreeland Act, and the newly-created Federal Reserve organized a fund to assure debts to foreign creditors. These efforts were largely successful, and the Aldrich-Vreeland notes were retired starting in November and the gold standard was restored when the New York Stock Exchange re-opened in December 1914.

As the United States remained neutral in the war, it remained the only country to maintain its gold standard, doing so without restriction on import or export of gold from 1915—1917. During the participation of the US as a belligerent(交战国), President Wilson banned gold export, thereby suspending the gold standard for foreign exchange. After the war, European countries slowly returned to their gold standards, though in somewhat altered form.

A gold-standard 1928 one-dollar bill. It is identified as a "United States Note" rather than a Federal Reserve note and by the words "Will Pay to the Bearer on Demand", which do not appear on today's currency. This clause became obsolete in 1933 but remained on new notes for 30 years thereafter.

During the Great Depression, every major currency abandoned the gold standard. Among the earliest, the Bank of England abandoned the gold standard in 1931 as speculators demanded gold in exchange for currency, threatening the solvency of the British monetary system. This pattern repeated throughout Europe and North America. In the United States, the Federal Reserve was forced to raise interest rates in order to protect the gold standard for the US dollar, worsening already severe domestic economic pressures. After bank runs became more pronounced in early 1933, people began to hoard gold coins as distrust for banks led to distrust for paper money, worsening deflation and gold reserves.

In early 1933, in order to fight severe deflation Congress and President Roosevelt implemented a series of Acts of Congress and Executive Orders which suspended the gold standard except for foreign exchange, revoked gold as universal legal tender for debts, and banned private ownership of significant amounts of gold coin. These acts included Executive Order 6073, the Emergency Banking Act, Executive Order 6102, Executive Order 6111, the Agricultural Adjustment Act, 1933 Banking Act, House Joint Resolution 192, and later the Gold Reserve Act. These actions were upheld by the US Supreme Court in the "Gold Clause Cases" in 1935.

For foreign exchange purposes, the set $20.67 per ounce value of the dollar was lifted, allowing the dollar to float freely in foreign exchange markets with no set value in gold. This was terminated after one year. Roosevelt attempted first to restabilize falling prices with the Agricultural Adjustment Act, however, this did not prove popular, so instead the next politically popular option was to devalue the dollar on foreign exchange markets. Under the Gold Reserve Act the value of the dollar was fixed at $35 per ounce, making the dollar more attractive for foreign buyers (and making foreign currencies more expensive to those holding US dollars). The higher price increased the conversion of gold into dollars, allowing the U.S. to effectively corner the world gold market.

The suspension of the gold standard was considered temporary by many in markets and in the government at the time, but restoring the standard was considered a low priority to dealing with other issues.

Under the post-World War II Bretton Woods system, all other currencies were valued in terms of U. S. dollars and were thus indirectly linked to the gold standard. The need for the U. S. government to maintain both a \$35 per troy ounce (112.53 ¢/g) market price of gold and also the conversion to foreign currencies caused economic and trade pressures. By the early 1960s, compensation for these pressures started to become too complicated to manage.

In March 1968, the effort to control the private market price of gold was abandoned. A two-tier system began. In this system all central-bank transactions in gold were insulated from the free market price. Central banks would trade gold among themselves at \$35 per troy ounce (112.53 ¢/g) but would not trade with the private market. The private market could trade at the equilibrium market price and there would be no official intervention. The price immediately jumped to \$43 per troy ounce (138.25 ¢/g). The price of gold touched briefly back at \$35 (112.53 ¢/g) near the end of 1969 before beginning a steady price increase. This gold price increase turned steep through 1972 and hit a high that year of over \$70 (2.25 \$/g). By that time floating exchange rates had also begun to emerge, which indicated the de facto dissolution of the Bretton Woods system. The two-tier system was abandoned in November 1973. By then the price of gold had reached \$100 per troy ounce (3.22 \$/g).

In the early 1970s, inflation caused by rising prices for imported commodities, especially oil, and spending on the Vietnam War, which was not counteracted by cuts in other government expenditures, combined with a trade deficit to create a situation in which the dollar was worth less than the gold used to back it.

In 1972, the United States reset the value to 38 dollars per troy ounce (122.17 ¢/g) of gold. Because other currencies were valued in terms of the U. S. dollar, this failed to resolve the disequilibrium between the U. S. dollar and other currencies. In 1975 the United States began to float the dollar with respect to both gold and other currencies. With this the United States was, for the first time, on a fully fiat currency.

The sudden jump in the price of gold after central banks gave up on controlling it was a strong sign of a loss of confidence in the U. S. dollar. In the absence of a gold-market-valued U. S. dollar, investors were choosing to continue putting their faith in actual gold. Consequently, the price of gold rose from \$35 per troy ounce (1.125 \$/g) in 1969 to almost \$900 (29 \$/g) in 1980.

This graph shows the final closing value of the U. S. dollar for each calendar year. Value is measured in milligrams of gold. By this measure the U. S. dollar lost a great amount of value during the 1970s.

Shortly after the gold price started its ascent in the early 1970s, the price of other commodities such as oil also began to rise. While commodity prices became more volatile(不稳

定的), the average exchange rate between oil and gold remained much the same in the 1990s as it had been in the 1960s, 1970s and 1980s.

Fearing the emergence of a specie gold-based economy separate from central banking, and with the corresponding threat of the collapse of the U. S. dollar, the U. S. government approved several changes to the trading on the COMEX. These changes resulted in a steep decline in the traded value of precious metals from the early 1980s onward.

In September 1987 under the Reagan administration the U. S. Secretary of the Treasury James Baker made a proposal through the IMF to use a commodity basket (which included gold) as a reference point to manage national currencies. However, the stock market Crash of October 1987 followed by the Iran-Contra scandal distracted the administration from such plans, and political momentum was lost.

As of May 2004, the U. S. reserve assets include $11,045,000,000 of gold stock, valued at $42.2222 per fine troy ounce (1.36 $/g).

Fiat standard（不兑现纸币本位）

Today, like the currency of most nations, the dollar is fiat money, unbacked by any physical asset. A holder of a federal reserve note has no right to demand an asset such as gold or silver from the government in exchange for a note. Consequently, proponents of the intrinsic theory of value believe that the dollar has little intrinsic value (i. e., none except for the value of the paper) and is only valuable as a medium of exchange.

In 1963 the words "PAYABLE TO THE BEARER ON DEMAND" were removed from all newly issued Federal Reserve notes. Then, in 1968, redemption of pre-1963 Federal Reserve notes for gold or silver officially ended. The Coinage Act of 1965 removed all silver from quarters and dimes, which were 90% silver prior to the act. However, there was a provision in the act allowing some coins to contain a 40% silver consistency, such as the Kennedy Half Dollar. Later, even this provision was removed, and all coins minted for general circulation are now mostly clad. The content of the nickel has not changed since 1946.

All circulating notes, issued from 1861 to present, will be honored by the government at face value as legal tender. But this means only that the government will give the holder of the notes new federal reserve notes in exchange for the note (or will accept the old notes as payments for debts owed to the federal government). The government is not obligated to redeem the notes for gold or silver, even if the note itself states that it is so redeemable. Some bills may have a premium to collectors.

The only exception to this rule is the $10,000 gold certificate of Series 1900, a number of which were inadvertently released to the public because of a fire in 1935. A box of them was literally thrown out of a window. This set is not considered to be "in circulation" and in fact is stolen property. However, the government canceled these banknotes and removed them from official records. Their value, relevant only to collectors, is approximately one thousand dollars.

According to the Federal Reserve Bank of New York, there was $829 Billion in total US currency in worldwide circulation as of December 2007.

In September 2004, it was estimated that if all the gold held by the U. S. government (261.7 million ounces = 8.14 million kilograms) were again required to back the circulating U. S. currency ($733,170,953,704), gold would need to be valued at $2,800/ounce (90 $/g).

Greenbacks

The federal government began issuing currency that was backed by Spanish dollars during the American Civil War. As photographic technology of the day could not reproduce color, it was decided the back of the bills would be printed in a color other than black. Because the color green was seen as a symbol of stability, it was selected. These bills were known as "greenbacks" for their color and started a tradition of the United States' printing the back of its money in green. In contrast to the currency notes of many other countries, Federal Reserve notes of varying denominations are the same colors: predominantly black ink with green highlights on the front, and predominantly green ink on the back. Federal Reserve notes were printed in the same colors for most of the 20th century, although older bills called "silver certificates" had blue highlights on the front, and "United States notes" had red highlights on the front.

In 1929, sizing of the bills was standardized (involving a 25% reduction in their current sizes). Modern U. S. currency, regardless of denomination, is 2.61 inches (66.3 mm) wide, 6.14 inches (156 mm) long, and 0.0043 inches (0.109 mm) thick. A single bill weighs about one gram and costs approximately 4.2 cents for the Bureau of Engraving and Printing to produce.

Microprinting and security threads were introduced in the 1991 currency series.

Another series started in 1996 with the $100 note, adding the following changes:

- A larger portrait, moved off-center to create more space to incorporate a watermark.
- The watermark to the right of the portrait depicting the same historical figure as the portrait. The watermark can be seen only when held up to the light (and had long been a standard feature of all other major currencies).

- A security thread that will glow red when exposed to ultraviolet light in a dark environment. The thread is in a unique position on each denomination.
- Color-shifting ink that changes from green to black when viewed from different angles. This feature appears in the numeral on the lower right-hand corner of the bill front.
- Microprinting in the numeral in the note's lower left-hand corner and on Benjamin Franklin's coat.
- Concentric fine-line printing in the background of the portrait and on the back of the note. This type of printing is difficult to copy well.
- The value of the currency written in 14pt Arial font on the back for those with sight disabilities.
- Other features for machine authentication and processing of the currency.

Annual releases of the 1996 series followed. The $50 note on June 12, 1997, introduced a large dark numeral with a light background on the back of the note to make it easier for people to identify the denomination. The $20 note in 1998 introduced a new machine-readable capability to assist scanning devices. The security thread glows green under ultraviolet light, and "USA TWENTY" and a flag are printed on the thread, while the numeral "20" is printed within the star field of the flag. The microprinting is in the lower left ornamentation of the portrait and in the lower left corner of the note front. As of 1998, the $20 note was the most frequently counterfeited note in the United States.

On May 13, 2003, the Treasury announced that it would introduce new colors into the $20 bill, the first U.S. currency since 1905 to have colors other than green or black. The move was intended primarily to reduce counterfeiting, rather than to increase visual differentiation between denominations. The main colors of all denominations, including the new $20 and $50, remain green and black; the other colors are present only in subtle shades in secondary design elements. This contrasts with the euro and other currencies, in which the main banknote colors contrast strongly with one another.

The new $20 bills entered circulation on October 9, 2003, the new $50 bills on September 28, 2004. The new $10 notes were introduced in 2006, the new $5 bills on March 13, 2008. And the $100 note will eventually be redesigned, but a date has not been announced. Each will have subtle elements of different colors, though will continue to be primarily green and black. The Treasury said it will update Federal Reserve notes every 7 to 10 years to keep up with counterfeiting technology. In addition, there have been rumors that future banknotes will use embedded RFID microchips as another anti-counterfeiting tool.

The 2008 $5 bill contains significant new security updates. The obverse side of the bill includes patterned yellow printing that will cue digital image-processing software to prevent digital copying, watermarks, digital security thread, and extensive microprinting. The reverse side includes an oversized purple number 5 to provide easy differentiation from other denominations.

"The soundness of a nation's currency is essential to the soundness of its economy. And to uphold our currency's soundness, it must be recognized and honored as legal tender and counterfeiting must be effectively thwarted," Federal Reserve Chairman Alan Greenspan said at a ceremony unveiling the $20 bill's new design. Prior to the current design, the most recent redesign of the U.S. dollar bill was in 1996.

Large portrait

Date of first series: 1999; date of last series: 2006; obverse: President Abraham Lincoln; Great Seal of the United States

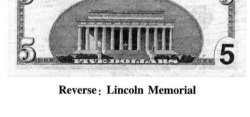

Reverse: Lincoln Memorial

Date of first series: 1999; date of last series: 2003; obverse: Secretary Alexander Hamilton; The phrase "We the People" from the United States Constitution and the torch of the Statue of Liberty

Reverse: United States Department of Treasury Building

Date of first series: 1996; date of last series: 2001 (current: 2006); obverse: Benjamin Franklin

Reverse: Independence Hall

Part Ⅲ CURRENCIES

Post-2004 Redesigned Series

Beginning in 2003, the Federal Reserve introduced a new series of bills, featuring images of the symbols of freedom. The new $20 bill was first issued on October 9, 2003; the new $50 on September 28, 2004; the new $10 bill on March 2, 2006; the new $5 on March 13, 2008 and the new $100 at a later time.

Date of first series: 2006; date of last series: March 13, 2008; obverse: President Abraham Lincoln; Great Seal of the United States; watermark: Two Watermarks of the Number "5"; main color: Purple

Reverse: Lincoln Memorial

Date of first series: 2004A; date of last series: March 2, 2006; obverse: Secretary Alexander Hamilton; The phrase "We the People" from the United States Constitution and the torch of the Statue of Liberty; watermark: As portrait; main color: orange

Reverse: United States Department of Treasury Building

Date of first series: 2004; date of last series: October 9, 2003; obverse: President Andrew Jackson; Eagle; main color: green

Reverse: White House

Date of first series: 2004; date of last series: September 28, 2004; obverse: President Ulysses S. Grant; Flag of the United States; main color: pink

Reverse: United States Capitol

(FROM: http://en.wikipedia.org/wiki/History_of_the_United_States_dollar)

( ) 1. The history of the United States dollar covers more than _____ years.
  A. 100 B. 200 C. 150 D. 250

( ) 2. Though several monetary systems were proposed for the early republic, the dollar was approved by _____ in a largely symbolic resolution on August 8, 1786.
  A. treasury department B. President
  C. Minister D. Congress

( ) 3. The term "dollar" was widely used in reference to a _____ coin at the time it was adopted by the United States.
  A. Portuguese B. Spanish C. British D. French

( ) 4. Bimetallism persisted until March 14, _____, with the passage of the Gold Standard Act.
  A. 1890 B. 1910 C. 1900 D. 1920

( ) 5. The gold standard was suspended twice during _____, once fully and then for foreign exchange.
  A. World War II B. Civil War
  C. war between the states D. World War I

( ) 6. During the _____, every major currency abandoned the gold standard.
  A. Great War B. Great Depression
  C. World War I D. World War II

( ) 7. In _____ the words "PAYABLE TO THE BEARER ON DEMAND" were removed from all newly issued Federal Reserve notes.
  A. 1963 B. 1964 C. 1965 D. 1968

( ) 8. In the sentence "All circulating notes, issued from 1861 to present, will be honored by the government at face value as legal tender.", the word HONORED means _____.
  A. paid B. pay C. cover D. settle

FURTHER READING

THE FEDERAL RESERVE SYSTEM
SUPERVISION AND REGULATION

The Federal Reserve has supervisory and regulatory authority over a wide range of financial institutions and activities. It works with other federal and state supervisory authorities to ensure the safety and soundness of financial institutions, stability in the financial markets, and fair and equitable treatment of consumers in their financial transactions. As the U.S. central bank, the Federal Reserve also has extensive and well-established relationships with the central banks and financial supervisors of other countries, which enables it to coordinate its actions with those of other countries when managing international financial crises and supervising institutions with a substantial international presence.

The Federal Reserve has responsibility for supervising and regulating the following segments of the banking industry to ensure safe and sound banking practices and compliance with banking laws:

- bank holding companies, including diversified financial holding companies formed under the Gramm-Leach-Bliley Act of 1999 and foreign banks with U.S. operations
- state-chartered banks that are members of the Federal Reserve System (state member banks)
- foreign branches of member banks
- Edge and agreement corporations, through which U.S. banking organizations may conduct international banking activities
- U.S. state-licensed branches, agencies, and representative offices of foreign banks
- nonbanking activities of foreign banks

Although the terms bank supervision and bank regulation are often used interchangeably, they actually refer to distinct, but complementary, activities. Bank supervision involves the monitoring, inspecting, and examining of banking organizations to assess their condition and their compliance with relevant laws and regulations. When a banking organization within the Federal Reserve's supervisory jurisdiction is found to be noncompliant or to have other problems, the Federal Reserve may use its supervisory authority to take formal or informal action to have the organization correct the problems.

Bank regulation entails issuing specific regulations and guidelines governing the operations, activities, and acquisitions of banking organizations.

Responsibilities of the Federal Banking Agencies

The Federal Reserve shares supervisory and regulatory responsibilities for domestic banking institutions with the Office of the Comptroller of the Currency (OCC)(货币监理局), the Federal Deposit Insurance Corporation (FDIC), and the Office of Thrift Supervision (OTS) at the federal level, and with the banking departments of the various states. The primary supervisor of a domestic banking institution is generally determined by the type of institution that it is and the governmental authority that granted it permission to commence business (commonly referred to as a charter). Banks that are chartered by a state government are referred to as state banks; banks that are chartered by the OCC, which is a bureau of the Department of the Treasury, are referred to as national banks.

The primary supervisor of a domestic banking institution is generally determined by the type of institution that it is and the governmental authority that granted it permission to commence business.

The Federal Reserve has primary supervisory authority for state banks that elect to become members of the Federal Reserve System (state member banks). State banks that are not members of the Federal Reserve System (state nonmember banks) are supervised by the FDIC. In addition to being supervised by the Federal Reserve or FDIC, all state banks are supervised by their chartering state. The OCC supervises national banks. All national banks must become members of the Federal Reserve System. This dual federal-state banking system has evolved partly out of the complexity of the U.S. financial system, with its many kinds of depository institutions and numerous chartering authorities. It has also resulted from a wide variety of federal and state laws and regulations designed to remedy problems that the U.S. commercial banking system has faced over its history.

Banks are often owned or controlled by another company. These companies are referred to as **bank holding companies**(银行控股公司). The Federal Reserve has supervisory authority for all bank holding companies, regardless of whether the subsidiary bank(分行) of the holding company is a national bank, state member bank, or state nonmember bank.

Savings associations, another type of depository institution, have historically focused on **residential mortgage lending**(住宅抵押借款). The OTS, which is a bureau of the Department of the Treasury, charters and supervises federal savings associations and also supervises companies that own or control a savings association. These companies are referred to as thrift holding companies.

The FDIC insures the deposits of banks and savings associations up to certain limits established by law. As the insurer, the FDIC has special examination authority to determine the condition of an insured bank or savings association for insurance purposes.

Table 1 summarizes the supervisory responsibilities of the Federal Reserve and other federal banking agencies.

Table 1 Federal supervisor and regulator of corporate components of banking organizations in the United States

Component	Supervisor and regulator
Bank holding companies (including financial holding companies)	FR
Nonbank subsidiaries of bank holding companies	FR Functional regulator
National banks	OCC
State banks 　　Members 　　Nonmembers	 FR FDIC
Thrift holding companies(储蓄机构控股公司)	OTS
Savings banks(储蓄银行)	OTS
FDIC Savings and loan associations(储蓄借款社)	OTS
Edge and agreement corporations(艾奇及协议公司)	FR
Foreign banks 　　Branches and agencies State-licensed 　　Federally licensed 　　Representative offices	 FRFDIC OCCFDIC FR

NOTE: FR = Federal Reserve; OCC = Office of the Comptroller of the Currency; FDIC = Federal Deposit Insurance Corporation; OTS = Office of Thrift Supervision

1. Nonbank subsidiaries engaged in securities, commodities, or insurance activities are supervised and regulated by their appropriate functional regulators. Such functionally regulated subsidiaries include a broker, dealer, investment adviser, and investment company registered with and regulated by the Securities and Exchange Commission (or, in the case of an investment adviser, registered with any state); an insurance company or insurance agent subject to supervision by a state insurance regulator; and a subsidiary engaged in commodity activities regulated by the Commodity Futures Trading Commission.

2. Applies to direct operations in the United States. Foreign banks may also have indirect operations in the United States through their ownership of U.S. banking organizations.

3. The FDIC has responsibility for branches that are insured.

Federal Financial Institutions Examination Council

To promote consistency in the examination and supervision of banking organizations, in 1978 Congress created the Federal Financial Institutions Examination Council (FFIEC). The FFIEC is composed of the chairpersons of the FDIC and the National Credit Union Administration, the comptroller of the currency, the director of the OTS, and a governor of the Federal Reserve Board appointed by the Board Chairman. The FFIEC's purposes are to prescribe uniform federal principles and standards for the examination of depository institutions, to promote coordination of bank supervision among the federal agencies that regulate financial institutions, and to encourage better coordination of federal and state regulatory activities. Through the FFIEC, state and federal regulatory agencies may exchange views on important regulatory issues. Among other things, the FFIEC has developed uniform financial reports for federally supervised banks to file with their federal regulator.

Supervisory Process

The main objective of the supervisory process is to evaluate the overall safety and soundness of the banking organization.

The main objective of the supervisory process is to evaluate the overall safety and soundness of the banking organization. This evaluation includes an assessment of the organization's risk-management systems(风险管理体系), financial condition, and compliance with applicable banking laws and regulations.

The supervisory process entails both on-site examinations and inspections and off-site surveillance and monitoring. Typically, state member banks must have an on-site examination at least once every twelve months. Banks that have assets of less than $250 million and that meet certain management, capital, and other criteria may be examined once every eighteen months. The Federal Reserve coordinates its examinations with those of the bank's chartering state and may alternate exam cycles with the bank's state supervisor.

The Federal Reserve generally conducts an annual inspection of large bank holding companies (companies with consolidated assets of $1 billion or greater) and smaller bank holding companies that have significant nonbank assets. Small, noncomplex bank holding companies are subject to a special supervisory program that permits a more flexible approach that relies on off-site monitoring and the supervisory ratings of the lead subsidiary depository institution. When evaluating the consolidated condition of the holding company, Federal Reserve examiners rely heavily on the results of the examination of the company's subsidiary banks by the primary federal or state banking authority, to minimize duplication of efforts and reduce burden on the banking organization.

Risk-Focused Supervision

With the largest banking organizations growing in both size and complexity, the Federal Reserve has moved towards a risk-focused approach to supervision that is more a continuous process than a **point-in-time examination** (即时检查). The goal of the risk-focused supervision process is to identify the greatest risks to a banking organization and assess the ability of the organization's management to identify, measure, monitor, and control these risks. Under the risk-focused approach, Federal Reserve examiners focus on those business activities that may pose the greatest risk to the organization.

Supervisory Rating System (监管评级体系)

The results of an on-site examination or inspection are reported to the board of directors and management of the bank or holding company in a report of examination or inspection, which includes a confidential supervisory rating of the financial condition of the bank or holding company. The supervisory rating system is a supervisory tool that all of the federal and state banking agencies use to communicate to banking organizations the agency's assessment of the organization and to identify institutions that raise concern or require special attention. This rating system for banks is commonly referred to as CAMELS, which is an acronym for the six components of the rating system: capital adequacy, asset quality, management and administration, earnings, liquidity, and sensitivity to market risk. The Federal Reserve also uses a supervisory rating system for bank holding companies, referred to as RFI/C(D), that takes into account risk management, financial condition, potential impact of the parent company and nondepository subsidiaries on the affiliated depository institutions, and the CAMELS rating of the affiliated depository institutions. (Note: The risk-management component has four subcomponents that reflect the effectiveness of the banking organization's risk management and controls: board and senior management oversight; policies, procedures, and limits; risk monitoring and management information systems; and internal controls. The financial-condition component has four subcomponents reflecting an assessment of the quality of the banking organization's capital, assets, earnings, and liquidity.)

Financial Regulatory Reports

In carrying out their supervisory activities, Federal Reserve examiners and supervisory staff rely on many sources of financial and other information about banking organizations, including reports of recent examinations and inspections, information published in the financial press and elsewhere, and the standard financial regulatory reports filed by institutions.

The financial report for banks is the Consolidated Reports of Condition and Income, often referred to as the Call Report(财政报告:美国金融当局每年要求银行提供的报表). It is used to prepare the Uniform Bank Performance Report, which employs ratio analysis to detect unusual or significant changes in a bank's financial condition that may warrant supervisory attention. The financial report for bank holding companies is the Consolidated Financial Statements for Bank Holding Companies (the FR Y-9 series).

The number and type of report forms that must be filed by a banking organization depend on the size of the organization, the scope of its operations, and the types of activities that it conducts either

Part III CURRENCIES

directly or through a subsidiary. The report forms filed by larger institutions that engage in a wider range of activities are generally more numerous and more detailed than those filed by smaller organizations.

Off-Site Monitoring

The Federal Reserve plays a significant role in promoting sound accounting policies and meaningful public disclosure by financial institutions.

In its ongoing off-site supervision of banks and bank holding companies, the Federal Reserve uses automated screening(审核) systems to identify organizations with poor or deteriorating financial profiles and to help detect adverse trends developing in the banking industry. The System to Estimate Examinations Ratings (SEER) statistically estimates an institution's supervisory rating based on prior examination data and information that banks provide in their quarterly Call Report filings. This information enables the Federal Reserve to better direct examiner resources to those institutions needing supervisory attention.

Accounting Policy and Disclosure

Enhanced market discipline is an important component of bank supervision. Accordingly, the Federal Reserve plays a significant role in promoting sound accounting policies and meaningful public disclosure by financial institutions. In 1991, Congress passed the Federal Deposit Insurance Corporation Improvement Act, emphasizing the importance of financial institution accounting, auditing, and control standards. In addition, the Sarbanes-Oxley Act of 2002 seeks to improve the accuracy and reliability of corporate disclosures and to detect and address corporate and accounting fraud. Through its supervision and regulation function, the Federal Reserve seeks to strengthen the accounting, audit, and control standards related to financial institutions. The Federal Reserve is involved in the development of international and domestic capital, accounting, financial disclosure, and other supervisory standards. Federal Reserve examiners also review the quality of **financial institutions' disclosure** (应行公告的财务事项) practices. Public disclosure allows market participants to assess the strength of individual institutions and is a critical element in market discipline.

Umbrella Supervision and Coordination with Other Functional Regulators

In addition to owning banks, bank holding companies also may own **broker-dealers**(经纪自营商) engaged in securities activities or insurance companies. Indeed, one of the primary purposes of the Gramm-Leach-Bliley Act (GLB Act), enacted in 1999, was to allow banks, securities broker-dealers, and insurance companies to affiliate with each other through the bank holding company structure. To take advantage of the expanded affiliations permitted by the GLB Act, a bank holding company must meet certain capital, managerial, and other requirements and must elect to become a "financial holding company". When a bank holding company or financial holding company owns a subsidiary broker-dealer or insurance company, the Federal Reserve seeks to coordinate its supervisory responsibilities with those of the subsidiary's functional regulator—the Securities and Exchange Commission (SEC) in the case of a broker-dealer and the state insurance authorities in the case of an insurance company.

The Federal Reserve's role as the supervisor of a bank holding company or financial holding company is to review and assess the consolidated organization's operations, risk-management systems, and capital adequacy to ensure that the holding company and its nonbank subsidiaries do not threaten the viability of the company's depository institutions. In this role, the Federal Reserve serves as the "umbrella supervisor" of the consolidated organization. In fulfilling this role, the Federal Reserve relies to the fullest extent possible on information and analysis provided by the appropriate supervisory authority of the company's bank, securities, or insurance subsidiaries.

Anti-Money-Laundering Program(反洗钱工程)

To enhance domestic security following the terrorist attacks of September 11, 2001, Congress passed the USA Patriot Act, which contained provisions for fighting international money laundering and for blocking terrorists' access to the U.S. financial system. The provisions of the act that affect banking organizations were generally set forth as amendments to the Bank Secrecy Act (BSA), which was enacted in 1970.

The BSA requires financial institutions doing business in the United States to report large currency transactions and to retain certain records, including information about persons involved in large currency transactions and about suspicious activity related to possible violations of federal law, such as money laundering, terrorist financing, and other financial crimes. The BSA also prohibits the use of foreign bank accounts to launder illicit funds or to avoid U.S. taxes and statutory restrictions.

The Department of the Treasury maintains primary responsibility for issuing and enforcing regulations to implement this statute. However, Treasury has delegated to the federal financial regulatory agencies responsibility for monitoring banks' compliance with the BSA. The Federal Reserve Board's Regulation H requires banking organizations to develop a written program for BSA compliance. During examinations of state member banks and U.S. branches and agencies of foreign banks, Federal Reserve examiners verify an institution's compliance with the recordkeeping and reporting requirements of the BSA and with related regulations, including those related to economic sanctions(经济制裁) imposed by Congress against certain countries, as implemented by the Office of Foreign Assets Control.

Business Continuity

After September 11, 2001, the Federal Reserve implemented a number of measures to promote the continuous operation of financial markets and to ensure the continuity of Federal Reserve operations in the event of a future crisis. The process of strengthening the resilience of the private-sector financial system—focusing on organizations with systemic elements—is largely accomplished through the existing regulatory framework. In 2003, responding to the need for further guidance for financial institutions in this area, the Federal Reserve Board, the OCC, and the SEC issued the "Interagency Paper on Sound Practices to Strengthen the Resilience of the U.S. Financial System". The paper sets forth sound practices for the financial industry to ensure a rapid recovery of the U.S. financial system in the event of a wide-scale disruption that may include loss or inaccessibility of staff. Many of the concepts in the paper amplify long-standing and well-recognized principles relating to safeguarding information and the ability to recover and resume essential financial services.

Other Supervisory Activities

The Federal Reserve conducts on-site examinations of banks to ensure compliance with consumer protection laws as well as compliance in other areas, such as **fiduciary activities**(信用活动), transfer agency, securities clearing agency, government and municipal securities dealing, securities credit lending, and information technology. Further, in light of the importance of information technology to the safety and soundness of banking organizations, the Federal Reserve has the authority to examine the operations of certain independent organizations that provide information technology services to supervised banking organizations.

Enforcement

If the Federal Reserve determines that a state member bank or bank holding company has problems that affect the institution's safety and soundness or is not in compliance with laws and regulations, it may take a supervisory action to ensure that the institution undertakes corrective measures. Typically, such findings are communicated to the management and directors of a banking organization in a written report. The management and directors are then asked to address all identified problems voluntarily and to take measures to ensure that the problems are corrected and will not recur. Most problems are resolved promptly after they are brought to the attention of an institution's management and directors. In some situations, however, the Federal Reserve may need to take an informal supervisory action, requesting that an institution adopt a board resolution or agree to the provisions of a memorandum of understanding to address the problem.

If necessary, the Federal Reserve may take formal enforcement actions to compel the management and directors of a troubled banking organization, or persons associated with it, to address the organization's problems. For example, if an institution has significant deficiencies or fails to comply with an informal action, the Federal Reserve may enter into a written agreement with the troubled institution or may issue a **cease-and-desist order**[结束和停止命令;禁止商业欺诈行为的通知(美国)] against the institution or against an individual associated with the institution, such as an officer or director. The Federal Reserve may also assess a fine, remove an officer or director from office and permanently bar him or her from the banking industry, or both. All final enforcement orders issued by the Board and all written agreements executed by Reserve Banks are available to the public on the Board's web site.

Supervision of International Operations of U.S. Banking Organizations

Under federal law, U.S. banking organizations generally may conduct a wider range of activities abroad than they may conduct in this country.

The Federal Reserve also has supervisory and regulatory responsibility for the international operations of member banks (that is, national and state member banks) and bank holding companies. These responsibilities include

- authorizing the establishment of foreign branches of national banks and state member banks and regulating the scope of their activities;
- chartering and regulating the activities of Edge and agreement corporations, which are specialized institutions used for international and foreign business;
- authorizing foreign investments of member banks, Edge and agreement corporations, and bank holding companies and regulating the activities of foreign firms acquired by such investors; and
- establishing supervisory policy and practices regarding foreign lending by state member banks.

Under federal law, U.S. banking organizations generally may conduct a wider range of activities abroad than they may conduct in this country.

The Board has broad discretionary powers(自行决定权;斟酌决定权) to regulate the foreign activities of member banks and bank holding companies so that, in financing U.S. trade and investments abroad, U.S. banking organizations can be fully competitive with institutions of the host country. U.S. banks also may conduct deposit and loan business in U.S. markets outside their home states through Edge and agreement corporations if the operations of the corporations are related to international transactions.

The Federal Reserve examines the international operations of state member banks, Edge and agreement corporations, and bank holding companies principally at the U.S. head offices of these organizations. When appropriate, the Federal Reserve will conduct an examination at the foreign operations of a U.S. banking organization in order to review the accuracy of financial and operational information maintained at the head office as well as to test the organization's adherence to safe and sound banking practices and to evaluate its efforts to implement corrective measures. Examinations abroad are conducted in cooperation with the responsible foreign-country supervisor.

Supervision of U. S. Activities of Foreign Banking Organizations

Although foreign banks have been operating in the United States for more than a century, before 1978 the U.S. branches and agencies of these banks were not subject to supervision or regulation by any federal banking agency. When Congress enacted the International Banking Act of 1978 (IBA), it created a federal regulatory structure for the activities of foreign banks with U.S. branches and agencies. The IBA established a policy of "**national treatment**"(国民待遇) for foreign banks operating in the United States to promote competitive equality between them and domestic institutions. This policy generally gives foreign banking organizations operating in the United States the same powers as U. S. banking organizations and subjects them to the same restrictions and obligations that apply to the domestic operations of U.S. banking organizations.

The Foreign Bank Supervision Enhancement Act of 1991 (FBSEA) increased the Federal Reserve's supervisory responsibility and authority over the U.S. operations of foreign banking organizations and eliminated gaps in the supervision and regulation of foreign banking organizations. The FBSEA amended the IBA to require foreign banks to obtain Federal Reserve approval before establishing branches, agencies, or commercial lending company subsidiaries in the United States. An application by a foreign bank to establish such offices or subsidiaries generally may be approved only if the Board determines that the foreign bank and any foreign-bank parents engage in banking business outside the United States and are subject to comprehensive supervision or regulation on a consolidated basis by their home-country supervisors. The Board may also take into account other factors, such as whether the home-country supervisor has consented to the proposed new office or subsidiary, the financial and managerial resources of the foreign bank, the condition of any existing U. S. offices, the bank's compliance with U.S. law, the extent of access by the Federal Reserve to information on the foreign bank from the bank and its home-country supervisor, and whether both the foreign bank and its home-country supervisor have taken actions to combat money laundering. The Board's prior approval is also required before a foreign bank may establish a representative office and, in approving the establishment of such an office, the Board takes the above-mentioned standards into account to the extent deemed appropriate.

The FBSEA also increased the responsibility and the authority of the Federal Reserve to regularly examine the U.S. operations of foreign banks. Under the FBSEA, all branches and agencies of foreign banks must be examined on-site at least once every twelve months, although this period may be extended to eighteen months if the branch or agency meets certain criteria. Supervisory actions resulting from examinations may be taken by the Federal Reserve alone or with other agencies. Representative offices are also subject to examination by the Federal Reserve.

The Federal Reserve evaluates transactions between a bank and its affiliates to determine the effect of the transactions on the bank's condition.

The Federal Reserve coordinates the supervisory program for the U.S. operations of foreign banking organizations with the other federal and state banking agencies. Since a foreign banking organization may have both federally and state-chartered offices in the United States, the Federal Reserve plays a key role in assessing the condition of the organization's entire U.S. operations and the foreign banking organization's ability to support its U.S. operations. In carrying out their supervisory responsibilities, the Federal Reserve and other U.S. supervisors rely on two supervisory tools: SOSA rankings and ROCA ratings. SOSA (the Strength of Support Assessment) is the examiners' assessment of a foreign bank's ability to provide support for its U.S. operations. The ROCA rating is an assessment of the organization's U.S. activities in terms of its risk management, operational controls, compliance, and asset quality.

Under the Bank Holding Company Act and the IBA, the Federal Reserve is also responsible for approving, reviewing, and monitoring the U.S. nonbanking activities of foreign banking organizations that have a branch, agency, commercial lending company, or subsidiary bank in the United States. In addition, such foreign banks must obtain Federal Reserve's approval to acquire more than 5 percent of the shares of a

U.S. bank or bank holding company.

Supervision of Transactions with Affiliates

As part of the supervisory process, the Federal Reserve also evaluates transactions between a bank and its affiliates to determine the effect of the transactions on the bank's condition and to ascertain whether the transactions are consistent with sections 23A and 23B of the Federal Reserve Act, as implemented by the Federal Reserve Board's Regulation W. Since the GLB Act increased the range of affiliations permitted to banking organizations, sections 23A and 23B play an increasingly important role in limiting the risk to depository institutions from these broader affiliations. Among other things, section 23A prohibits a bank from purchasing an affiliate's low-quality assets. In addition, it limits a bank's loans and other extensions of credit to any single affiliate to 10 percent of the bank's capital and surplus, and it limits loans and other extensions of credit to all affiliates in the aggregate to 20 percent of the bank's capital and surplus. Section 23B requires that all transactions between a bank and its affiliates be on terms that are substantially the same, or at least as favorable, as those prevailing at the time for comparable transactions with nonaffiliated companies. The Federal Reserve Board is the only banking agency that has the authority to exempt any bank from these requirements. During the course of an examination, examiners review a banking organization's intercompany transactions for compliance with these statutes and Regulation W.

Regulatory Functions

As a bank regulator, the Federal Reserve establishes standards designed to ensure that banking organizations operate in a safe and sound manner and in accordance with applicable law. These standards may take the form of regulations, rules, policy guidelines, or supervisory interpretations and may be established under specific provisions of a law or under more general legal authority. Regulatory standards may be either restrictive (limiting the scope of a banking organization's activities) or permissive (authorizing banking organizations to engage in certain activities).

In many cases, the Federal Reserve Board's regulations are adopted to implement specific legislative initiatives or requirements passed by Congress. These statutory provisions may have been adopted by

Congress to respond to past crises or problems or to update the nation's banking laws to respond to changes in the marketplace. For example, in response to the savings and loan crisis and financial difficulties in the banking industry in the late 1980s and early 1990s, Congress enacted several laws to improve the condition of individual institutions and of the overall banking industry, including the Competitive Equality Banking Act of 1987; the Financial Institutions Reform, Recovery, and Enforcement Act of 1989; and the Federal Deposit Insurance Corporation Improvement Act of 1991. These legislative initiatives restricted banking practices, limited supervisors' **discretion**(自行处理) in dealing with weak banks, imposed new regulatory requirements—including prompt corrective action—and strengthened supervisory oversight(失察;疏忽) overall.

More recently, Congress has adopted other laws to respond to the growing integration of banking markets, both geographically and functionally, and the increasing convergence of banking, securities, and insurance activities. The Riegle-Neal Interstate Banking and Branching Efficiency Act of 1994 significantly reduced the legal barriers that had restricted the ability of banks and bank holding companies to expand their activities across state lines. In 1999, Congress passed the GLB Act, which repealed certain Depression-era banking laws and permitted banks to affiliate with securities and insurance firms within financial holding companies.

Acquisitions and Mergers(并购)

Under the authority assigned to the Federal Reserve by the Bank Holding Company Act of 1956 as amended, the Bank Merger Act of 1960, and the Change in Bank Control Act of 1978, the Federal Reserve Board maintains broad authority over the structure of the banking system in the United States.

The Bank Holding Company Act assigned to the Federal Reserve primary responsibility for supervising and regulating the activities of bank holding companies. Through this act, Congress sought to achieve two basic objectives: (1) to avoid the creation of a monopoly or the restraint of trade in the banking industry through the acquisition of additional banks by bank holding companies and (2) to keep banking and commerce separate by restricting the nonbanking activities of bank holding companies. Historically, bank holding companies could engage only in banking activities and other activities that the Federal Reserve determined to be closely related to banking. But since the passage of the GLB Act, a bank holding company that qualifies to become a financial holding company may engage in a broader range of financially related activities, including full-scope securities underwriting and dealing, insurance underwriting and sales, and merchant banking. A bank holding company seeking financial holding company status must file a written declaration with the Federal Reserve System, certifying that the company meets the capital, managerial, and other requirements to be a financial holding company.

Bank Acquisitions

Under the Bank Holding Company Act, a firm that seeks to become a bank holding company must first obtain approval from the Federal Reserve. The act defines a bank holding company as any company that directly or indirectly owns, controls, or has the power to vote 25 percent or more of any class of the voting shares of a bank; controls in any manner the election of a majority of the directors or trustees of a bank; or is found to exercise a controlling influence over the management or policies of a bank. A bank holding company must obtain the approval of the Federal Reserve before acquiring more than 5 percent of the shares of an additional bank or bank holding company. All bank holding companies must file certain reports with the Federal Reserve System.

When considering applications to acquire a bank or a bank holding company, the Federal Reserve is required to take into account the likely effects of the acquisition on competition, the convenience and needs of the communities to be served, the financial and managerial resources and future prospects of the companies and banks involved, and the effectiveness of the company's policies to combat money laundering. In the case of an interstate bank acquisition, the Federal Reserve also must consider certain other factors and may not approve the acquisition if the resulting organization would control more than 10 percent of all deposits held by insured depository institutions. When a foreign bank seeks to acquire a U.S. bank, the Federal Reserve also must consider whether the foreign banking organization is subject to comprehensive supervision or regulation on a consolidated basis by its home-country supervisor.

Bank Mergers

Another responsibility of the Federal Reserve is to act on proposed bank mergers when the resulting institution would be a state member bank. The Bank Merger Act of 1960 sets forth the factors to be considered in evaluating merger applications. These factors are similar to those that must be considered in reviewing bank acquisition proposals by bank holding companies. To ensure that all merger applications are evaluated in a uniform manner, the act requires that the responsible agency request reports from the Department of Justice and from the other approving banking agencies addressing the competitive impact of the transaction.

Other Changes in Bank Control

The Change in Bank Control Act of 1978 authorizes the federal bank regulatory agencies to deny proposals by a single "person" (which includes an individual or an entity), or several persons acting in concert, to acquire control of an insured bank or a bank holding company. The Federal Reserve is responsible for approving changes in the control of bank holding companies and state member banks, and the FDIC and the OCC are responsible for approving changes in the control of insured state nonmember and national banks, respectively. In considering a proposal under the act, the Federal Reserve must review several factors, including the financial condition, competence, experience, and integrity of the acquiring person or group of persons; the effect of the transaction on competition; and the adequacy of the information provided by the acquiring party.

Formation and Activities of Financial Holding Companies

As authorized by the GLB Act, the Federal Reserve Board's regulations allow a bank holding company or a foreign banking organization to become a financial holding company and engage in an expanded array of financial activities if the company meets certain capital, managerial, and other criteria. Permissible activities for financial holding companies include conducting securities underwriting and dealing, serving as an insurance agent and underwriter, and engaging in merchant banking. Other permissible activities include those that the Federal Reserve Board, after consulting with the Secretary of the Treasury, determines to be financial in nature or incidental to financial activities. Financial holding companies also may engage to a limited extent in a nonfinancial activity if the Board determines that the activity is complementary to one or more of the company's financial activities and would not pose a substantial risk to the safety or soundness of depository institutions or the financial system.

Capital Adequacy Standards

A key goal of banking regulation is to ensure that banks maintain sufficient capital to absorb reasonably likely losses. In 1989, the federal banking regulators adopted a common standard for measuring capital adequacy that is broadly based on the risks of an institution's investments. This common standard, in turn, was based on the 1988 agreement "International Convergence of Capital Measurement and Capital Standards" (commonly known as the Basel Accord) developed by the Basel Committee on Banking Supervision. This committee, which is associated with the Bank for International Settlements headquartered in Switzerland, is composed of representatives of the central banks or bank supervisory authorities from Belgium, Canada, France, Germany, Italy, Japan, Luxembourg, the Netherlands, Spain, Sweden, Switzerland, the United Kingdom, and the United States.

The risk-based capital standards require institutions that assume greater risk to hold higher levels of capital. Moreover, these standards take into account risks associated with activities that are not included on a bank's balance sheet, such as the risks arising from commitments to make loans. Because they have been accepted by the bank supervisory authorities of most of the countries with major international banking centers, these standards promote safety and soundness and reduce competitive inequities among banking organizations operating within an increasingly global market.

Recognizing that the existing risk-based capital standards were in need of significant enhancements to address the activities of complex banking organizations, the Basel Committee began work to revise the Basel Accord in 1999 and, in June 2004, endorsed a revised framework, which is referred to as Basel II. Basel II has three "pillars" that make up the framework for assessing capital adequacy. Pillar I, minimum regulatory capital requirements, more closely aligns banking organizations' capital levels with their underlying risks. Pillar II, supervisory oversight, requires supervisors to evaluate banking organizations' capital adequacy and to encourage better risk-management techniques. Pillar Ⅲ, market discipline, calls for enhanced public disclosure of banking organizations' risk exposures.

Financial Disclosures by State Member Banks

State member banks that issue securities registered under the Securities Exchange Act of 1934 must disclose certain information of interest to investors, including annual and quarterly financial reports and **proxy statements**(股东签署的委托书). By statute, the Federal Reserve administers these requirements and has adopted financial disclosure regulations for state member banks that are substantially similar to the SEC's regulations for other public companies.

Securities Credit

The Securities Exchange Act of 1934 requires the Federal Reserve to regulate the extension of credit used in connection with the purchase of securities. Through its regulations, the Board establishes the minimum amount the buyer must put up when purchasing a security. This minimum amount is known as the **margin requirement**(保证金). In fulfilling its responsibility under the act, the Federal Reserve limits the amount of credit that may be provided by securities brokers and dealers (Regulation T) and the amount of securities credit extended by banks and other lenders (Regulation U). These regulations generally apply to **credit-financed**(信贷融资) purchases of securities traded on securities exchanges and certain securities traded over the counter when the credit is collateralized by such securities. In addition, Regulation X prohibits borrowers who are subject to U.S. laws from obtaining such credit overseas on terms more favorable than could be obtained from a domestic lender.

In general, compliance with the Federal Reserve's margin regulations is enforced by several federal regulatory agencies. The federal agencies that regulate financial institutions check for Regulation U compliance during examinations. The Federal Reserve checks for Regulation U compliance on the part of securities credit lenders not otherwise regulated by federal agencies. Compliance with Regulation T is verified during examinations of broker-dealers by the securities industry's self-regulatory organizations under the general oversight of the SEC.

(*FROM*: *http*://*www.federalreserve.gov*)

BACKGROUND KNOWLEDGE

▶ *Basel Committee on Banking Supervision* 巴塞尔银行监督委员会

An international committee of bank supervisors, associated with the BIS, that is headquartered in Basel, Switzerland, and is composed of bank supervisors from Belgium, Canada, France, Germany, Italy, Japan, Luxembourg, the Netherlands, Spain, Sweden, Switzerland, the United Kingdom, and the United States.

Part III CURRENCIES

CHAPTER 8
THE EUROPEAN CENTRAL BANK & THE EUROSYSTEM

Learning Objectives

1. The road to economic and monetary union;
2. Structure and tasks;
3. Monetary policy;
4. The target 2 system;
5. Euro banknotes and coins;
6. Banking supervision.

FOREWORD

When speaking of a "central bank", the first idea which probably comes to mind is that it is the institution that issues money. And money is the instrument we use as a unit of account, a means of payment and a store of value. Granted, the key objective of any central bank is to ensure that the value of money is preserved over time. But there are many other lesser-known aspects of modern central banking. One of them is communication.

A central bank should not only do what it says it does but also explain what it is doing, thereby increasing the public's awareness and knowledge of the policies and services it provides.

This chapter forms part of our communication on the activities of the European Central Bank (ECB) at the heart of the European System of Central Banks (ESCB), along with the national central banks of the 27 European Union Member States. Since not all Member States have adopted the euro as their currency, the term Eurosystem is used to describe the entity composed of the ECB and the national central banks of those Member States that have adopted the euro, currently 15. Most of the tasks conferred upon the ESCB by the Treaty on European Union are handled by the Eurosystem.

1 THE ROAD TO ECONOMIC AND MONETARY UNION

1.1 EUROPEAN INTEGRATION

The idea of establishing an economic and monetary union in Europe goes back more than half a century. It was a vision of the political leaders who, in 1952, founded the European Coal and Steel Community (ECSC), which consisted of six countries—Belgium, Germany, France, Italy, Luxembourg and the Netherlands.

Gradual expansion of the European Union

Further steps were taken towards European integration in the 1950s and thereafter. The same six countries established the European Economic Community (EEC) and the European Atomic Energy Community (EURATOM) in 1958. This network of relationships strengthened and deepened over the years, becoming the European Communities (EC) and then, with the adoption of the Maastricht Treaty in 1993, the European Union (EU). The number of member countries increased too. Denmark, Ireland and the United Kingdom joined in 1973, followed by Greece eight years later. Portugal and Spain became members in 1986; Austria, Finland and Sweden joined in 1995. This expansion continued on 1 May 2004, when the Czech Republic, Estonia, Cyprus, Latvia, Lithuania, Hungary, Malta, Poland, Slovenia and Slovakia acceded to the European Union. Bulgaria and Romania are the latest members, having joined on 1 January 2007.

Criteria for accession to the EU

The conditions to be fulfilled before entering the EU are the Copenhagen criteria. These require the prospective members (ⅰ) to have stable institutions guaranteeing democracy, the rule of law, human rights and the respect for and protection of minorities, and (ⅱ) to have a functioning market economy as well as the capacity to cope with competitive pressure, in order to be able to take on the obligations of membership, including the aims of political, economic and monetary union.

1.2 ECONOMIC INTEGRATION

The first attempt to create an economic and monetary union was described in the Werner Report of 1970, which envisaged three stages to be completed by 1980. However, these first plans for an economic and monetary union were never realised amid the considerable international currency unrest after the collapse of the Bretton Woods system in the early 1970s, and the international recession in the wake of the first oil crisis in 1973.

To counter this instability, the then nine Member States of the EEC created the European Monetary System (EMS) in 1979. Its main feature was the exchange rate mechanism (ERM), which introduced fixed but adjustable exchange rates among the currencies of the nine countries.

Maastricht Treaty signed in 1992

In the second half of the 1980s the idea of an economic and monetary union was revived in the Single European Act of 1986, which created a single market. But it was realised that the full benefits of a single market could only be reaped with the introduction of a single currency for the participating countries. In 1988 the European Council instructed the Delors Committee to examine ways of realising Economic and Monetary Union (EMU). The 1989 Delors Report led to the negotiations for the Treaty on European Union, which established the European Union (EU) and amended the Treaty establishing the European Community. It was signed in Maastricht in February 1992 (so it is sometimes called the Maastricht Treaty) and entered into force on 1 November 1993.

Three stages towards EMU: I. Single European Market; II. European Monetary Institute; III. ECB and the euro

Progress towards EMU in Europe took place in three stages. Stage One (1990—1993) was characterised mainly by the full achievement of a single European market through the dismantling of all internal barriers to the free movement of persons, goods, capital and services within Europe.

Stage Two (1994—1998) started with the creation of the European Monetary Institute, and was dedicated to the technical preparations for the single currency, the avoidance of excessive deficits, and enhanced convergence of the economic and monetary policies of the Member States (to ensure stability of prices and sound public finances).

Stage Three began on 1 January 1999 with the irrevocable fixing of exchange rates, the transfer of monetary policy competence to the ECB and the introduction of the euro as the single currency. On 1 January 2002 euro banknotes and coins became legal tender in the participating countries and by the end of February 2002 national banknotes and coins ceased to be legal tender.

1.3 CONVERGENCE CRITERIA

Stability-oriented economic policies and independent central banks

Countries wishing to adopt the euro as their currency must achieve a high degree of "sustainable convergence". The degree of convergence is assessed on the basis of several criteria in the Maastricht Treaty, which require a country to have:

- a high degree of price stability
- sound public finances
- a stable exchange rate
- low and stable long-term interest rates.

The criteria are designed to ensure that only countries with stability-oriented economic policies and a track record in price stability are admitted to Stage

Three of EMU. The Treaty also requires the central bank of the respective country to be independent (see Article 108 of the Treaty).

1.4 MEMBER STATES HAVE ADOPTED THE EURO

In May 1998 an EU summit meeting in Brussels confirmed that 11 of the then 15 EU Member States Belgium, Germany, Spain, France, Ireland, Italy, Luxembourg, the Netherlands, Austria, Portugal and Finland had met the criteria for the adoption of the single currency. On 1 January 1999 these countries adopted the euro as their common currency. Greece joined this group of countries on 1 January 2001 after fulfilling the criteria. Other Member States have since complied with the convergence criteria and also joined the euro area Slovenia on 1 January 2007, and Cyprus and Malta on 1 January 2008. One member state, Sweden, did not fulfill all the conditions. Moreover, Denmark and the United Kingdom are "Member States with a special status". In protocols annexed to the Treaty establishing the European Community, the two countries were granted the right to choose whether or not to participate in Stage Three of EMU, i. e. to adopt the euro. They both made use of this so-called "opt-out clause" by notifying the EU Council that they do not intend for the time being to move to Stage Three, i. e. they do not yet wish to become part of the euro area.

Sweden as well as nine of the 12 countries that have joined since 2004 count as members with a "derogation" since they have not yet met all the requirements to adopt the euro. Having a derogation means that a Member State is exempt from some, but not all, of the provisions which normally apply from the beginning of Stage Three of EMU. It includes all provisions which transfer responsibility for monetary policy to the Governing Council of the ECB.

Two Member States have "opted out"

Like Sweden, the other Member States of the EU which have not yet adopted the euro have no "opt-out" clauses, such as those negotiated by the United Kingdom and Denmark.

New EU Member States are committed to ultimately adopting the euro

This implies that, by joining the EU, the new Member States commit themselves to ultimately adopting the euro when they fulfill the convergence criteria. The ECB and the European Commission prepare reports every other year—or at the request of a Member State with a derogation—on progress made towards fulfilling the convergence criteria. These convergence reports also take account of other factors that might influence the integration of the country into the euro area economy. The reports provide the basis for the EU Council's decision on whether to allow a new country to become part of the euro area.

1.5 KEY CHARACTERISTICS OF THE EURO AREA

The individual countries that now comprise the euro area were relatively open economies before they joined the euro area. However, they are now part of a larger, much more self-contained economy. The size of the euro area makes it comparable with major economies such as the United States and Japan.

One of the world's largest economies

The euro area is one of the largest economies in the world, with a population of 318 million in 2006. The European Union as a whole has 27 Member States and a population of 493 million. By comparison, the United States and Japan have 299 and 128 million inhabitants respectively.

In terms of gross domestic product (GDP) expressed in purchasing power parities, the United States was the largest economy in 2006, with 19.7% of world GDP, followed by the euro area with 14.3%. Japan's share was 6.3%. The shares of the individual euro area countries are significantly smaller: the largest accounted for 3.9% of world GDP in 2006.

Limited dependence on foreign trade

Although the euro area can be significantly affected by developments in the global economy, the fact that the euro area has a less open economy means that movements in prices of foreign goods have only a limited impact on domestic prices. However, it is more open than either the United States or Japan. Euro area exports of goods and services as a share of GDP were significantly higher in 2006 (21.6%) than the corresponding figures for the United States (11%) and Japan (16.8%).

1.6 BENEFITS OF THE EURO

A real single market for goods and services

With the establishment of Economic and Monetary Union (EMU), the EU has made an important step towards completing the internal market. Consumers and firms can now easily compare prices and find the most competitive suppliers in the euro area. Moreover, EMU is providing an environment of economic and monetary stability all over Europe which is favourable to sustainable growth and job creation, and the single currency has done away with disruptions caused by sharp movements in the exchange rates of the former national currencies.

The introduction of euro banknotes and coins on 1 January 2002 has made travelling simpler within the euro area. Prices for goods and services can be compared at a glance and payments can be made with the same money in all the countries.

Foreign exchange risks and transaction costs eliminated

With the birth of the euro, foreign exchange transaction costs and foreign exchange risks were eliminated within the euro area. In the past, these costs and risks hindered competition across borders. Increased competition makes it more likely that available resources will be used in the most efficient way. With a single currency, investment decisions are much easier, as fluctuations in the exchange rate can no longer influence the return on investment across national borders within the euro area.

Integration of financial markets

Before the introduction of the euro, financial markets were, as a rule, national in character. Financial instruments, such as government bonds and shares were denominated in national currencies. The launch of the euro was a major step towards the integration of the financial markets in the euro area. It will continue to influence the structure of the euro area economy. Evidence of integration can be found, to varying degrees, in all parts of the financial structure:

- The euro area's interbank money market is fully integrated.
- The euro-denominated bond market is well integrated, deep and liquid, and provides a wide choice of investments and funding.
- The euro area equity market is increasingly viewed as a single market.
- Domestic and cross-border mergers and acquisitions have increased among banks in the euro area.

The depth and quality of an integrated financial market facilitate the financing of economic growth and thereby the creation of jobs. People have a broader range of choices for their decisions on savings and investments. Companies can tap a very large capital market to finance their business and use new financial instruments to protect themselves against various financial risks and to enhance the management of their investments.

MILESTONES

1952 European Coal and Steel Community (ECSC) is established by Belgium, Germany, France, Italy, Luxembourg and the Netherlands.

1958 Treaties of Rome enter into force; European Economic Community (EEC) and European Atomic Energy Community (EURATOM) are set up.

1967 Merger Treaty combines three existing Communities (ECSC, EEC, EURATOM).

1970 Werner Report, first "blueprint" for a monetary union, is presented.

1973 Denmark, Ireland and the United Kingdom join the European Communities (EC).

1979 Establishment of European Monetary System (EMS).

1981 Greece joins the European Communities.

1986 Spain and Portugal join EC.

1987 Single European Act enters into force, paving the way for the single market.

1989 Delors Committee presents report on Economic and Monetary Union.

1990 Start of Stage One of EMU.

1993 Treaty on European Union (Maastricht Treaty) enters into force.

1994 Start of Stage Two of EMU. European Monetary Institute (EMI) is established in Frankfurt am Main.

1995 Austria, Finland and Sweden join EU

1998 EMI is liquidated; European Central Bank is established in Frankfurt am Main

1999 Start of Stage Three of EMU with 11 participating countries; introduction of the euro as a single currency.

　　　Amended Treaty on European Union (Treaty of Amsterdam) enters into force.

2001 Greece joins euro area as the 12th country.

2002 Euro banknotes and coins are put into circulation.

2003 Amended Treaty on European Union (Treaty of Nice) enters into force.

2004 Ten more countries join EU on 1 May.

2007 EU grows to 27 members with accession of Bulgaria and Romania. Slovenia joins euro area. Treaty of Lisbon is signed in December.

2008 Cyprus and Malta join euro area, which now has 15 members.

2 STRUCTURE AND TASKS

2.1 THE EUROPEAN SYSTEM OF CENTRAL BANKS AND THE EUROSYSTEM

The European System of Central Banks (ESCB) was established in accordance with the Maastricht Treaty and the Statute of the European System of Central Banks and of the European Central Bank. It comprises the European Central Bank (ECB) and the national central banks (NCBs) of all EU Member States.

The Eurosystem comprises the ECB and the NCBs of the EU Member States which have adopted the euro (currently 15).

The ECB's decision-making bodies are the Governing Council(行长理事会) and the Executive Board(执行董事会). The ECB's monetary policy decisions are taken by the Governing Council. The Executive Board implements the decisions and is responsible for the daily management of the ECB. The third decision-making body of the ECB is the General Council(总理事会), which will continue to exist as long as there are EU Member States which have not yet adopted the euro as their currency.

2.2 THE EUROPEAN CENTRAL BANK

The ECB is a supra-national organisation

The ECB was established in June 1998 in Frankfurt am Main, taking over from its predecessor, the European Monetary Institute (EMI). It is a supra-national institution with its own legal personality. The ECB is based in three buildings in the heart of Frankfurt but will move to its new headquarters, currently under construction in the eastern part of the city, in 2011.

The staff of the ECB is truly European; its members come from all 27 countries of the European Union.

2.3 TASKS OF THE EUROSYSTEM

Governing Council decides on key interest rates

The Eurosystem has four main tasks. The first task is to carry out the monetary policy adopted by the Governing Council of the ECB e. g. , decisions on the key ECB interest rates (the minimum bid rate on the main refinancing operations as well as interest rates on the marginal lending facility and the deposit facility and, where appropriate, decisions relating to monetary objectives and the supply of reserves). The Executive Board is responsible for implementing the monetary policy, a responsibility it exercises by giving instructions to the NCBs. For example, the Executive Board decides once a week on the allotment of liquidity to the banking sector via the main refinancing operations.

The second and third tasks of the Eurosystem are to conduct foreign exchange operations and to hold and manage the official reserves of the euro area countries.

Foreign reserve assets held by the ECB and by NCBs

The Eurosystem NCBs have transferred foreign reserve assets to the ECB totalling some 40 billion (85% in foreign currency holdings and 15% in gold). In exchange, the NCBs have received interest-bearing claims on the ECB, denominated in euro. Eurosystem NCBs are involved in the management of the ECB's foreign reserves: they act as agents for the ECB, in accordance with portfolio management guidelines set by the ECB. The remaining Eurosystem foreign reserve assets are owned and managed by the NCBs. Transactions in those reserve assets are regulated by the Eurosystem. In particular, transactions above certain thresholds require prior approval from the ECB.

A fourth main task of the Eurosystem is to promote the smooth operation of payment systems. Furthermore, the Eurosystem contributes to the conduct of financial supervision: it advises legislators in its field of competence and it compiles monetary and financial statistics. The Maastricht Treaty also specifies that the ECB has the exclusive right to authorise the issue of euro banknotes.

2.4 INDEPENDENCE

When performing Eurosystem-related tasks, the ECB and the national central banks must not seek or take instructions from Community institutions or bodies, from any government of an EU country or from any other body. Likewise, the Community institutions and bodies and the governments of the Member States must not seek to influence the members of the decision-making bodies of the ECB or of the NCBs in the performance of their tasks.

Personal independence

The Statute of the ESCB and of the ECB provides for security of tenure for governors of NCBs and members of the Executive Board as follows:

- a minimum term of office for NCB governors of five years;
- a non-renewable term of office of eight years for members of the Executive Board of the

ECB;

• removal of the Members of the Executive Board from office only in the event of incapacity or serious misconduct; in this respect the Court of Justice of the European Communities is competent to settle any disputes.

Functional independence

The Eurosystem is also functionally independent. The ECB and the NCBs have at their disposal all instruments and competencies necessary for the conduct of an efficient monetary policy and are authorised to decide autonomously how and when to use them.

The Eurosystem is prohibited from granting loans to Community bodies or national public sector entities, which further enhances its independence by shielding it from any influence exercised by public authorities. Moreover, the ECB's Governing Council has the right to adopt binding regulations to carry out the tasks of the ESCB and in certain other cases, as laid down in specific acts of the EU Council.

2.5 NATIONAL CENTRAL BANKS

The national central banks of the Eurosystem have a legal personality (under the law of their respective country) which is separate from that of the ECB. At the same time, they are an integral part of the Eurosystem, which is responsible for price stability in the euro area; they operate in line with the ECB's guidelines and instructions in the performance of the Eurosystem's tasks.

NCBs carry out monetary policy operations

The NCBs are involved in conducting the single monetary policy of the euro area. They carry out monetary policy operations, such as providing central bank money to credit institutions, and they ensure settlement of cashless domestic and cross-border payments. Moreover, they undertake foreign reserve management operations on their own account and as agents for the ECB.

In addition, the NCBs are largely responsible for collecting national statistical data and for issuing and handling euro banknotes in their respective countries. The NCBs also perform functions outside the scope of the Statute, unless the Governing Council deems them to be incompatible with the objectives and tasks of the Eurosystem.

Under national laws, the NCBs can be assigned other functions that are not related to monetary policy functions: some NCBs are involved in banking supervision and/or act as the government's principal banker.

2.6 DECISION-MAKING BODIES OF THE ECB

Governing Council meets every second Thursday

The Governing Council of the ECB comprises the members of the Executive Board of the ECB and the governors of the NCBs of the euro area countries. The Statute of the ESCB states that the Governing Council of the ECB must meet at least ten times a year. The dates of its meetings are decided by the Governing Council itself on the basis of a proposal from the Executive Board. Unless at least three governors object, meetings may also be held by teleconference. The Governing Council currently meets twice a month, usually on the first and third Thursday of each month. Monetary policy issues are normally discussed at the first meeting of the month only.

The President of the EU Council and a member of the European Commission may attend the meetings, although only the members of the Governing Council have the right to vote. Each member of the Governing Council has one vote and, except for decisions on the ECB's financial matters, the Governing Council takes its decisions by a simple majority. In the event of a tie, the President has the casting vote. As regards financial matters—for example, the subscription to the ECB's capital, the transfer of foreign exchange reserves, or the distribution of monetary income—the votes are weighted according to the NCBs' shares in the subscribed capital of the ECB.

The Treaty on European Union and the Statute of the ESCB and the ECB empower the Governing Council to take the most strategically significant decisions for the Eurosystem.

The main responsibilities of the Governing Council are:

- to formulate the monetary policy of the euro area; i.e. to take decisions on the level of the key ECB interest rates;

- to adopt the guidelines and take the decisions necessary to ensure the performance of the Eurosystem's tasks.

Focus on the euro area

When taking decisions on monetary policy and other tasks of the Eurosystem, the Governing Council takes into account the developments in the euro area as a whole.

Executive Board meets every Tuesday

The Executive Board comprises the President and the Vice-President of the ECB and four other members. They are appointed from among persons of recognised standing and professional experience in monetary and banking matters by common accord of the governments of the euro area at the level of the Heads of State or Government, on a recommendation from the EU Council after it has consulted the European Parliament and the Governing Council of the ECB. The Executive Board normally meets every Tuesday.

The President of the ECB or, in his absence, the Vice-President, chairs the meetings of the Governing Council, the Executive Board and the General Council of the ECB. The President is invited to the meetings of the Eurogroup, the informal group of the euro area economics and finance ministers, and he may participate in EU Council meetings on topics relating to the objectives and tasks of the Eurosystem.

The main responsibilities of the Executive Board are:

- to prepare the meetings of the Governing Council;

- to implement monetary policy in the euro area in accordance with the guidelines and decisions laid down by the Governing Council and, in so doing, to give instructions to the NCBs;
- to manage the day-to-day business of the ECB;
- to exercise certain powers, including regulatory powers, delegated to it by the Governing Council.

General Council meets four times every year

The General Council comprises the President and the Vice-President of the ECB and the governors of the national central banks of all EU Member States.

The other members of the Executive Board, the President of the EU Council and a member of the European Commission may attend the meetings of the General Council but they do not have the right to vote. Meetings of the General Council may be convened whenever the President deems it necessary or at the request of at least three of its members. The General Council usually meets in Frankfurt once every three months.

The General Council has no responsibility for monetary policy decisions in the euro area. It has taken over tasks from the EMI which the ECB has to perform in Stage Three of EMU as long as some EU Member States have not adopted the euro. This implies that it is responsible primarily for reporting on the progress made towards convergence by EU Member States which have not yet adopted the euro, and for giving advice on the preparations necessary for adopting the euro as their currency. It contributes to the advisory functions of the ESCB and helps to collect statistical information.

2.7 ESCB COMMITTEES

Expert committees support decision-making bodies

The decision-making bodies of the ECB are supported by ESCB Committees. These Committees are also important for intra-ESCB cooperation. They consist of members from the ECB and the national central banks (NCBs) of the Eurosystem, as well as from other competent bodies, such as national supervisory authorities in the case of the Banking Supervision Committee. The NCBs of the non-euro area countries have each appointed experts to take part in ESCB Committee meetings whenever a Committee is dealing with matters which fall within the field of competence of the General Council. The mandates of the Committees are laid down by the Governing Council, to which the Committees report via the Executive Board.

At present, the Committees are as follows: the Accounting and Monetary Income Committee, the Banking Supervision Committee, the Banknote Committee, the Committee on Cost Methodology, the Eurosystem/ESCB Communications Committee, the Eurosystem IT Steering Committee, the Information Technology Committee, the Internal Auditors Committee, the International Relations Committee, the Legal Committee, the Market Operations Committee, the Monetary Policy Committee, the Payment and Settlement Systems Committee and the

Statistics Committee.

In 1998 the Governing Council also established a Budget Committee, composed of members coming from the ECB and the Eurosystem NCBs. The Budget Committee assists the Governing Council in matters related to the ECB's budget.

Finally, in 2005 a Human Resources Conference was established, consisting of members from the ESCB. This Conference aims to further promote the cooperation and team spirit among Eurosystem/ESCB central banks in the field of human resources management.

3 MONETARY POLICY

3.1 PRICE STABILITY

The primary objective of the Eurosystem is to maintain price stability. Without prejudice to the objective of price stability, the Eurosystem shall support the general economic policies of the European Community.

Price stability is the top priority

Article 2 of the Treaty on European Union states that the European Union aims to promote "economic and social progress and a high level of employment and to achieve balanced and sustainable development". The Eurosystem contributes to these objectives by maintaining price stability. In addition, in the pursuit of price stability, it takes these objectives into account. Should there be any conflict between the objectives, the maintenance of price stability must always be given priority by the ECB.

The Eurosystem acts in accordance with the principle of an open market economy with free competition, favouring an efficient allocation of resources.

3.2 MONETARY POLICY STRATEGY OF THE ECB

The ECB must influence conditions in the money market, and thereby the level of short-term interest rates, in order to achieve price stability.

The ECB has adopted a strategy to ensure that a consistent and systematic approach is applied to monetary policy decisions. Consistency helps to stabilize inflation expectations and enhance the credibility of the ECB.

A main element of the ECB Governing Council's monetary policy strategy is its quantitative definition of price stability: "a year-on-year increase in the Harmonised Index of Consumer Prices (HICP) for the euro area of below 2%". Price stability must be maintained over the medium term, which reflects the need for monetary policy to be forward-looking. In the pursuit of price stability, the ECB aims to maintain inflation rates below but close to 2% over the medium term. This underlines its commitment to provide a sufficient safety margin to guard against the risks of deflation.

Forward-looking monetary policy

Monetary policy needs to be forward-looking since there are significant lags in the transmission mechanism. In addition, monetary policy should anchor inflation expectations and help to reduce volatility in economic developments.

In addition to the definition of price stability, the monetary policy strategy consists of a comprehensive assessment of the risks to price stability consisting of an economic analysis and a monetary analysis. Every decision on monetary policy is preceded by a thorough cross-checking of the information coming from the two analyses.

3.3 MONETARY POLICY INSTRUMENTS

Money market is the first to be affected

The transmission mechanism of monetary policy starts with the central bank's management of liquidity and steering of short-term interest rates.

The money market, as part of the financial market, plays a crucial role in the transmission of monetary policy decisions, since it is the first market to be affected by changes in monetary policy. A deep and integrated money market is essential for an efficient monetary policy, since it ensures an even distribution of central bank liquidity and a homogeneous level of short-term interest rates throughout the single currency area. This precondition was met almost immediately from the start of Stage Three of EMU when the national money markets were successfully integrated into an efficient euro area money market.

To steer short-term interest rates, the Eurosystem has at its disposal a set of monetary policy instruments, namely open market operations, standing facilities and reserve requirements.

Open market operations can be divided into:

- main refinancing operations; these are regular liquidity-providing transactions with a frequency and maturity of one week;
- longer-term refinancing operations; these are liquidity-providing transactions with a monthly frequency and a maturity of three months;
- fine-tuning operations; these can be executed on an ad hoc basis to manage the liquidity situation in the market and to steer interest rates. In particular, they aim to smooth the effects on interest rates of unexpected liquidity imbalances; and
- structural operations can be carried out by the Eurosystem through reverse transactions, outright transactions and issuance of debt certificates.

Standing facilities

The Eurosystem also offers two standing facilities, which set boundaries for overnight market interest rates by providing and absorbing liquidity:

- the marginal lending facility, which allows credit institutions to obtain overnight liquidity from the national central banks against eligible assets; and
- the deposit facility, which can be used by credit institutions to make overnight deposits with the national central banks in the Eurosystem.

Minimum reserve requirements

Finally, the Eurosystem requires credit institutions to hold minimum reserves on accounts with the national central banks. Each credit institution must keep a certain percentage of some of its own customer deposits (as well as of some other bank liabilities) in a deposit account with the relevant national central bank on average over a reserve maintenance period of around one month. The Eurosystem pays a short-term interest rate on these accounts. The purpose of the minimum reserve system is to stabilize money market interest rates and create (or enlarge) a structural liquidity deficit in the banking system.

3.4 COMMUNICATION

Efficient external communication is an essential part of a central bank's job. Communication contributes to the effectiveness and credibility of monetary policy. In order to increase the public's understanding of monetary policy and other central bank activities, the ECB must be open and transparent. This is the main guiding principle for the Eurosystem in its external communication, which involves close cooperation between the ECB and the NCBs.

To make its communication effective, the ECB and the NCBs use many different tools. The most important are:

- regular press conferences after the first Governing Council meeting in each month;
- publication of a Monthly Bulletin containing a detailed description of economic developments in the euro area and articles on topics relevant to the ECB's activities;
- public hearings of the ECB's President and other members of the ECB's Executive Board in the European Parliament;
- speeches and interviews given by members of the ECB's decision-making bodies;
- press releases explaining the decisions and views of the Governing Council;
- the websites of the ECB and the NCBs, which give access to all published material, including a very large collection of statistical data;
- working papers;
- occasional papers.

3.5 MONETARY AND FINANCIAL STATISTICS

The ECB compiles and publishes financial and monetary statistics in close cooperation with the NCBs. This statistical information supports the monetary policy of the euro area and the decision-making of the ECB.

ECB compiles aggregates for the euro area

The NCBs (and, in some cases, other national authorities) collect data from financial institutions and other sources in their respective countries and calculate aggregates at the national level, which they send to the ECB. The ECB then compiles the aggregates for the euro area.

The legal basis for the development, collection, compilation and dissemination of statistics by the ECB is laid down in the Statute of the European System of Central Banks and of the

European Central Bank annexed to the Treaty. While ensuring that its statistical requirements are met, the ECB seeks to minimise the burden which statistical reporting places on financial institutions and other reporting agents.

Responsibility for statistics at the European level is shared between the ECB and the European Commission (through Eurostat, the Statistical Office of the European Communities). The ECB is primarily or jointly responsible for euro area monetary, financial institutions and financial markets statistics, external statistics (including the balance of payments), financial accounts and the development of quarterly non-financial accounts for institutional sectors (households, corporations and government). Responsibility for the statistical infrastructure (including seasonal adjustment, the design of a quality framework and data transmission standards) at the European level is also shared between both institutions. Wherever possible, ESCB statistics conform to international standards.

4 THE TARGET2 SYSTEM

Real-time gross settlement in euro

TARGET2 (Trans-European Automated Real-time Gross Settlement Express Transfer) is now replacing the first generation TARGET system, which has been in operation since January 1999, when the euro was launched. By the summer of 2008, the new system will be available for all transactions in euro between and within the euro area countries as well as several other EU countries.

Like its predecessor, TARGET2 is used for the settlement of central bank operations, large-value euro interbank transfers as well as other euro payments. It provides real-time processing, settlement in central bank money and immediate finality. However, unlike its predecessor, in which all payments were processed decentrally by the national central banks, the new system uses a single shared platform with no intervention by the central banks. This platform makes the provision of an enhanced and harmonised service possible and, via economies of scale (economy of scale), permits lower fees and better cost-efficiency. There is no upper or lower value limit for TARGET2 payments.

By using TARGET2 for all large-value payments, in particular those related to interbank operations, market participants receive a premium service and make a substantial contribution to reducing systemic risk throughout the EU, i.e. the risk of "contagion" to other areas due to the high number and value of interactions between banks.

Another development in this context is the launch in 2008 of the Single Euro Payments Area (SEPA), in which all non-cash euro payments are treated as domestic payments; the difference between national and cross-border transactions is disappearing. TARGET2 together with SEPA will transform the payments market in the euro area, making it more dynamic and cost-efficient.

5 EURO BANKNOTES AND COINS

5.1 BANKNOTES

Euro banknotes were put into circulation on 1 January 2002. There are seven denominations: € 5, € 10, € 20, € 50, € 100, € 200 and € 500. The higher the denomination, the larger the banknote. The banknotes depict the architectural styles of seven periods in Europe's cultural history—classical, Romanesque, Gothic, Renaissance, baroque and rococo, the age of iron and glass architecture, and modern twentieth century architecture and show three main architectural elements: windows, gateways and bridges. None of the designs depicts actual buildings or monuments.

2002 Series

Image		Dimensions (mm)	Main Colour	Design		Printer code position
Obverse	Reverse			Architecture	Century	
		120 × 62	Grey	classical	<5th	Left image edge
		127 × 67	Red	Romanesque	11—12th	8 o'clock star
		133 × 72	Blue	Gothic	12—14th	9 o'clock star
		140 × 77	Orange	Renaissance	15—16th	Right image edge
		147 × 82	Green	Baroque & Rococo	17—18th	Right of 9 o'clock star
		153 × 82	Yellow-Brown	The age of iron and glass	19—20th	Above 7 o'clock star
		160 × 82	Purple	Modern 20th century	20—21st	9 o'clock star

Europa Series

Obverse	Reverse	Year	Color	Architecture	Century	Printer code position
		2013	Grey	classical	<5th	Top right
		2014	Red	Romanesque	11—12th	Top right
		2015	Blue	Gothic	12—14th	Top right

2002 Series

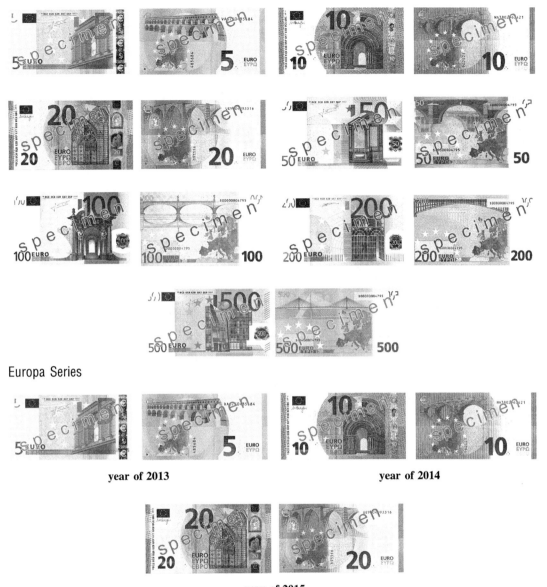

year of 2013

year of 2014

year of 2015

　　The windows and gateways on the front of each banknote symbolise the spirit of openness and cooperation in Europe. The reverse of each banknote features a bridge. These bridges are used as a metaphor for communication between the nations of Europe and between Europe and the rest of the world.

　　A number of security features, such as a watermark, a hologram, a security thread and colour-changing ink, have been incorporated into the banknote designs to protect them against counterfeiting and enable people to recognise genuine banknotes. Special design features, e. g. raised print and large numerals, have also been included to help blind and partially sighted people.

Strict quality controls ensure that all banknotes produced are identical in quality and appearance. The banknotes do not have individual national designs.

The planning of a new series of euro banknotes is under way. It will incorporate new security features but in other respects it will represent a continuation of the current series: the banknotes will have the same denominations—from €5 to €500—and they will be based on the current designs, making them immediately recognisable as euro banknotes.

Now the Europa series banknote, similarly to the first series, bears the EU Flag, a map of Europe on the reverse and the signature of Mario Draghi, current president of the ECB and the 12 stars from the EU Flag are also incorporated into the note.

The banknote also has the name "euro", but in three scripts, in Latin, Greek and Cyrillic script (EURO/EYPΩ/EBPO).

5.2 COINS

One euro is divided into 100 cent. There are eight euro coins: 1, 2, 5, 10, 20 and 50 cent, €1 and €2. Each one has a "European" side and a national side. Of course, all euro coins can be used in all euro area countries, irrespective of their national side.

The eight euro coins vary in size, weight, material, colour and thickness. Some additional innovative features have also been included to help users, particularly blind and partially sighted people, to recognise the different denominations. For instance, each consecutive coin in the series has a different edge. A detailed quality management system ensures that all euro coins are interchangeable throughout the euro area and conform to the standards necessary for their use in vending machines.

Particular care has been taken in the production of the higher-value euro coins (€1 and €2) to protect them against counterfeiting. Their sophisticated two-colour design makes them difficult to counterfeit, as do the embossed characters around the edge of the €2 coin.

6 BANKING SUPERVISION

The direct responsibility for banking supervision and financial stability remains with the competent authorities in each EU Member State, but the Treaty has assigned to the ESCB the task of "contributing to the smooth conduct of policies pursued by the competent authorities relating to the prudential supervision of credit institutions and the stability of the financial system".

This task is mainly carried out in three ways.

Monitoring financial stability

First, the ESCB monitors and assesses the financial stability at the euro area/EU level. This activity complements and supports the corresponding activity at the national level, carried out by the national central banks and supervisory authorities in order to maintain financial stability in their respective country.

Second, the ESCB gives advice on the design and review of regulatory and supervisory requirements for financial institutions. Much of this advice is provided through the ECB's participation in the relevant international and European regulatory and supervisory bodies, such as the Basel Committee on Banking Supervision, the European Banking Committee and the Committee of European Banking Supervisors.

Third, the ECB promotes cooperation between central banks and supervisory authorities on issues of common interest (e. g. payment system oversight, financial crisis management).

These activities are carried out with the assistance of the Banking Supervision Committee (one of the ESCB committees mentioned in section 2.7), which brings together experts from the EU central banks and supervisory authorities.

(*FROM*: http://www.ecb.int/pub/pdf/other/escb_en.pdf)

WORDS AND EXPRESSIONS

• ***price stability*** *n.* It is the primary objective of the Eurosystem. The Governing Council (行长理事会) defined price stability as a year-on-year increase in consumer prices (measured by HICP) for the euro area of below 2%. In the pursuit of price stability the Governing Council aims to maintain inflation rates below but close to 2% over the medium term. 价格稳定

• ***summit meeting*** *n.* A summit meeting (or summit) is a meeting of heads of state or government, usually with considerable media exposure, tight security and a prearranged agenda. 最高级会议,首脑会议,峰会

• ***opt-out clause*** *n.* a clause in an agreement that gives people the choice not to be involved in one part of that agreement 退出/脱离条款

• ***purchasing power parities*** (PPPs) *n.* Purchasing power parities (PPPs) are the rates of currency conversion that equalise the purchasing power of different currencies by eliminating the differences in price levels between countries. In their simplest form, PPPs show the ratio of the prices in national currencies of the same goods or service in different countries. 购买力平价

• ***denominate*** /dɪˈnɒmɪneɪt/ *vt.* to issue or express in terms of a given monetary unit. 以……面值发行

• ***equity market*** *n.* It's the market for shares in companies listed on a stock exchange. Equities are normally considered more risky investments than bonds, since the holders of equities are entitled to receive a dividend(股息,红利) from the issuing companies, while bond holders are entitled to an interest payment independent of the companies' profits. 股票市场

• ***Governing Council*** *n.* It's the supreme decision-making body of the ECB, comprising the six members of the ECB's Executive Board and the governors of the national central banks of the EU Member States which have adopted the euro. 行长理事会

• ***Executive Board*** *n.* It's one of the decision-making bodies of the ECB, comprising the President and the Vice-President of the ECB and four other members appointed by common accord by the heads of state or government of the countries that have adopted the euro. 执行董事会

• ***General Council*** *n.* It's one of the decision-making bodies of the ECB, comprising the President and the Vice-President of the ECB and the governors of the national central banks of all EU Member States. 总理事会

• ***minimum bid rate*** *n.* It is the lower limit to the interest rates at which counterparties may submit bids in the variable rate tenders of the main refinancing operations. This is one of the key ECB interest rates reflecting the stance of monetary policy. 最低竞标价格

• *the main refinancing operations* n. It is a regular open market operation executed by the Eurosystem in the form of reverse transactions. The main refinancing operations are conducted through weekly standard tenders and normally have a maturity of one week. 主要再融资业务：央行以拍卖的方式将货币注入银行系统

• *the marginal lending facility* n. a standing facility of the Eurosystem which counterparties may use to receive overnight credit from an NCB at a pre-specified interest rate against eligible assets 边际贷款工具：欧洲央行借给私人银行的隔夜贷款（standing facility：a central bank facility available to counterparties on their own initiative；The Eurosystem offers two overnight standing facilities：the marginal lending facility and the deposit facility. 常用便利，即订约方可主动获得的央行便利。欧元系统提供两种隔夜常用便利：边际贷款便利和存款便利。）

• *security of tenure* n. It is a term used in political science to describe a constitutional or legal guarantee that an office-holder cannot be removed from office except in exceptional and specified circumstances. 职位/地位的稳定性（或保证）

• *Court of Justice of the European Communities* n. It's the judicial branch of the European Community. Located in Luxembourg, it was founded in 1958 as the joint court for the three treaty organizations that were consolidated into the European Community in 1967. By the early 1990s, the court was composed of 9 advocates general and 15 judges—one judge from each of the EU nations. All members of the court are appointed for renewable six-year terms by agreement among the EC nations. 欧洲法院

• *be incompatible with* adj. be opposed in nature or quality；be inconsistent with 与……相反的；不相容的

• *in the event of a tie* adv. on the chance that a situation in a game or competition when two or more players have the same score happens 如果出现平局（不分胜负）

• *casting vote* n. the deciding vote used by the presiding officer of an assembly when votes cast on both sides are equal in number （反对与赞成票数相等时会议主持人所投的）决定性的一票，决定票

• *mandate* /ˈmændeɪt/ n. an authoritative command or instruction （书面）命令

• *the Accounting and Monetary Income Committee* (AMICO) n. This committee advises on all Eurosystem matters relating to accounting, financial reporting and the allocation of monetary income. 会计与货币收入委员会

• *the Banking Supervision Committee* (BSC) n. This committee provides assistance regarding the prudential supervision and secure operations of credit institutions and the stability of the financial system. 银行监督委员会

• *the Banknote Committee* (BANCO) n. This committee advises on all banknote matters and assists in the strategic planning of banknote production and issuance. 纸币委员会

• *the Committee on Cost Methodology* (COMCO) n. 成本方法委员会

- *the Eurosystem/ESCB Communications Committee* (ECCO) *n.* This committee assists in external and intra-system communication policy. 欧元系统/欧洲各国中央银行通信委员会
- *the Eurosystem IT Steering Committee* (EISC) *n.* 欧元系统信息技术筹划指导委员会
- *the Information Technology Committee* (ITC) *n.* This committee assists in the development, implementation and maintenance of IT networks and communications infrastructures which support joint operational systems. 信息技术委员会
- *the Internal Auditors Committee* (IAC) *n.* This committee develops common standards for auditing Eurosystem operations and audits joint projects and joint operational systems at the Eurosystem/ESCB level. 内部审计员委员会
- *the International Relations Committee* (IRC) *n.* This committee assists in the performance of the ECB's statutory tasks with regard to international cooperation and acts as a forum for exchanging views on matters of common interest in the field of international relations. 国际关系委员会
- *the Legal Committee* (LEGCO) *n.* This committee provides legal advice for the fulfilment of the ECB's statutory tasks and prepares the legal acts for the operation of the Eurosystem. 法律委员会
- *the Market Operations Committee* (MOC) *n.* This committee assists in the execution of monetary policy operations and foreign exchange transactions, including those related to the operation of ERM Ⅱ, and to the management of the ECB's foreign reserves. 市场运作委员会
- *the Monetary Policy Committee* (MPC) *n.* This committee mainly advises on strategic and longer-term issues relating to the formulation of the monetary and exchange rate policy and is responsible for the Eurosystem staff projections. 货币政策委员会
- *the Payment and Settlement Systems Committee* (PSSC) *n.* This committee advises on the operation and maintenance of TARGET, general payment systems policy and oversight issues and issues of interest for central banks in the field of securities clearing and settlement. 支付与结算系统委员会
- *the Statistics Committee* (STC) *n.* This committee mainly advises on the design and compilation of statistical information collected by the ECB with the assistance of the national central banks. 统计委员会
- *team spirit n.* the spirit of a group that makes the members want the group to succeed 合作精神,团队精神
- *top priority n.* something that you think is the most important and should be dealt with first 应予最优先考虑的事
- *sustainable development n.* It is a pattern of resource use that aims to meet human

Part III CURRENCIES

needs while preserving the environment so that these needs can be met not only in the present, but in the indefinite future. 可持续发展

- *Harmonised Index of Consumer Prices* (HICP) *n.* The measure of prices used by the Governing Council to assess price stability in the euro area. It is calculated and published by Eurostat, the Statistical Office of the European Communities. 零售价格矫正指数
- *volatility* /ˌvɒləˈtɪlətɪ/ *n.* instability 不稳定性；流动性
- *homogeneous level n.* of the same or similar level 相似水平,均一水平
- *guiding principle n.* a rule that exerts control or influence 指导原则
- *press conference n.* an interview held for news reporters by a political figure or famous person; also called news conference 记者招待会
- *press release n.* an announcement of an event, performance, or other newsworthy item that is issued to the press 新闻稿
- *working papers n.* a report written by a group of people chosen to study an aspect of law, education health, etc.; legal documents certifying the right to employment of a minor or an alien. 雇用证书:证明有权雇用少数民族或外国人的法律文件;委员会等的研究报告
- *occasional papers n.* essays or reports that the Institute considers should be made available as a contribution to the debate on specific issues 不定期论文
- *data transmission n.* also called digital transmission or digital communications, it is the physical transfer of data (a digital bit stream) over a point-to-point or point-to-multipoint transmission medium. 信息传输,数据传输
- *Real-time gross settlement system* (RTGS) A real-time gross settlement system, such as TARGET2 is a payment system in which processing and settlement take place continuously ("in real time") rather than in batch processing mode. Like this, transactions can be settled with immediate finality. "Gross settlement" means that each transfer is settled individually rather than on a net basis. 实时支付结算系统
- *economy of scale n.* the decrease in unit manufacturing cost that is due to mass production 规模经济:因为大量生产而导致单位生产成本降低
- *contagion* /kənˈteɪdʒən/ *n.* the tendency to spread, as of a doctrine, influence, or emotional state 传染,蔓延
- *cost-efficient* /ˈkɒstɪˈfɪʃənt/ *adj.* (= cost-effective) providing adequate financial return in relation to outlay 有成本效益的,值得花钱的,合算的,划算的
- *iron-and-glass architecture n.* (in Western architecture: Construction in iron and glass) The Industrial Revolution in Britain introduced new building types and new methods of construction. Marshall, Benyou, and Bage's flour mill (now Allied Breweries) at Ditherington, Shropshire (1796—97), is one of the first iron-frame buildings, though brick walls still carry part of the load and there are no longitudinal beams. 钢铁玻璃建筑
- *hologram* /ˈhɒləɡræm/ *n.* the pattern produced on a photosensitive medium that has

been exposed by holography and then photographically developed; the photosensitive medium so exposed and so developed 全息摄影，全息图

• **counterfeit** /ˈkaʊntəfɪt/ *vt.* to make a copy of, usually with the intent to defraud; forge; to make a pretense of; feign 赝造，伪造：复制，通常目的为了诈骗；假装；伪装

BACKGROUND KNOWLEDGE

1 *Eurosystem* 欧元体系

The Eurosystem is the monetary authority of the Eurozone, the collective of European Union member states that have adopted the euro as their sole official currency. The Eurosystem consists of the European Central Bank (it decides the monetary policy) and the central banks of the member states that belong to the Eurozone (their function is to apply the monetary policy decided by the ECB). The primary objective of the Eurosystem is price stability. Secondary objectives are financial stability and financial integration. The mission statement of the Eurosystem says that the ECB and the national central banks jointly contribute to achieving the objectives.

2 *Copenhagen criteria* (accession criteria) 哥本哈根标准（加入欧盟标准）

Any country seeking membership of the European Union (EU) must conform to the conditions set out by Article 49 and the principles laid down in Article 6(1) of the Treaty on European Union. Relevant criteria were established by the Copenhagen European Council in 1993 and strengthened by the Madrid European Council in 1995.

To join the EU, a new Member State must meet three criteria:

• political: stability of institutions guaranteeing democracy, the rule of law, human rights and respect for and protection of minorities;

• economic: existence of a functioning market economy and the capacity to cope with competitive pressure and market forces within the Union;

• acceptance of the Community acquis: ability to take on the obligations of membership, including adherence to the aims of political, economic and monetary union.

For the European Council to decide to open negotiations, the political criterion must be satisfied.

Any country that wishes to join the Union must meet the accession criteria. The pre-accession strategy and accession negotiations provide the necessary framework and instruments.

3 *European Monetary System* (EMS) 欧洲货币体系

Before the euro was introduced a number of currencies of EU Member States were linked together in the EMS, which existed from 1979 until 1999. It had three main components: the ECU, which was a basket of the currencies of the Member States; the exchange-rate and intervention mechanisms, which gave each currency a central exchange rate linked to the ECU (bilateral exchange rate), and the credit mechanisms, which allowed central banks to intervene if bilateral exchange rates exceeded a threshold. On 1 January 1999 the EMS was replaced by the Exchange Rate Mechanism Ⅱ.

4 *Maastricht Treaty* (formally, the Treaty on European Union, TEU) 马斯特里赫特条约

Maastricht Treaty or Treaty on European Union, is the treaty that created the European Union (EU). The treaty was approved at Maastricht in the Netherlands by the heads of government of the 12 members of the European Community (EC) in December 1991 and was signed on February 7, 1992. The 12 nations were Belgium, Denmark, France, Germany, the United Kingdom, Greece, Ireland, Italy, Luxembourg, the Netherlands, Portugal, and Spain. The treaty reflected the intention of the EC nations to broaden the scale of monetary and economic union and begin serious consideration of joint policies in regard to defense, citizenship, and the protection of the environment. Under the Maastricht Treaty, European citizenship was granted to citizens of each member state. Customs and immigration agreements were enhanced to allow European citizens greater freedom to live, work, or study in any of the member states, and border controls were relaxed. The treaty created joint foreign and monetary policies. It called for the eventual creation of a single currency, the European Currency Unit (ECU), and a central bank, which would coordinate the monetary policies of the central banks of the respective nations.

5 *Single European Act of* 1986 单一欧洲法案(1986)

The Single European Act (SEA) was the first major revision of the Treaty of Rome that formally established the single European market and the European Political Cooperation.

6 *Treaty* 条约

Treaty refers specifically to the Treaty establishing the European Community. The original Treaty was signed in Rome on 25 March 1957 and entered into force on 1 January 1958. It established the European Economic Community (EEC), which is now the European Community (EC), and is often referred to as the Treaty of Rome. Treaty on European Union (which is often referred to as the Maastricht Treaty) was signed on 7 February 1992 and entered into force on 1 November 1993. The Treaty on European Union amended the Treaty establishing the European Community and established the European Union. Treaty of Amsterdam, which was signed in Amsterdam on 2 October 1997 and entered into force on 1 May 1999, and the Treaty of Nice, which was signed on 26 February 2001 and entered into force on 1 February 2003, amended both the Treaty establishing the European Community and the Treaty on European Union. Treaty of Lisbon was signed on 13 December 2007, but will only enter into force once it has been ratified by all Member States. It amends both the Treaty establishing the European Community and the Treaty on European Union. These two Treaties will continue to be the basis on which the EU functions. The Treaty of Lisbon simplifies the structure of the EU, which currently consists of three "pillars": the Community, the common foreign and security policy, and justice and home affairs. In the new Treaty, the pillars cease to exist and the Community is replaced by the Union, which will have legal personality. The Treaty establishing the European Community is renamed the Treaty on the Functioning of the Union.

7 European Monetary Institute (EMI) 欧洲货币机构

It is an organization set up by the Maastricht Treaty in 1991 in order to coordinate the economic and monetary policy of members of the European Union before the introduction of a single European currency in accordance with the objectives of European Monetary Union. The members of the EMI council are the governors of the central banks of the 15 EU countries.

Convergence criteria (融合标准, also known as the Maastricht criteria) are the criteria for European Union member states to enter the third stage of European Economic and Monetary Union (EMU) and adopt the euro. The four main criteria are based on Article 121(1) of the European Community Treaty. Those member countries who are to adopt the euro need to meet four criteria:

(1) Inflation rate: No more than 1.5 percentage points higher than the three lowest inflation member states of the EU.

(2) Government finance:

Annual government deficit:

The ratio of the annual government deficit to gross domestic product (GDP) must not exceed 3% at the end of the preceding fiscal year. If not, it is at least required to reach a level close to 3%. Only exceptional and temporary excesses would be granted for exceptional cases.

Government debt:

The ratio of gross government debt to GDP must not exceed 60% at the end of the preceding fiscal year. Even if the target cannot be achieved due to the specific conditions, the ratio must have sufficiently diminished and must be approaching the reference value at a satisfactory pace.

(3) Exchange rate: Applicant countries should have joined the exchange-rate mechanism (ERM II) under the European Monetary System (EMS) for 2 consecutive years and should not have devaluated its currency during the period.

(4) Long-term interest rate: The nominal long-term interest rate must not be more than two percentage points higher than the three lowest inflation member states.

The purpose of setting the criteria is to maintain the price stability within the Eurozone even with the inclusion of new member states.

8 EU Council (Council of Ministers) 欧共体理事会(部长会议)

It is an institution of the European Community made up of representatives of the governments of the Member States, normally the ministers responsible for the matters under consideration (therefore often referred to as the Council of Ministers). The EU Council meeting in the composition of the ministers of economy and finance is often referred to as the Council. In addition, for decisions of particular importance, the EU Council meets in the composition of the Heads of States or Governments. This should not be confused with the European Council, which also brings together the heads of state or government but which provides the Union with the necessary impetus for its development and defines the general political guidelines.

9 *European Commission* 欧洲委员会

As one of the five European institutions, the European Commission was created in 1967 for the three European Communities. It drafts proposals for new European laws, which it presents to the European Parliament and the Council. The Commission makes sure that EU decisions are properly implemented and supervises the way EU funds are spent. It also monitors compliance with the European treaties and Community law. As the guardian of the Treaties, it ensures, together with the Court of Justice of the European Communities, that the legislation applying to all EU Member States is properly implemented. At the moment, the Commission consists of a president and 26 commissioners. Its departments, called Directorates General, are responsible for the implementation of common policies and general administration in a specific area. It represents the general interest of the EU and is independent of the Member States. The Commission is appointed for a five-year term, but it can be dismissed by Parliament.

10 *Eurogroup* 欧洲集团

It's an informal gathering of the ministers of economics and finance of the euro area member countries. The ministers discuss issues connected with their shared responsibilities in respect of the single currency. The European Commission and the ECB are invited to take part in the meetings. The Eurogroup usually meets immediately before an ECOFIN meeting.

11 *TARGET*2: Trans-European Automated Real-time Gross settlement Express Transfer 第二代泛欧自动实时全额结算快速转账;泛欧自动转账系统

It's the system for the euro, which is used for the settlement of central bank operations, large-value euro interbank transfers and other euro payments. TARGET2 provides settlement in central bank money and immediate finality. It is available for all transactions in euro between and within the euro area countries as well as several other EU countries. TARGET2 is now replacing the first generation of TARGET system, which has been in operation since January 1999, when the euro was launched.

After the proposed European Monetary Union, this system will allow banks to transfer euros instantaneously between accounts held at their central bank. At present, instantaneous transfers can only be made for domestic currencies, e.g. via the Clearing House Automated Payments System CHAPS. (Clearing House Automated Payment System) A British company that provides fund transfers for both the British Pound and the Euro. CHAPS is used to transfer funds from one banking institution to another. 票据交换所自动支付系统。

12 *SEPA*：单一欧元支付区

It is an area in Europe where individuals, companies and other organisations can make and receive noncash payments in euro, both within and across national borders, under the same basic conditions, rights and obligations, regardless of their location.

Since 1 January 2002, consumers have been paying with euro banknotes and coins everywhere in the euro area, irrespective of the country. But non-cash payments between two countries continued to be expensive and complicated. Further integration was needed.

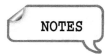

1 *exchange rate mechanism*（*ERM*）汇率机制

The mechanism formerly used in the European Monetary System in which participating governments committed themselves to maintain the values of their currencies in relation to the ECU.

It also refers to Exchange Rate Mechanism Ⅱ. The mechanism used to stabilize the currencies of European Union states that have not adopted the euro but wish to maintain the value of their currency in relation to it.

2 *Derogation* 法律的部分撤回,与法律的取消或彻底废除相对

Derogation is the partial revocation（撤回）of a law, as opposed to abrogation（废除,取消）or the total abolition of a law. The term is used in both civil law（民法）and canon law（教会法规）. It is sometimes used, loosely, to mean abrogation, as in the legal maxim: Lex posterior derogat priori, i. e. a subsequent law imports the abolition of a previous one.

Derogation differs from dispensation（豁免,免除法律责任）in that it applies to the law, where dispensations applies to specific people affected by the law. 就其应用法律而言,此词不同于 dispensation,后者意为"豁免,免除法律责任",应用于受法律影响特种人群。

In terms of European Union legislation, a derogation can also imply that a member state delays the implementation of an element of an EU Regulation（etc）into their legal system over a given timescale, such as five years; or that a member state has opted not to enforce a specific provision in a treaty due to internal circumstances（typically a state of emergency）. 就欧盟立法而言,此词亦指某成员国可以延迟执行欧盟规定(等),即超过特定的时间表而纳入其法律体系,或者某成员国因其国内形势(尤其是紧急状态)而选择不执行某特殊规定。

According to Article 122 of the EC Treaty, Member States with a derogation are the ones which are preparing to adopt, but have not yet adopted, the euro. This status refers to 10 Member States（Sweden and nine of the new Member States）: rights and obligations relating to the introduction of the euro as a single currency are not applicable to them. The case of Denmark and the United Kingdom is different: they have an exemption from participating in the third stage of Economic and Monetary Union. 根据《欧盟条约》第122条规定,"部分豁免"成员国是指那些准备采用、但仍未采用欧元的国家。这种情况是指10个成员国(瑞典及9个新成员国):有关将欧元用作单一货币的权利和义务不适用于这些国家。丹麦和(不列颠)联合王国则是另一种情形:他们免于参与经济和货币同盟第三阶段进程。

3 *the deposit facility* 存款工具(私人银行在央行的隔夜存款。)

It is a standing facility of the Eurosystem which counterparties may use to make overnight deposits, remunerated at a pre-specified interest rate, at an NCB. 存款工具

4 *portfolio management* 证券管理

The act or practice of making investment decisions in order to make the largest possible return. Portfolio management takes two basic forms: active and passive. Active management involves using technical, fundamental, or some other analysis to make trade on a fairly regular basis. For example, one may sell stock A in order to buy stock B. Then, a few days or weeks later, one may sell stock B to buy bond C. Passive management, on the other hand, involves buying an index, an exchange-traded fund, or some other investment vehicle with securities the investor does not directly choose. For example, one may buy an exchange-traded fund that holds all the stocks on the S&P 500.

5 *money market* 金融市场,货币市场,短期资金市场

In finance, the money market is the global financial market for short-term borrowing and lending. It provides short-term liquid funding for the global financial system. The money market is where short-term obligations such as Treasury bills, commercial paper and bankers' acceptances are bought and sold.

The money market consists of financial institutions and dealers in money or credit who wish to either borrow or lend. Participants borrow and lend for short periods of time, typically up to thirteen months. Money market trades in short term financial instruments commonly called "paper". This contracts with the capital market for longer-term funding, which is supplied by bonds and equity.

6 *transmission mechanism of monetary policy* 货币政策的传导机制

Any of several channels by which a change in the money supply of a country can cause changes in real variables. Most operate primarily within a country, but some, as through the exchange rate, operate through international transactions.

Any of several ways that real and monetary shocks in one economy can be transmitted to another through monetary channels involving interest rates, exchange rates, and international capital flows.

7 *minimum reserve* 最低准备/储备

The ECB requires credit institutions established in the euro area to hold deposits on accounts with their national central bank. These are called "minimum" or "required" reserves. The minimum reserve is a mix-effective (liquidity-political) instrument of the monetary policy. It makes it for the central bank possible to make the business banks dependent during its credit distribution on their own credits with the central bank by increasing or lowering the minimum reserve obligation. The business banks are in response dependent on central bank money, for example by the main refinancing instrument of the European central bank.

8 *European regulatory and supervisory bodies* n. 欧洲管理与监督机构

EXERCISES

I. Decide whether the following statements are true(T) or false(F).

1. The idea of establishing an economic and monetary union in Europe dated back to 1958 when the European Economic Community and the European Atomic Energy Community were founded. (　)
2. The Treaty on European Union, which established the European Union is also called the Maastricht Treaty. (　)
3. Countries wishing to adopt the euro as their currency must achieve "sustainable convergence", which require a country to have a high degree of price stability, sound public finances, and low and stable long-term interest rates. (　)
4. The euro area is the largest economies in the world, with a population of 318 million in 2006. (　)
5. The European System of Central Banks comprises the ECB and the NCBs of the EU Member States which have adopted the euro as their common currency. (　)
6. The NCBs are prohibited from carrying out responsibilities that are not related to monetary policy functions. (　)
7. The purpose of the minimum reserve system which is required by the Eurosystem is to stabilize money market interest rates and create (or enlarge) a structural liquidity deficit in the banking system. (　)
8. TARGET2 is used for the settlement of central bank operations and large-value euro interbank transfers as well as other euro payments. (　)
9. The windows, gateways and bridges on the surface of each Euro banknote symbolise the spirit of openness and cooperation in Europe. (　)
10. The ESCB monitors and assesses the financial stability of all EU Member States at the national level, carried out by the national central banks and supervisory authorities in order to maintain financial stability in their respective country. (　)

II. Translate the following expressions into Chinese.

1. to ensure that the value of money is preserved over time
2. envisaged three stages to be completed by 1980
3. dismantling of all internal barriers to the free movement of persons, goods, capital and services within Europe
4. enhanced convergence of the economic and monetary policies of the Member States (to ensure stability of prices and sound public finances)
5. to be part of a larger, much more self-contained economy
6. in terms of gross domestic product (GDP) expressed in purchasing power parities
7. domestic and cross-border mergers and acquisitions
8. to tap a very large capital market to finance their business and use new financial instruments to protect themselves against various financial risks and to enhance the management of their investments
9. a supra-national institution with its own legal personality
10. the minimum bid rate on the main refinancing operations as well as interest rates on the marginal lending facility and the deposit facility
11. providing for security of tenure for governors of NCBs and members of the Executive Board
12. undertake foreign reserve management operations on their own account and as agents for the ECB
13. to implement monetary policy in the euro area in accordance with the guidelines and decisions laid down by the Governing Council
14. underline its commitment to provide a sufficient safety margin to guard against the risks of deflation
15. an even distribution of central bank liquidity and a homogeneous level of short-term interest rates throughout the single currency area
16. a set of monetary policy instruments, namely open market operations, standing facilities and reserve requirements
17. on an ad hoc basis to manage the liquidity situation in the market and to steer interest rates
18. requires credit institutions to hold minimum reserves on accounts with the national central banks
19. be available for all transactions in euro between and within the euro area countries as well as several other EU countries
20. the launch in 2008 of the Single Euro Payments Area (SEPA)

Ⅲ. Translate the following paragraphs into Chinese.
1. The conditions to be fulfilled before entering the EU are the Copenhagen criteria. These require the prospective members (ⅰ) to have stable institutions guaranteeing democracy, the rule of law, human rights and the respect for and protection of minorities, and (ⅱ) to have a functioning market economy as well as the capacity to cope with competitive pressure, in order to be able to take on the obligations of membership, including the aims of political, economic and monetary union.

2. In the second half of the 1980s the idea of an economic and monetary union was revived in the Single European Act of 1986, which created a single market. But it was realised that the full benefits of a single market could only be reaped with the introduction of a single currency for the participating countries. In 1988 the European Council instructed the Delors Committee to examine ways of realising Economic and Monetary Union (EMU). The 1989 Delors Report led to the negotiations for the Treaty on European Union, which established the European Union (EU) and amended the Treaty establishing the European Community. It was signed in Maastricht in February 1992 (so it is sometimes called the Maastricht Treaty) and entered into force on 1 November 1993.

3. Countries wishing to adopt the euro as their currency must achieve a high degree of "sustainable convergence". The degree of convergence is assessed on the basis of several criteria in the Maastricht Treaty, which require a country to have:
    - a high degree of price stability
    - sound public finances
    - a stable exchange rate
    - low and stable long-term interest rates.

4. Sweden as well as nine of the 12 countries that have joined since 2004 count as members with a "derogation" since they have not yet met all the requirements to adopt the euro. Having a derogation means that a Member State is exempt from some, but not all, of the provisions which normally apply from the beginning of Stage Three of EMU. It includes all provisions which transfer responsibility for monetary policy to the Governing Council of the ECB.

5. Efficient external communication is an essential part of a central bank's job. Communication contributes to the effectiveness and credibility of monetary policy. In order to increase the public's understanding of monetary policy and other central bank activities, the ECB must be open and transparent. This is the main guiding principle for the Eurosystem in its external communication, which involves close cooperation between the ECB and the NCBs.

6. Like its predecessor, TARGET2 is used for the settlement of central bank operations, large-value euro interbank transfers as well as other euro payments. It provides real-time

processing, settlement in central bank money and immediate finality. However, unlike its predecessor, in which all payments were processed decentrally by the national central banks, the new system uses a single shared platform with no intervention by the central banks. This platform makes the provision of an enhanced and harmonised service possible and, via economies of scale, permits lower fees and better cost-efficiency. There is no upper or lower value limit for TARGET2 payments.

Ⅳ. **Read the passage and fill in the blanks.**

Three Pillars of the European Union

The Treaty of Maastricht, which established the European Union, divided EU policies into three main areas called pillars.

1. The first or "Community" pillar concerns economic, social and environmental policies.

2. The second or "Common Foreign and Security Policy" (CFSP) pillar concerns foreign policy and military matters.

3. The third or "Police and Judicial Co-operation in Criminal Matters" (PJCC) pillar concerns co-operation in the fight against crime. This pillar was originally named "Justice and Home Affairs".

• Research (e.g. Sixth Framework Programme)		
• Asylum policy		
• Schengen treaty		
• Immigration policy		

Within each pillar, a different balance is struck between the supranational and intergovernmental principles.

Supranationalism is strongest in the first pillar. Its function generally corresponded at first to the three European Communities (European Coal and Steel Community, ECSC; European Economic Community, EEC and Euratom) whose organisational structure had already been unified in 1965-67 through the Merger Treaty. Later, through the Treaty of Maastricht the word "Economic" was removed from the EEC, so it became simply the EC. Then with the Treaty of Amsterdam additional areas would be transferred from the third pillar to the first. In 2002, the ECSC (which had a life time of 50 years) ceased to exist because the treaty which established it, the Treaty of Paris, had expired.

In the CFSP and PJCC pillars the powers of the European Parliament, the Commission and European Court of Justice with respect to the Council are significantly limited, without however being altogether eliminated. The balance struck in the first pillar is frequently referred to as the "community method", since it is that used by the European Community.

Origin of the three pillars structure

The pillar structure had its historical origins in the negotiations leading up to the Maastricht Treaty. It was desired to add powers to the Community in the areas of foreign policy, security and defense policy, asylum and immigration policy, criminal co-operation, and judicial co-operation.

However, some member-states opposed the addition of these powers to the Community on the grounds that they were too sensitive to national sovereignty for the community method to be used, and that these matters were better handled intergovernmentally. To the extent that at that time the Community dealt with these matters at all, they were being handled intergovernmentally, principally in European Political Cooperation (EPC).

As a result, these additional matters were not included in the European Community; but were tacked on externally to the European Community in the form of two additional "pillars". The first additional pillar (Common Foreign and Security Policy, CFSP) dealt with foreign policy, security and defence issues, while the second additional pillar (JHA, Justice and Home Affairs), dealt with the remainder.

Recent amendments in the Treaty of Amsterdam and the Treaty of Nice have made the additional pillars increasingly supranational. Most important among these has been the transfer of policy on asylum, migration and judicial co-operation in civil matters to the Community pillar, effected by the Amsterdam Treaty. Thus the third pillar has been renamed Police and Judicial Co-operation in Criminal Matters, or PJCC. The term Justice and Home Affairs is still used to cover both the third pillar and the transferred areas.

Abolition of the pillar structure

In a speech before the Nice Conference, Joschka Fischer, then Foreign Minister of Germany, called for a simplification of the European Union, resulting in the draft of a European Constitution. Though this constitution failed due to referenda in France and the Netherlands, the main ideas remained the same. One of these core ideas was the de facto abolition of the pillar structure. Therefore the draft Treaty of Lisbon, if ratified by all member states, will simplify and unify the legal structure of the European Union. As such the current three pillar structure will be replaced as all functions will be merged into the European Union which will have a legal personality of its own for the first time.

1. Among the three pillars of the European Union, _____ is responsible for cultural issues while _____ concerns security policy.
2. The pillar structure originated from the Maastricht Treaty which was desired to add power to the Community concerning _____ policy, security and defense policy, asylum and policy, criminal co-operation, and _____ co-operation.
3. The three-pillar structure will cease to function if the draft _____ is ratified by all members.

FURTHER READING

THE EUROSYSTEM

The European System of Central Banks (ESCB)

The European System of Central Banks (ESCB) comprises
- the European Central Bank (ECB) and
- the national central banks (NCBs) of all 27 EU Member States.

This means that the ESCB includes the national central banks of those EU Member States that have not yet adopted the euro, be it due to their special status (Denmark, United Kingdom) or because they have a derogation. The latter currently applies to Sweden as well as 9 of the 12 Member States that have joined the EU since May 2004. This means in consequence: these countries still have their own national currency, for which they still conduct their own monetary policy and their respective central banks keep for the time being their monetary sovereignty. This also means, of course, that they are not involved in the performance of the core activities of Monetary Union, such as the conduct of the monetary policy for the euro area.

The non-euro area NCBs are nevertheless committed to the principles of monetary policies which aim at price stability. Furthermore, ESCB membership implies at varying degrees active cooperation with the Eurosystem in several fields of activity, such as participation in the TARGET payment system and support in the collection of statistics. In addition, the European Exchange Rate Mechanism II (ERM II) provides a framework for monetary and exchange rate policy cooperation with the Eurosystem. The institutional forum for such cooperation is the General Council of the ECB.

The legal basis for the ESCB is the Treaty establishing the European Community (EC Treaty) and the Statute of the European System of Central Banks and of the European Central Bank (ESCB Statute). The Treaty entrusts the ESCB in general with the performance of the central banking functions for the euro. The ESCB Statute defines more specifically the relative roles and functions of the ECB and the NCBs, respectively.

The Eurosystem

Members

The legal texts which establish the European System of Central Banks (ESCB)—the Treaty establishing the European Community and the Statute of the ESCB—were written on the assumption that all EU Member States will adopt the euro and that therefore the ESCB will conduct all the tasks involved in the single currency. However, until all EU countries have introduced the euro, it is the "Eurosystem" which is the key actor. The term "Eurosystem" therefore serves to facilitate understanding of the structure of central banking in the euro area.

The Eurosystem as the central banking system of the euro area comprises:

- the ECB, and
- the national central banks (NCBs) of the 15 EU Member States whose common currency is the euro.

The Eurosystem is thus a sub-set of the ESCB. Since the ECB's policy decisions, such as on monetary policy, naturally apply only to the euro area countries, it is in reality the Eurosystem which as a team carries out the central bank functions for the euro area. In doing so, the ECB and the NCBs jointly contribute to attaining the common goals of the Eurosystem.

Why a system instead of a single central bank?

There are three main reasons for having a system of central banking in Europe:

- The Eurosystem approach builds on the existing competencies of the NCBs, their institutional set-up, infrastructure, expertise and excellent operational capabilities. Moreover, several central banks perform additional tasks besides those of the Eurosystem.
- Given the geographically large euro area and the long-established relationships between the national banking communities and their NCB, it was deemed appropriate to give the credit institutions an access point (接入点) to central banking in each participating Member State.
- Given the multitude of nations, languages and cultures in the euro area, the NCBs (instead of a supranational one) were best located to serve as access points of the Eurosystem.

The national central banks as integral part of the Eurosystem

Each national central bank (NCB) has legal personality according to the national law of its respective country.

The euro area NCBs, which form an integral part of the Eurosystem, carry out the tasks conferred upon the Eurosystem in accordance with the rules established by the ECB's decision-making bodies. The NCBs also contribute to the work of the Eurosystem and the European System of Central Banks (ESCB) through their participation in the various Eurosystem/ESCB Committees (see also separate slide "Eurosystem/ESCB Committees").

They may perform non-Eurosystem functions on their own responsibility, unless the Governing Council finds that such functions interfere with the objectives and tasks of the Eurosystem.

Such non-Eurosystem functions vary according to countries and mainly consist of various types of financial and administrative services to the governments of the respective countries. Most NCBs for example are involved in the supervision of financial institutions in their respective countries and some NCBs run their own printing works for the production of banknotes.

The European Central Bank

The European Central Bank (ECB) is the organisation for the conduct of monetary policy and the performance of other central banking functions for the euro. It carries out these tasks together with the national central banks of the euro area. The ECB is at the heart of the Eurosystem and the European System of Central Banks (ESCB). It was established in June 1998, replacing its precursor(先驱), the European Monetary Institute (EMI).

The legal basis of the ESCB and the ECB is provided for in Article 8 of the Treaty. The Treaty limits the ECB's activities to a clearly defined area: the central bank functions for the euro.

The ECB has its seat in Frankfurt am Main, Germany. Due to initial growth, the staff of the ECB is currently located in three different sites. However, new headquarters will be built in the eastern part of the city of Frankfurt. The construction is estimated to be completed at the end of 2011.

The number of staff of the ECB amounts to around 1,350 (in 2006) and it is truly European: its members come from all 27 countries of the

European Union (EU). In the early days, the EMI and the ECB recruited many staff from the national central banks of the EU Member States, but nowadays the ECB also attracts staff members from other sectors.

Independence

A cornerstone(基础) of the monetary order of the euro area is the independence of the ECB and the national central banks (NCBs) of the Eurosystem, which has been given "constitutional" status, as it has been **enshrined in**[庄严载入(宣告),明文昭示] both the Treaty establishing the European Community (EC Treaty) and the Statute of the European System of Central Banks (ESCB Statute), rather than in secondary legislation. Independence is an indispensable element which facilitates the pursuit of price stability.

The concept of independence includes:

Functional independence

Functional independence requires a primary objective determined by clarity and legal certainty that provides the central bank with the necessary means and instruments to achieve this objective, independently of any other authority. The primary objective of the ESCB, as enshrined in the EC Treaty and the ESCB Statute, is the maintenance of price stability.

Institutional independence

The principle of institutional independence is expressly referred to in Article 108 of the EC Treaty and Article 7 of the ESCB Statute. These provisions prohibit the ECB, the NCBs and members of their decision-making bodies from seeking or taking instructions from Community institutions or bodies, from any government of a Member State or from any other body. In addition, they also prohibit such institutions, governments and bodies from seeking to influence the members of the decision-making bodies of the ECB or the NCBs.

Personal independence

The Statute's provisions on **security of tenure**[职/地位的稳定性(或保证)] for members of the ECB's decision-making bodies further safeguard central bank independence. Such provisions stipulate a minimum term of office of five years for NCB governors (renewable), and a non-renewable term of office of eight years for the members of the ECB's Executive Board. Furthermore, members of the decision-making bodies may not be dismissed for reasons other than those stipulated in the ESCB Statute.

Financial independence

The ECB and the NCBs must be able to autonomously avail themselves of sufficient financial resources to fulfil their mandates. The ECB has its own capital, subscribed and paid up by the NCBs. It also has its own budget independent from that of the other European institutions. As regards the NCBs, Member States may not put their NCBs in the position of not having sufficient financing resources to carry out their ESCB-related and own national tasks.

Accountability

Accountability is a core element of democratic structures. The Eurosystem has the exclusive competence for the monetary policy of the euro area and thus has been entrusted with monetary sovereignty. Respect for the fundamental principles of democratic societies requires that the ECB is held accountable to the citizens and their democratically elected representatives, in order to balance the substantial degree of independence that it has been granted.

Consequently, both the Treaty establishing the European Community (EC Treaty) and the Statute of the European System of Central Banks (ESCB Statute) contain a number of provisions that require the ECB, just like any other independent central bank, to subject its actions and decisions to public scrutiny. It is of course also in the ECB's own interest to ensure that its decisions are properly explained and justified so as to foster public support for its policies.

The **legitimacy**[合法(性),正统(性),正确(性),合理(性)] of the independent ECB rests on a comprehensive framework for holding it accountable. Thus, the ECB is called on to explain and justify to the European citizens and their elected representatives how it uses the powers and prerogatives(特权) it has been entrusted with.

Reporting: publications and press conferences

The Treaty lays down a number of reporting requirements for the ECB, ranging from the publication of an annual report, a quarterly report and a weekly consolidated financial statement to appearances before the European Parliament.

The ECB fully complies with these requirements and even exceeds them, for instance by publishing a Monthly Bulletin rather than a quarterly report, by holding monthly press conferences to explain its monetary policy decisions and, since December 2004, by making public on a monthly basis other decisions taken by the Governing Council in addition to interest rate decisions.

Public speeches and testimonies

The members of the Governing Council deliver numerous speeches and give interviews throughout the euro area in order to explain the ECB's policies to the public. In line with the provisions of Article 113 of the Treaty, the ECB also reports regularly to the European Parliament on the decisions taken in the field of monetary policy and on its other tasks. Quarterly testimonies by the President of the ECB before Parliament's Committee on Economic and Monetary Affairs serve as the main forum for these regular exchanges of views. The President also presents the ECB's Annual Report to the plenary of the European Parliament.

Beyond the scope of its Treaty obligations, the ECB has the voluntary practice of replying to written questions submitted by members of the European Parliament on issues related to the ECB's mandate.

Financial controls

The accounts of the ECB and the national central banks (NCBs) are also subject, under Article 27 of the ESCB Statute, to the audit review by independent external auditors recommended by the Governing Council and approved by the EU Council. Such auditors have the full power to examine all books and accounts of the ECB and the NCBs and obtain full information on their transactions.

In addition, the European Court of Auditors is entrusted with examining the operational efficiency of the management of the ECB and publishes the results of such examination in its annual report. Finally, the ECB is also subject to control by OLAF, the European **Anti-Fraud**(反欺诈) Office.

Basic tasks of the Eurosystem

The Treaty establishing the European Community entrusts the European System of Central Banks (ESCB) with the task of performing the central bank function for the Community. Since some EU Member States do not participate in Economic and Monetary Union, the terms "ESCB" and "Community" are to be read as "Eurosystem" and "euro area", respectively.

Monetary policy

The Eurosystem is responsible for defining and implementing the monetary policy of the euro area. This is a public policy function that is implemented mainly by financial market operations. Important for this task is the full control of the Eurosystem over the monetary base. As part of that, the ECB and the national central banks (NCBs) are the only institutions that are entitled to actually issue legal tender banknotes in the euro area. Given the dependency of the banking system on base money, the Eurosystem is thus in a position to exert a dominant influence on money market conditions and money market interest rates.

Foreign exchange operations

Foreign exchange operations influence exchange rates and domestic liquidity conditions; both are important variables for monetary policy. Assigning this task to the Eurosystem is therefore logical, also because central banks have the necessary operational facilities. Secondly, if the central bank carries out this task, it ensures that the foreign exchange operations remain consistent with the aims of the central bank's monetary policy.

Promote smooth operation of payment systems

Payment systems are a means to transfer money between credit and other monetary institutions. This function places them at the heart of an economy's financial infrastructure. Assigning the task of promoting their smooth operation to the Eurosystem acknowledges the importance of having sound and efficient payment systems—not only for the conduct of monetary policy but also for the stability of the financial system and as such for the economy as a whole.

Hold and manage foreign reserves

One of the most important reasons for managing the foreign reserves portfolio is to ensure that the ECB has sufficient liquidity to conduct its foreign exchange operations. The ECB's foreign reserves are currently managed in a decentralised manner by the NCBs that opt to take part in operational ECB foreign reserve management activities. These NCBs act on behalf of the ECB in accordance with instructions received from the ECB. Although the NCBs manage their own foreign reserves independently, their operations on the foreign exchange market are, above a certain limit, subject to the approval of the ECB, in order to ensure consistency with the exchange rate and monetary policy of the Eurosystem.

Other tasks of the Eurosystem

Advisory functions

The ECB has to be consulted within certain limits and conditions
- on any proposed Community act in its field of competence,
- by national authorities regarding any draft legislative provision in the ECB's field of competence.

The ECB gives its advice in the form of "ECB opinions" which are published, for example, on its website.

Collection and compilation of statistics

The ECB, assisted by the national central banks, collects a wide range of statistical information necessary for the fulfilment of its tasks. Statistics are essential, for example for the monthly decision on the key interest rates, because they mirror the current situation of the euro area economy.

Contribution to prudential supervision and financial stability

Whereas direct responsibility for the pursuit of financial stability and prudential supervision has remained with the national competent authorities, the Treaty has assigned to the Eurosystem the important task of contributing to the smooth conduct of policies in these fields. This task—which evolves in relation to market and institutional developments—encompasses three main activities: first, the monitoring of financial stability, which aims at identifying sources of **vulnerabilities**(弱点) and assessing **the degree of resilience**(恢复力) of the financial system in the euro area. Second, the provision of advice to the competent authorities on the design and amendment of financial rules and supervisory requirements. Third, the promotion of arrangements for the maintenance of financial stability and the effective management of financial crises, including the smooth cooperation between central banks and supervisory authorities.

Issuance of euro banknotes and ensuring their integrity

Only euro banknotes have the status of legal tender in the euro area. In addition, the euro banknotes are used on an international scale. It is the Eurosystem's task to ensure a smooth and efficient supply of banknotes and to preserve the general public's confidence in the legal tender. Ensuring the integrity of the euro banknotes is achieved by conducting research and development activities, by counterfeit deterrence and monitoring and by applying common quality and authentication standards for banknote processing by NCBs, credit institutions and other professional cash handlers, such as cash-in-transit companies.

International cooperation

A number of issues (such as global imbalances and systemic macroeconomic and financial stability) that are of relevance to the ECB's basic tasks (in particular monetary policy) have implications beyond the euro area and therefore need to be addressed at the international level. Against this background, the ECB participates in meetings of international **fora** (forum 的复数) in which issues of relevance to the Eurosystem are addressed in order to present the Eurosystem's views. The Statute of the European System of Central Banks stipulates that the President of the ECB shall decide how the Eurosystem shall be represented in the field of international cooperation.

Division of labour in the Eurosystem

The Eurosystem consists of the ECB and the national central banks (NCBs) of those EU countries that have adopted the euro. Under Article 8 of the Statute of the European System of Central Banks (ESCB Statute), it is the ECB's decision-making bodies that govern the Eurosystem. Within their respective responsibilities, these bodies take all the decisions that are necessary to enable the Eurosystem to carry out its tasks.

Except for the statutory tasks that have been exclusively assigned to the ECB, the ESCB Statute does not indicate to what extent ECB policies are to be implemented through activities of the ECB or the NCBs. For the bulk of the Eurosystem's activities, the actual intra-System division of labour has been guided by the principle of **decentralization**(分权), with the ECB having recourse to the NCBs, to the extent deemed possible and appropriate, to carry out operations which form part of the tasks of the Eurosystem (cf. Article 12.1 of the ESCB Statute).

Thus, the ECB and the NCBs jointly contribute to attaining the Eurosystem's common goals. However, according to Article 9.2 of the Statute, the ECB has to ensure that all tasks are carried out properly and consistently. To ensure this across the euro area, the ECB has the power to issue guidelines and instructions to the NCBs.

Tasks of the ECB

In contrast to the national central banks (NCBs), the ECB carries out only few operations. Instead, it focuses on **formulating**(明确地叙述) the policies and on ensuring that the decisions are implemented consistently by the NCBs.

In particular, the ECB is responsible for

- **Defining Eurosystem policies**: the Governing Council of the ECB is in charge of monetary policy for the single currency. This includes the definition of price stability, how inflationary risks are analysed, etc.

- **Deciding, coordinating and monitoring the monetary policy operations**: the ECB instructs the NCBs on the details of the required operations (value, time, date, etc.) and checks their successful execution.

- **Adopting legal acts**: within closely defined limits, the decision-making bodies have the power to issue intra-Eurosystem binding legal acts, such as Guidelines and Instructions, to ensure that decentralised operations are carried out consistently by the NCBs. Moreover, within defined limits, they can adopt Regulations and Decisions, which are binding outside the Eurosystem.

- **Authorising the issuance of banknotes**: this encompasses(包含) the strategic planning and coordination of the production and issuance of euro banknotes. Furthermore, the ECB coordinates the Eurosystem's research and development activities and the security and quality of the euro banknote production. In addition, the ECB hosts the Counterfeit Analysis Centre for the analysis and classification of euro counterfeits, the central database for euro banknote counterfeits, and the International Counterfeit Deterrence Centre, which contributes to global central bank cooperation on counterfeit deterrence under the auspices of the G10 Governors.

- **Interventions on the foreign exchange markets**: if needed, also jointly with individual NCBs. This involves the buying and/or selling of securities on foreign exchange markets.

- **International and European cooperation**: in order to present its views at the international and European level, the ECB participates in the meetings of various international and European fora. In December 1998, the ECB became the only central bank in the world to be granted observer status at the International Monetary Fund (IMF) and it now participates in all meetings of the IMF's Executive Board on issues relevant to Economic and Monetary Union. For this reason, the ECB has established a permanent representation in Washington D. C. Moreover, the ECB participates in meetings of the G7, the G20 and the Financial Stability Forum. At the European level, the President of the ECB is regularly invited to attend meetings of the Eurogroup, the monthly informal gatherings of euro area finance ministers. Moreover, the ECB may participate in meetings of the EU Council whenever issues relating to the objectives and tasks of the Eurosystem are discussed.

Further, the ECB is responsible for

• **Statutory reports**: the reporting obligations are laid down in the Statute of the European System of Central Banks (Article 15). The ECB produces a Monthly Bulletin, a consolidated weekly financial statement of the Eurosystem and an Annual Report.

• **Monitoring financial risks**: this involves assessing the risks of securities, either those purchased in the context of the investment of the ECB's own funds and foreign reserves or of those securities that have been accepted as collateral in Eurosystem credit operations.

• **Fulfilling advisory functions to Community institutions and national authorities**: the ECB adopts "Opinions" on draft EU and national legislation, where it concerns the ECB's field of competence.

• **Running the IT systems**: the ECB and the NCBs have established a number of common operational systems to make it easier to carry out decentralised operations. These systems provide the "logistical" support for the Eurosystem's functional integrity. These systems encompass information systems, applications and procedures. They are organised according to a "hub-and-spokes" approach, with the hub located at the ECB.

• **Strategic and tactical management (战略和战术的管理) of the ECB's foreign reserves**: this involves the definition of the long-term risk return preferences of the foreign reserve assets (strategic asset allocation), the steering of the risk-return profile against the background of prevailing market conditions (tactical asset allocation) and the setting of the investment guidelines and the overall operational framework.

Tasks of the national central banks

The operational set-up of the Eurosystem takes account of the principle of decentralization. The national central banks (NCBs) perform almost all operational tasks of the Eurosystem. In doing so, they enact the decisions made centrally by the Governing Council of the ECB.

The NCBs are responsible for

- **Execution of monetary policy operations**: this means that the NCBs carry out the actual transactions, such as providing the commercial banks with central bank money.
- **Operational management of the ECB's foreign reserves**: this includes the execution and the settlement of the market transactions necessary to invest the ECB's foreign reserves.
- **Management of their own foreign reserves**: planned NCB operations in this area are subject to approval from the ECB, if such transactions may affect exchange rates or domestic liquidity conditions and if they exceed certain limits established by ECB guidelines. The aim is to ensure consistency with the monetary and exchange rate policy of the ECB.
- **Operation and supervision of payment systems**: payment systems are a means to transfer money within the banking system. Each NCB operates and supervises its own national system. These are all interlinked and form TARGET, the payment system for the euro. Besides, other private payment and security settlement systems exist, which are supervised to ensure their smooth functioning.
- **Joint issuance of banknotes together with the ECB**: both the ECB and the NCBs are issuers of euro banknotes. All banknotes are put into circulation by the NCBs, which accommodate any demand for euro banknotes by launching annual banknote production orders and by operating a Eurosystem-wide stock management system. Both activities are coordinated by the ECB. NCBs take measures to achieve a high quality of banknotes in circulation and to analyse counterfeits.
- **Collection of statistics and providing assistance to the ECB**: the ECB requires a wide range of economic and financial data to support the conduct of its monetary policy and the fulfilment of other Eurosystem tasks. The main areas where the NCBs help by collecting data from the national financial institutions are ⅰ) money, banking and financial markets, ⅱ) balance of payments statistics and on the Eurosystem's international reserves, and ⅲ) financial accounts.

- **Functions outside the European System of Central Banks (ESCB)**: national central banks may also perform functions other than those specified in the Statute unless the Governing Council finds, by a majority of two-thirds of the votes cast, that these interfere with the objectives and tasks of the ESCB. Such functions shall be performed on the responsibility and liability of national central banks and shall not be regarded as being part of the functions of the ESCB.

Decision-making bodies of the ECB

Fulfilling the ECB's mission

The ECB's mission is to keep inflation low and stable. To achieve this goal, it closely follows economic developments in the euro area and seeks to influence the state of the economy through its decision-making. The ECB has three bodies which take all the decisions in this respect:

- the Governing Council,
- the Executive Board, and
- the General Council.

The General Council will exist only as long as there are EU Member States which have not yet adopted the euro as their currency. Both the decision-making procedures and the various tasks are specified in the Statute of the European System of Central Banks (ESCB Statute).

Centralised decision-making

The ECB is the centre of decision-making in the Eurosystem. Thus, the Governing Council, the Executive Board and the General Council of the ECB each take all the decisions necessary to enable the Eurosystem and the ESCB to carry out their respective tasks. This includes the formulation of policies, such as the monetary policy for the euro area, but also how they should be implemented.

Principle of decentralization

The ESCB Statute does not specify who should implement the ECB's policies and decisions: the ECB itself or the national central banks. Article 12.1 states merely that the ECB should have recourse to the national central banks (NCBs), where possible and appropriate, to carry out operations.

This principle of decentralisation should not be confused with the "principle of subsidiarity", as set out in Article 5 of the Treaty on European Union. Subsidiarity means that the need for centralisation must be proven conclusively before action at Union level can be taken. In Stage Three of Economic and Monetary Union, however, monetary policy is conducted exclusively at Union level—under the authority of the ECB's Governing Council. Therefore it is centralised by definition and does not need to be justified. Instead, it is for the ECB to evaluate the extent to which decentralised implementation is possible and appropriate.

Decentralised operations

For the bulk of the Eurosystem's activities, there is indeed a division of labour guided by the principle of decentralisation.

The NCBs perform almost all operational tasks of the Eurosystem. In particular, they carry out the monetary policy operations and, as agents of the ECB, most foreign exchange operations, provide payment and securities settlement facilities, and ensure the procurement, issue and post-issue handling of euro banknotes. They also collect statistics for the ECB, collaborate with the ECB on translation and the production of publications and contribute to economic analysis and research.

By contrast, the ECB carries out few operations while it oversees all of them, in order to ensure that the operations of the Eurosystem are performed consistently by the euro area NCBs.

Governing Council

Members

The Governing Council of the ECB is the main decision-making body of the Eurosystem. It comprises

- all the members of the Executive Board of the ECB, and
- the governors/presidents of all the national central banks (NCBs) of the euro area, that is those EU Member States that have adopted the euro.

The Treaty establishing the European Community and the Statute of the European System of Central Banks (ESCB Statute) assign to the Governing Council the power to take the most important and strategically significant decisions for the Eurosystem. When taking decisions on monetary policy and on other tasks of the Eurosystem, the members of the Governing Council act not as national representatives but in a fully independent capacity.

The Governing Council currently meets twice a month, usually on the first and third Thursday. Interest rate decisions are normally discussed at the first meeting of the month only. The President of the EU Council/Eurogroup and a member of the European Commission may attend the meetings, but without having the right to vote. Each member of the Governing Council has one vote and, unless otherwise provided for in the ESCB Statute, the Governing Council acts by simple majority. In the event of a tie, the President has the casting vote. Although the proceedings of the meetings are confidential, the Governing Council makes the outcome of its deliberations public, primarily those about setting the key interest rates, via a press conference which is held after the first Governing Council meeting of each month. Since December 2004 decisions taken by the Governing Council other than those setting interest rates have also been published every month on the websites of the Eurosystem central banks.

Tasks

The main responsibilities of the Governing Council are:
- formulating the monetary policy of the euro area by taking the necessary decisions and adopting the Guidelines needed for its implementation;
- adopting the Regulations which the ECB may make in application of the Treaty or by delegation from the EU Council;
- acting as second and last instance for appeals of third parties to ECB Decisions adopted by the Executive Board;
- issuing Guidelines for operations of the NCBs with remaining foreign reserve assets and for the transactions of euro area member countries in their foreign exchange working balances;
- taking the necessary steps to ensure compliance with ECB Guidelines and Instructions and defining any necessary information to be provided by the NCBs;
- exercising the right of initiative for Community legislation and fulfilling the advisory role of the ECB;
- authorising the issuance of euro banknotes and the volume of issue of the euro coins within the euro area;
- establishing the necessary rules for the standardisation of the accounting and reporting of operations undertaken by the national central banks;
- adopting the rules governing the allocation of monetary income

among the Eurosystem NCBs; and
- adopting the Annual Report of the ECB.

In addition, the Governing Council is the supreme decision-making body for the administration and functioning of the ECB itself. In particular, the Governing Council adopts the Rules of Procedure of the ECB and is competent with regard to its finances, budget and appropriation of the annual financial results.

Executive Board

The Executive Board of the ECB is the operational decision-making body of the ECB and of the Eurosystem. It assumes the responsibility for all the decisions which need to be taken on a day-to-day basis. The ECB must be able to react and adapt to quickly changing conditions in the money and capital markets, to address specific cases and to deal with matters of urgency. This function can only be performed by a body whose members are permanently and exclusively involved in the implementation of the ECB's policies. The Executive Board usually meets once a week.

Members

The Executive Board comprises
- the President of the ECB,
- the Vice-President of the ECB, and
- four other members.

All of the Executive Board members are chosen from among people of recognised standing and with professional experience in monetary or banking matters. They are appointed by common accord of the governments of the participating Member States at the level of the Heads of State or Government, on a recommendation from the EU Council after it has consulted the European Parliament and the Governing Council of the ECB.

As a member of the Executive Board, the President of the ECB has a prominent status and exercises certain functions exclusively devoted to him/her (or in his/her absence to the Vice-President): chairing meetings of the Governing Council, the General Council and the Executive Board of the ECB; representing the ECB externally; and presenting the Annual Report of the ECB to the EU Council and the European Parliament. Furthermore, the President is invited to participate in EU Council meetings in which matters relating to the objectives and tasks of the Eurosystem are discussed. In addition, he/she is invited to the meetings of the Eurogroup, the informal group of the euro area ministers of finance and economy.

Tasks

The main responsibilities of the Executive Board are to:
- prepare the meetings of the Governing Council;
- implement monetary policy in the euro area in accordance with the guidelines and decisions laid down by the Governing Council and, in so doing, give the necessary instructions to the national central banks;
- manage the day-to-day business of the ECB;
- exercise certain powers, including regulatory powers, delegated to it by the Governing Council.

General Council

Members

The General Council of the ECB comprises
- the President and Vice-President of the ECB, and
- the governors/presidents of the national central banks of all 27 EU Member States.

The General Council usually meets once every three months. Decisions are taken by a simple majority unless otherwise stipulated in the Statute of the European System of Central Banks (ESCB Statute). The President of the ECB has to keep the General Council informed of decisions taken by the Governing Council.

In accordance with the ESCB Statute, the General Council will exist only as long as there are EU Member States which have not adopted the euro.

Tasks

The General Council can be regarded as a "transitional body" since it carries out the tasks, taken over from the European Monetary Institute, which the ECB is required to perform in Stage Three of Economic and Monetary Union (EMU) because some EU Member States have not adopted the euro.

The General Council is primarily responsible for
- reporting on the progress made towards convergence by EU Member States which have not yet adopted the euro;
- giving advice on the preparations necessary for irrevocably fixing the exchange rates of those Member States;
- monitoring the functioning of the Exchange Rate Mechanism II (ERM II) and the sustainability of bilateral exchange rate relations

between each participating non-euro area currency and the euro;

• serving as a forum for monetary and exchange rate policy coordination in the EU;

• the administration of the intervention and financing mechanism of ERM II;

• contributing to particular activities, such as the ECB's advisory functions, and

• the collection of statistical information.

Moreover, the General Council is also consulted inter alia on changes to the rules on accounting and financial reporting, the determination of the ECB's capital key and the conditions of employment of ECB staff.

Eurosystem/ESCB Committees

The Committees assist the work of the decision-making bodies of the ECB, which can request them to provide any information in their fields of expertise in order to facilitate the decision-making process and the implementation of decisions.

Participation is usually restricted to experts of the Eurosystem central banks. However, the national central banks (NCBs) of the EU Member States which have not yet adopted the euro take part in the meetings of a Committee whenever appropriate. Moreover, representatives of other competent bodies may also be invited, such as national supervisory authorities in the case of the Banking Supervisory Committee.

• The **Accounting and Monetary Income Committee** (**AMICO**) advises on all intra-Eurosystem issues relating to accounting, financial reporting and the allocation of monetary income.

• The **Banknote Committee** (**BANCO**) advises on all banknote policy-related matters and assists in the strategic planning of banknote production and issuance.

• The **Banking Supervision Committee** (**BSC**) assists regarding the contribution to prudential supervision of credit institutions and the stability of the financial system.

• The **Eurosystem/ESCB Communications Committee** (**ECCO**) assists in external and intra-system communication policy.

• The **Information Technology Committee** (**ITC**) assists in the development, implementation and maintenance of IT networks and communications infrastructures which support the joint operational systems.

- The **Internal Auditors Committee** (**IAC**) develops common standards for auditing Eurosystem operations and audits joint projects and joint operational systems at the Eurosystem/ESCB level.
- The **International Relations Committee** (**IRC**) assists in the performance of the ECB's statutory tasks with regard to international cooperation and acts as a forum for exchanging views on matters of common interest in the field of international relations.
- The **Legal Committee** (**LEGCO**) provides legal advice for the fulfilment of the ECB's statutory task and prepares the legal acts for the operation of the Eurosystem.
- The **Market Operations Committee** (**MOC**) assists in the execution of monetary policy operations and foreign exchange transactions, including those related to the operation of ERM II, and to the management of the ECB's foreign reserves.
- The **Monetary Policy Committee** (**MPC**) mainly advises on strategic and longer-term issues relating to the formulation of the monetary and exchange rate policy and is responsible for the Eurosystem staff projections.
- The **Payment and Settlement Systems Committee** (**PSSC**) advises on the operation and maintenance of TARGET, general payment systems policy and oversight issues and issues of interest for central banks in the field of securities clearing and settlement.
- The **Statistics Committee** (**STC**) mainly advises on the design and compilation of statistical information collected by the ECB with the assistance of the NCBs.
- In 1998, the Governing Council also established a **Budget Committee** (**BUCOM**), composed of representatives of the ECB and the Eurosystem NCBs, which assists and reports directly to the Governing Council in matters related to the ECB's budget.
- The **Human Resources Conference** (**HRC**) was established in 2005 and includes the heads of personnel of all EU central banks.

(*FROM*: *http://www.ecb.int/ecb/educational/facts/orga/html/or_001.en.html*)

CHAPTER 9
HISTORY OF RENMINBI (RMB)

Learning Objectives

1. Basic information about Renminbi;
2. Five series of Renminbi;
3. Value of Renminbi.

Etymology

The renminbi (simplified Chinese 人民币; traditional Chinese 人民幣; pinyin: rénmínbì; literally "people's currency"; sign: ; code: CNY) is the currency of the People's Republic of China (PRC), whose principal unit is the *yuan* (simplified Chinese: 元 or 圆; traditional Chinese: 圓; *pinyin*: *yuán*; Wade-Giles: yüan), subdivided into 10 *jiao* (角), each of 10 *fen* (分). The *renminbi* is issued by the People's Bank of China, the monetary authority of the PRC. The ISO 4217 abbreviation is CNY, although it is also commonly abbreviated as "RMB". The Latinized symbol is ¥.

A variety of currencies circulated in China during the Republic of China (ROC) era, most of which were denominated in the unit "*yuan*". Each was distinguished by a currency name, such as the *fabi* ("legal tender"), the "*gold yuan*", and the "*silver yuan*". The word *yuan* in

Chinese literally means *round*, after the shape of the coins. The Korean and Japanese currency units, *won* and *yen* respectively, are cognates of the *yuan* and have the same Chinese character (*hanja/kanji*) representation, but in different forms (respectively, 원/圓 and 円/圓), also meaning *round* in Korean and Japanese. However, they do not share the same names for the subdivisions. (See also New Taiwan dollar, referred to as 元 or 圓, for the currency of Taiwan.)

As the Communist Party of China took control of ever larger territories in the latter part of the China's War of Liberation (1945—1949), its People's Bank of China began in 1948 to issue a unified currency for use in communist-controlled territories. Also denominated in yuan, this currency was identified by different names, including "People's Bank of China banknotes" (traditional

fabi

Chinese: 中國人民銀行鈔票; simplified Chinese: 中国人民银行钞票; from November 1948), "New Currency" (traditional Chinese: 新幣; simplified Chinese: 新币; from December 1948), "People's Bank of China notes" (traditional Chinese: 中國人民銀行券; simplified Chinese: 中国人民银行券; from January 1949), "People's Notes" (人民券, as an abbreviation of the last name), and finally "People's Currency", or "renminbi", from June 1949.

Production and minting

Renminbi currency production is carried about by a state owned corporation, China Banknote Printing and Minting Corporation (CBPMC) headquartered in Beijing. CBPMC uses a network of printing and engraving and minting facilities around the country to produce banknotes and coins for subsequent distribution. Banknote printing facilities are based in Beijing, Shanghai, Chengdu, Xi'an, Shijiazhuang, and Nanchang. Mints are located in Nanjing, Shanghai, and Shenyang. Also, high grade paper for the banknotes is produced at two facilities in Baoding and Kunshan. The Baoding facility is the largest facility in the world dedicated to developing banknote material according to its website. In addition, the People's Bank of China has its own printing technology research division which researches new techniques for creating banknotes and making counterfeiting more difficult.

First series, 1948—1955

The first series of renminbi banknotes was introduced by the People's Bank of China in December 1948, about a year before the Chinese Communist Party's victory in China's War of Liberation. It was issued only in paper money form and replaced the various currencies circulating in the areas controlled by the communists. One of the first tasks of the new government was to end the hyperinflation that had plagued China in the final years of the Kuomintang (KMT) era. That achieved, a revaluation occurred in 1955, at the rate of 1 new yuan = 10,000 old yuan.

Banknotes

On December 1, 1948, the newly-founded People's Bank of China introduced notes in denominations of 1, 5, 10, 20, 50, 100 and 1000 *yuan*. Notes for 200,500,5000 and 10,000 *yuan* followed in 1949, with 50,000 *yuan* notes added in 1950. A total of 62 different designs were issued. The notes were officially withdrawn on various dates from April 1, 1955 to May 10, 1955.

These first renminbi notes were printed with the words "People's Bank of China", "Republic of China", and the denomination, written in Chinese characters by Dong Biwu.

The name *renminbi* was first recorded as an official name in June 1949. After work began in 1950 to design the second series of the *renminbi*, the previous series were retroactively dubbed the "first series of the *renminbi*".

Second series, 1955—present

Part Ⅲ   CURRENCIES

The second series of *renminbi* banknotes was introduced in 1955. During the era of the command economy, the value of the *renminbi* was set to unrealistic values in exchange with western currency and severe currency exchange rules were put in place. With the opening of the mainland Chinese economy in 1978, a dual-track currency system was instituted, with renminbi usable only domestically, and with foreigners forced to use foreign exchange certificates. The unrealistic levels at which exchange rates were pegged led to a strong black market in currency transactions.

In the late 1980s and early 1990s, the PRC worked to make the RMB more convertible. Through the use of swap centers, the exchange rate was brought to realistic levels and the dual track currency system was abolished.

The *renminbi* is convertible on current accounts but not capital accounts. The ultimate goal has been to make the RMB fully convertible. However, partly in response to the Asian financial crisis in 1998, the PRC has been concerned that the mainland Chinese financial system would not be able to handle the potential rapid cross-border movements of hot money, and as a result, as of 2007, the currency trades within a narrow band specified by the Chinese central government.

The *fen* and *jiao* have become increasingly unnecessary as prices have increased. Chinese retailers tend to avoid decimal values (such as 9.99), opting instead for integer values of *yuan* (such as 9 or 10).

Coins

In 1955, aluminium 1, 2 and 5 *fen* coins were introduced. In 1980, brass 1, 2, and 5 *jiao* and cupro-nickel 1 *yuan* coins were added, although the 1 and 2 *jiao* were only produced until 1981, with the last 5 *jiao* and 1 *yuan* issued in 1985. In 1991, a new coinage was introduced, consisting of an aluminium 1 *jiao*, brass 5 *jiao* and nickel-clad-steel 1 *yuan*. Issuance of the 1 and 2 *fen* coins ceased in 1991, with that of the 5 *fen* halting a year later. The small coins were still made for annual mint sets, and from the beginning of 2005 again for general circulation. New designs of the 1 and 5 *jiao* and 1 *yuan* were introduced in between 1999 and 2002.

The use of coins varies from place to place. For example, coins are more often used for values less or equal to 1 *yuan* in Shanghai and Shenzhen but banknotes of the lower value are more often used than coins in Beijing and Xi'an. Coins are used far less than banknotes in China nowadays, this is mainly because of the inflation in China, in which most everyday expenses cost around 5 to 10 *yuan* such as buying a drink or going by taxi.

Banknotes

"People's Bank of China" written in 5 different languages. From top to bottom and left to right: Mandarin *pinyin*, Mongol, Tibetan, Uyghur, and Zhuang languages.

In 1955, notes (dated 1953), were introduced in denominations of 1, 2 and 5 *fen*, 1, 2 and 5 *jiao*, and 1, 2, 3, 5 and 10 *yuan*. Except for the three *fen* denominations and the 3 *yuan*, notes in these denominations continue to circulate, with 50 and 100 *yuan* notes added in 1980 and 20 *yuan* notes added in or after 1999.

The denomination of each banknote is printed in Chinese. The numbers themselves are printed in financial Chinese numeral characters, as well as Arabic numerals. The denomination and the words "People's Bank of China" are also printed in Mongol, Tibetan, Uyghur and Zhuang on the back of each banknote. The right front of the note has a tactile representation of the denomination in Chinese braille starting from the fourth series.

Second series

Second series of *renminbi* banknotes was introduced on 1 March 1955. Each note has the words "People's Bank of China" as well as the denomination in the Uyghur, Tibetan, Mongol and Zhuang languages on the back, which has since appeared in each series of *renminbi* notes. The denominations available in banknotes were ¥0.01, ¥0.02, ¥0.05, ¥0.1, ¥0.2, ¥0.5, ¥1, ¥2, ¥3, ¥5 and ¥10.

Third series

The third series of *renminbi* banknotes was introduced on April 15, 1962. For the next two decades, the second and third series banknotes were used concurrently. The denominations were of ￥0.1, ￥0.2, ￥0.5, ￥1, ￥2, ￥5 and ￥10. The third series was phased out during the 1990s and then was recalled completely on July 1, 2000.

Fourth series

Part Ⅲ CURRENCIES

The fourth series was introduced between 1987 and 1997, although the banknotes were dated 1980, 1990, or 1996. They are still legal tender. Banknotes are available in denominations of ￥0.1, ￥0.2, ￥0.5, ￥1, ￥2, ￥5, ￥10, ￥50 and ￥100.

Fifth series

In 1999, a new series of *renminbi* banknotes and coins was progressively introduced. The fifth series consists of banknotes for ￥1, ￥5, ￥10, ￥20, ￥50 and ￥100. Significantly, the fifth series uses the portrait of Mao Zedong on all banknotes, in place of the various leaders and workers which had been featured previously.

A new 100 banknote of the fifth series was issued on Nov. 12, 2015.

Commemorative designs

In 1999, a commemorative red ￥50 note was issued in honor of the 50th anniversary of the establishment of the People's Republic of China. This note features Mao Zedong on the front and various animals on the back.

An orange polymer note, and so far, China's only polymer note, commemorating the new millennium was issued in 2000 with a face value of ￥100. This features a dragon on the obverse and the reverse has a sundial.

For the 2008 Beijing Olympics, a green ￥10 note was issued featuring the Bird's Nest on the front with the back showing a classical Olympic discus thrower and various other athletes.

Possible future design

On March 13, 2006, some delegates to an advisory body at the National People's Congress proposed to include Sun Yat-sen and Deng Xiaoping on the *renminbi* banknotes. However, the proposal is a long way from becoming law.

Use outside mainland China

The two special administrative regions, Hong Kong and Macau, have their own respective currencies. According to the "one country, two systems" principle and the basic laws of the two territories, national laws generally do not apply. Therefore, the Hong Kong dollar and the Macanese pataca remain the legal tenders in the two territories, and renminbi, although accepted, is not legal tender. Banks in Hong Kong allow people to maintain accounts in RMB.

The RMB had a presence in Macau even before the 1999 return to the People's Republic of China from Portugal. Banks in Macau can issue credit cards based on the *renminbi* but not loans. *Renminbi* based credit cards cannot be used in Macau's casinos.

The *renminbi* is circulated in some of China's neighbors, such as Pakistan, Mongolia and northern part of Thailand. Cambodia welcomes the *renminbi* as an official currency and Laos and Myanmar allow it in border provinces. Though unofficial, Vietnam recognizes the exchange of *renminbi* to đồng.

Value

For most of its early history, the RMB was pegged to the U. S. dollar at 2.46 yuan per USD (note: during the 1970s, it was appreciated until it reached 1.50 *yuan* per USD in 1980). When China's economy gradually opened during the 1980s, the RMB was devalued in order to reflect its true market price and to improve the competitiveness of Chinese export. Thus, the official RMB/USD exchange rate declined from 1.50 *yuan* in 1980 to 8.62 *yuan* by 1994 (lowest ever on the record). Improving current account balance during the latter half of the 1990s enabled the Chinese government to maintain a peg of 8.27 *yuan* per USD from 1997 to 2005. On 21 July 2005, the peg was finally lifted, which saw an immediate one-off RMB revaluation to 8.11 per USD. The exchange rate against the euro stood at 10.07060 *yuan* per euro. The RMB is now moved to a managed floating exchange rate based on market supply and demand with reference to a basket of foreign currencies. The daily trading price of the U. S. dollar against the RMB in the inter-bank foreign exchange market would be allowed to float within a narrow band of 0.3% around the central parity published by the People's Bank of China (PBC); in a later announcement published on 18 May 2007, the band was extended to 0.5%. The PRC has stated that the basket is dominated by the United States dollar, euro, Japanese yen and South Korean won, with a smaller proportion made up of the British pound, Thai baht, Russian ruble, Australian dollar, Canadian dollar and Singapore dollar.

On April 10, 2008, it traded at 6.9920 *yuan* per U. S. dollar, which is the first time in more than a decade that a dollar bought less than seven *yuan*, and at 11.03630 *yuan* per euro.

On September 30, 2008, the *renminbi* traded at 6.7899 *yuan* per U. S. dollar, which is a 21.9% increase and the highest rate since the removal of the peg. On the other hand, on

October 27, 2008 it traded at 8.52812 *yuan* per euro, which corresponds roughly to the rate at the time of the lifting of the peg against the US-Dollar. In fact, the *renminbi* has remained at a value of around 6.83 per U. S. dollar since July 2008, oscillating around a narrow band, which in practice amounts to a re-pegging of the *renminbi* against the dollar.

Purchasing power parity

Scholarly studies suggest that the *yuan* is undervalued on the basis of purchasing power parity analysis.

• The World Bank estimated that, by purchasing power parity, one International dollar was equivalent to approximately ¥1.9 in 2004.

• The International Monetary Fund estimated that, by purchasing power parity, one United States dollar was equivalent to approximately ¥3.462 in 2006, ¥3.621 in 2007, and ¥3.798 in 2008.

(*FROM*：http://en.wikipedia.org/wiki/Renminbi)

WORDS AND EXPRESSIONS

• *cognate* /ˈkɒgneɪt/ *n.* a word related to one in another language 同字源的字

adj. related in origin, as certain words in genetically related languages descended from the same ancestral root; for example, English name and Latin nōmen from Indo-European nō-men- 同词源的：来源相关的，如在有关的语言中，一些词来自相同的词根；例如，英语 name 与拉丁文 nōmen 源自印欧语 nō-men-；

related by blood; having a common ancestor 同族的：有血缘关系的；有共同祖先的

• *Chinese character* *n.* also called Han character or Hanzi, is a logogram used in writing Chinese (hanzi) 汉字

• *China's War of Liberation* *n.* The war was fought between the Kuomintang (KMT or Chinese Nationalist Party) and the Communist Party of China (CPC). The war represented an ideological split between the Western-supported Nationalist KMT and the Soviet-supported Communist CPC. 解放战争,亦称第三次国内革命战争(the Third Civil Revolutionary War),是 1945 年 8 月至 1949 年 9 月中国人民解放军在中国共产党的领导和广大人民群众的支援下,为推翻国民党统治、解放全中国而进行的战争

• *China Banknote Printing and Minting Corporation* (CBPMC) *n.* It is a state-owned corporation which carries out the minting of all renminbi coins and printing of renminbi banknotes for the People's Republic of China headquartered in Beijing. 中国印钞造币总公司

• *counterfeiting* /ˈkaʊntəfɪtɪŋ/ *n.* an exact copy of something, especially currencies, to trick people into thinking that it is the real thing. 伪造；伪造货币

- *hyperinflation* /ˌhaɪpərɪnˈfleɪʃn/ *n.* extremely high monetary inflation 恶性通货膨胀
- *plague* /pleɪg/ *vt.* to afflict with or as if with a disease or calamity 使遭殃，困扰

  n. a widespread affliction or calamity 瘟疫，灾祸
- *retroactively* /ˌretrəʊˈæktɪvlɪ/ *adv.* retrospectively 逆动地，追溯地
- *dub* /dʌb/ *vt.* to honor with a new title or description 授予……新称号，把……称为；授予称号
- *command economy* *n.* an economy that is planned and controlled by a central administration 指令性（中央管制）经济；指标经济
- *integer* /ˈɪntɪdʒə(r)/ *n.* a member of the set of positive whole numbers (1,2,3,...), negative whole numbers (-1,-2,-3,...), and zero (0) 整数
- *cupro-nickel* /ˈkuːprəʊˈnɪkl/ *n.* an alloy of copper, nickel and strengthening impurities, such as iron and manganese 铜镍合金
- *nickel-clad-steel* *n.* 镀镍钢
- *tactile* /ˈtæktaɪl/ *adj.* perceptible to the sense of touch; tangible 可触知的；可触摸的
- *braille* /breɪl/ *n.* a system of writing and printing for visually impaired or sightless people, in which varied arrangements of raised dots representing letters and numerals are identified by touch. 盲人点字
- *pataca* /pəˈtɒkə/ *n.* a basic unit of currency in Macao Special Administrative Region of the People's Republic of China 澳元；帕塔卡（澳门特别行政区货币的基本单位）
- *casino* /kəˈsiːnəʊ/ *n.* (*pl.* casinos) a public room or building for gambling and other entertainment 娱乐场（供表演跳舞、赌博的地方）
- *one-off* /ˈwʌnˌɔːf,-ˌɒf/ *adj.* (chiefly British) happening, done, or made only once 一次性的

  n. something that is not repeated or reproduced. 一次性事物
- *baht* /ˈbɑːt/ *n.* a basic unit of currency in Thailand 铢，泰国货币单位
- *ruble* /ˈruːbl/ *n.* a basic unit of currency in Russia 卢布（俄罗斯货币单位）
- *đồng* /ˈdɒŋ/ (Vietnamese：/dôŋm/) It was the currency of North Vietnam from 3 November 1946 to 2 May 1978. It was subdivided into 10 *hào*, each itself divided into 10 *xu*.

The đồng (sign：đ; code：VND) is the currency of Vietnam since May 3, 1978. It is issued by the State Bank of Vietnam. It has the symbol đ. It is subdivided into 10 *hào*. However, the *hào* is now worth so little that it is no longer issued.

The word đồng is from the term "đồng tiền" (lit. money) which is a cognate of the Chinese "Tong Qian" (Traditional Chinese：銅錢; Simplified Chinese：铜钱). The term refers to Chinese bronze coins which were used as currency during the dynastic periods of China and Vietnam. The term *hào* is a cognate of the Chinese "halo" (Traditional Chinese：毫) which

means 1/10th a currency unit. 盾,越南货币单位

• ***undervalue*** /ˌʌndəˈvæljuː/ *vt.* to assign too low a value to; underestimate. 定值低,低估;对应词:overvalue 定值高,高估

BACKGROUND KNOWLEDGE

1 *Simplified Chinese or simplified Chinese Characters* 简化字

Each is one of the two standard sets of Chinese characters of the contemporary Chinese written language. They are based mostly on popular cursive (caoshu) forms embodying graphic or phonetic simplifications of the traditional forms that were used in printed text for over a thousand years. The government of the People's Republic of China has promoted them for use in printing in an attempt to increase literacy. They are officially used in the People's Republic of China (Mainland China), Singapore, and the United Nations.

Simplified character forms were created by decreasing the number of strokes and simplifying the forms of a sizable proportion of traditional Chinese characters. Some characters were simplified by applying regular rules; for example, by replacing all occurrences of a certain component with a simpler variant. Some characters were simplified irregularly, however, and some simplified characters are very dissimilar to and unpredictable from traditional characters. Finally, many characters were left untouched by simplification, and are thus identical between the traditional and simplified Chinese orthographies.

In August 2009, the PRC began collecting public comments for a modified list of simplified characters.

2 *Traditional Chinese characters* 繁体字

Each of them refers to one of two standard sets of printed Chinese characters. The modern shapes of traditional Chinese characters first appeared with the emergence of the clerical script during the Han Dynasty (206 B.C.—A.D. 220), and have been more or less stable since the 5th century (during the Southern and Northern Dynasties.) The retronym "traditional Chinese" is used to contrast traditional characters with another standardized set—simplified Chinese characters, introduced by the government of the People's Republic of China on Mainland China in the 1950s.

Traditional Chinese characters are currently used in Taiwan, Hong Kong and Macau. They were also used in mainland China before the People's Republic of China simplified them in the 1950s and 1960s. In overseas Chinese communities other than Singapore and Malaysia, traditional characters are most commonly used, although the number of printed materials in simplified characters is growing in Australia, USA and Canada, targeting or created by new arrivals from mainland China. A large number of overseas Chinese online newspapers allow users to switch between both sets. In contrast, simplified Chinese characters are used in mainland China, Singapore and Malaysia in official publications. The debate on traditional and simplified Chinese characters has been a long-running issue among Chinese communities.

3 *Wade-Giles* 威妥玛拼音, 韦氏拼音

It is a Romanization (*n.* 用罗马字体书写) system for the Mandarin language used in Beijing. It developed from a system produced by Thomas Wade during the mid-19th century, and was given completed form with Herbert Giles' Chinese-English dictionary of 1892.

Wade-Giles' was the main system of transcription in the English-speaking world for most of the 20th century, used in several standard reference books and in all books about China published before 1979. It replaced the Nanjing-based Romanization systems that had been common until late in the 19th century. It has mostly been replaced by the pinyin system (developed by the Chinese government and approved during 1958) nowadays, but parts of it, especially the names of individuals and certain cities remain in use in Taiwan region.

4 *ISO 4217* 国际标准化组织 4217 货币代码

It is the international standard describing three-letter codes (also known as the currency code) to define the names of currencies established by the International Organization for Standardization (ISO). The ISO 4217 code list is the established norm in banking and business all over the world for defining different currencies, and in many countries the codes for the more common currencies are so well known publicly, that exchange rates published in newspapers or posted in banks use only these to define the different currencies, instead of translated currency names or ambiguous currency symbols. ISO 4217 codes are used on airline tickets and international train tickets to remove any ambiguity about the price.

5 *Foreign exchange certificate* (FEC)

It is a type of currency. Foreign exchange certificates are sometimes used by governments as a surrogate for a national currency, where the national currency is usually subject to exchange controls or is not convertible. Most examples of foreign exchange certificate have an exchange rate higher than the national currency, being either pegged to a hard currency, or their exchange rate determined by the central bank.

Some countries which have employed FEC's in the past include: Soviet Union, China, Myanmar, East Germany, Ghana, North Korea, Cuba, Czechoslovakia and Poland.

在中国,中国银行外汇兑换券,俗称"外汇兑换券"、"外汇券",为中国银行发行,曾在中华人民共和国境内流通,特定场合使用,是面额与人民币等值的一种特定货币,但不是另一种货币,分为1979年和1988年两个版本,外汇兑换券自1980年4月1日开始流通,1995年1月1日停止使用。

Part III CURRENCIES

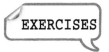

I. **Decide whether the following statements are true(T) or false(F) according to the text.**

1. Minting facilities of CBPMC are based in Beijing, Shanghai, Chengdu, Xi'an, Shijiazhuang, and Nanchang. (   )
2. The name *renminbi* was first recorded as an official name in 1948 when the first series of *renminbi* banknotes was introduced by the People's Bank of China. (   )
3. The *fen* and *jiao* of the second series of *renminbi* banknotes have become increasingly unnecessary as prices have increased. (   )
4. Issuance of the 5 *fen* ceased in 1992 while new designs of the 1 and 5 *jiao* and 1 *yuan* were introduced in between 1999 and 2002. (   )
5. The third series was introduced between 1987 and 1997, although the banknotes were dated 1980, 1990, or 1996. (   )
6. The fifth series uses the portrait of Mao Zedong on all banknotes, in place of the various leaders and workers which had been featured previously. (   )
7. For the 2008 Beijing Olympics, a green ¥10 note was issued featuring the Bird's Nest on the front with the back showing various athletes (   )
8. RMB, as well as the Hong Kong dollar and the Macanese pataca, is the legal tenders in Hong Kong and Macau. (   )
9. Full convertibility from RMB to the New Taiwan dollar has been realized in Taiwan. (   )
10. On April 10, 2008, RMB traded at 6.9920 *yuan* per U.S. dollar, which is the first time that a dollar bought less than seven *yuan*, and at 11.03630 *yuan* per euro. (   )

II. **Translate the following expressions into Chinese.**

1. after the shape of the coins
2. have its own printing technology research division which researches new techniques for creating banknotes and making counterfeiting more difficult
3. led to a strong black market in currency transactions
4. to feature a dragon on the obverse and the reverse has a sundial
5. to sign a bilateral foreign exchange settlement agreement
6. to be devalued in order to reflect its true market price and to improve the competitiveness of Chinese export
7. to enable the Chinese government to maintain a peg of 8.27 *yuan* per USD from 1997 to 2005
8. to move to a managed floating exchange rate based on market supply and demand with reference to a basket of foreign currencies

9. purchasing power parity
10. one United States dollar being equivalent to approximately ¥3.462 in 2006, ¥3.621 in 2007, and ¥3.798 in 2008

III. **Translate the following paragraphs into Chinese.**

1. *Renminbi* currency production is carried about by a state owned corporation, China Banknote Printing and Minting (CBPMC) headquartered in Beijing. CBPMC uses a network of printing and engraving and minting facilities around the country to produce banknotes and coins for subsequent distribution. Banknote printing facilities are based in Beijing, Shanghai, Chengdu, Xi'an, Shijiazhuang, and Nanchang. Mints are located in Nanjing, Shanghai, and Shenyang. Also, high grade paper for the banknotes is produced at two facilities in Baoding and Kunshan.

2. The first series of *renminbi* banknotes was introduced by the People's Bank of China in December 1948, about a year before the Chinese Communist Party's victory in China's War of Liberation. It was issued only in paper money form and replaced the various currencies circulating in the areas controlled by the communists. One of the first tasks of the new government was to end the hyperinflation that had plagued China in the final years of the Kuomintang (KMT) era.

3. The name *renminbi* was first recorded as an official name in June 1949. After work began in 1950 to design the second series of the *renminbi*, the previous series were retroactively dubbed the "first series of the *renminbi*".

4. The second series of *renminbi* banknotes was introduced in 1955. During the era of the command economy, the value of the *renminbi* was set to unrealistic values in exchange with western currency and severe currency exchange rules were put in place. With the opening of the mainland Chinese economy in 1978, a dual-track currency system was instituted, with *renminbi* usable only domestically, and with foreigners forced to use foreign exchange certificates.

5. The daily trading price of the U.S. dollar against the RMB in the inter-bank foreign exchange market would be allowed to float within a narrow band of 0.3% around the central parity published by the People's Bank of China (PBC); in a later announcement published on 18 May 2007, the band was extended to 0.5%. The PRC has stated that the basket is dominated by the United States dollar, euro, Japanese yen and South Korean won, with a smaller proportion made up of the British pound, Thai baht, Russian ruble, Australian dollar, Canadian dollar and Singapore dollar.

IV. **Read the passage and answer the questions.**

REVALUATION: A DOUBLE-EDGED SWORD FOR CHINA

The effect of a *renminbi* appreciation on each Chinese industry and on the country's overall economy is intricate and difficult to accurately predict. Due to the costs and profits that vary with each industry, economists to a large extent have different estimates when it comes to whether or not the *renminbi* should be allowed to appreciate.

At the "2005 International Currency Conference of the Forum of the Central Bank" on June 7, *Zhou Xiaochuan*, governor of the People's Bank of China, expressed his thoughts on the issue. The reform of foreign exchange policy in China must take into account its responsibility to the Chinese people, he says, and so before all else its influence on domestic industries needs to be researched thoroughly.

Since no one can claim to be able to fully predict the effects of an appreciation, the best one can do to effect an orderly and predictable management of the upward pressure on the *renminbi* is to thoroughly consider every angle as much as possible. For individual industries, it will clearly favour some, and cause worry for others.

Textile: grim situation

Amid the current wave of speculation over the *renminbi* appreciation, it is the textile industry that is on the frontline of the debate. If the *renminbi* were to rise, this industry would find itself in a difficult situation more than any other.

First, according to initial estimates, for each 1 per cent the *renminbi* rises, each sub-sector of the textile industry will see its profits from exports reduced, including a drop of 12 per cent in the cotton sector, 8 per cent in wool, and 13 per cent in garments. Smaller segments of the garment industry that depend more highly on exports will face even higher losses.

Large corporations with margins that are already high would see a smaller decrease in profits. At the same time, if a company already has a fixed proportion of the international market, although there will be more talk of raising prices, the overall negative effect will be relatively small. However, if the extent of the revaluation is too large or if the prices of exports continue to rise, then a slide in profits will be unavoidable. In addition to a weakened ability to negotiate prices abroad, as the range of the revaluation expands, the potential for other negative consequences rises considerably.

Professor Wang Kangmao, the honorary president and doctoral adviser of the East China University for Law and Politics, recently told reporters that if the *renminbi* were to appreciate by 3 per cent the textile industry could face export losses of up to 30 per cent mainly due to a lack of value-added products.

Uncompetitive small-and-medium-sized companies would then likely face bankruptcy, causing possible job losses for several hundred thousand workers. Since most of the employees in the textile industry come from low or medium income families, the loss of jobs could possibly trigger even greater social problems.

Real estate: fFlush with hot money; on the edge of a bubble

Real estate is another sensitive sector. A possible *renminbi* appreciation would cause a still-adjusting housing sector to confront the enormous pressures brought on by the massive influx of hot money.

Professor Yang Fan, a doctoral adviser in the China University of Law and Politics' Business School, recently explained to reporters that as a nation's or region's currency faces upward pressure or is on an extended rise, investors who exchange foreign currencies into the national currency will earn a profit proportional to the rise of the national currency. This will make capital in the country whose currency is being revalued attractive to investors, especially in stock and real estate. Thus investors will not only reap the benefits of the currency appreciation, but also see an increase in value of their corporate stock and real estate investments—something of a double return on their money. But since China's stock market continues to perform poorly it is likely that a large amount of hot money will be poured into real estate.

Professor Wang Kangmao also told reporters that it's possible that some 50 per cent of the Shanghai's housing market is currently being inflated by such foreign capital. For instance, he says, some Russian businessmen would buy 20 apartments at a time in some downtown or luxury districts. This clearly is a form of arbitrage and price manipulation(套利与价格操纵), with an aim that endangers the economic health of the nation.

If China does pull off a revaluation, there are two possible ways they could implement it: incremental or in one step. If it is done in one step, the danger of floating capital in the real estate market is relatively small as the country can employ a variety of methods to restrict the outflow and inflow of the capital over a short period of time. However, because it is impossible to forecast the magnitude of a single move towards appreciation, if there is an overestimation the danger to the economy is still great.

Looking at the recent experiences of other nations, a number of financial crises occurred due to an overestimation of currency. But, if the readjustment is gradual, the pressures that arise from floating capital are magnified. Each small readjustment will cause the market to anticipate even greater changes, attracting more hot money to flow in through all channels, creating an even bigger bubble. It seems that regardless of the method, the health and continued development of the real estate sector will soon face an unprecedented challenge.

Banking: risks of bad credit and outflow of hot money

For China's banking industry, the greatest risk associated with a revaluation is the possibility of deflation.

Zhang Weiguo, an associate professor in the social sciences department of Fudan University, says that an increased risk in the real estate sector implies an increased risk in banks' real estate financing activities. Over 60 per cent of the capital used for purchasing or building houses is lent from the banking system, and at present, the estimated amount of loan for individual home purchases totals around Rmb1,400 bn, with mortgages accounting for 70 per cent.

If the *renminbi* were to appreciate under these circumstances, it is fully possible that those who hold hot money will sell their property at a high price level, triggering an unavoidable price collapse, with the related loans, mortgages and properties possibly turning into bad debt. Professor Wang Kangmao points out that a banking crisis caused by growing real estate risks would be a threat to the stability of the overall national banking system and an obstacle to the reform of the state-owned banks—unfortunately, all in one chain reaction.

However, setting aside these real estate issues, we can see that there are yet other factors arising from a *renminbi* adjustment.

In an analysis done by Sun Lijian, associate professor of the international finance department of Fudan University, the initial effects of a *renminbi* revaluation on the banking system will not be large, and will be mainly centerd on two aspects: a contraction of bank's core capital, and a possible increase in bad debt of trade companies. For example, the core capital of Bank of China and China Construction Bank include $45bn in foreign exchange reserves, which will take a hit from a *renminbi* appreciation. Both banks are actively seeking strategic overseas investors, and a *renminbi* revaluation would directly affect the process, influence their listing schedule and finally affect the ability of the entire banking industry. Of course, the proportion of foreign exchange reserves of other banks is not very large, so the overall effect that this issue would have on the banking system is not entirely clear.

Trade companies will also be affected by a revaluation. When the *renminbi* weakens together with the US dollar, local labor will become cheaper and can achieve an advantage on the international market.

However, 60 per cent of the Chinese economy is dependent on foreign countries, meaning it will continue relying on the outside world to drive the economic development. If the *renminbi* were to appreciate, the competitiveness of trade companies would decrease, causing a squeeze in the margins, and the ability to repay loans would weaken, resulting in an increase in bad debt.

Furthermore, exports point out once the *renminbi* appreciates a large amount of the "hot money" would flow out, increasing downward pressure on the *renminbi*. This would result in another tough blow to the country's banking industry.

In 2004 alone over Rmb20bn of foreign assets that had no discernable background flew into the country, and according to the latest statistics of the central bank, these individual accounts actively engage in currency trade in the past six months. In the battle around *renminbi* revaluation it is this steady stream of foreign hot money that poses the greatest risk to damage China's economy. As foreign capital withdraws the bubble of prosperity will rapidly burst, causing bankruptcy of many investors. This will bring about a huge risk of bad debt as some mortgages will default, bringing considerable losses to the banking sector.

As a result of these predictions, experts in related fields suggest that trade companies should strive to shift toward self-sufficiency and more value-added products from dependence on price superiority in foreign markets.

On the other hand, the banking industry needs to develop more banking **derivative** products(衍生产品) to avoid the risks of a changing exchange rate. At the same time, to avoid increasing amount of bad debt after a revaluation, national banks should be on guard against the irrational speculation of foreign capital, including those that use property as **collateral for loans**(抵押贷款).

One other potential countermeasure is to speed up the development of channels of direct funding. Professor Sun says that a banking system using direct funding is far less affected than those using mainly secondary channels based on the lessons from the multinational financial crises of recent years. Direct channels for funding, he says, better distribute the risks that emerge when hot money is withdrawn from a market, thus resulting in a less serious challenge for the banking system.

Energy industry: enormous effect in the medium and long term

According to analysts, if the *renminbi* appreciates within the range of 5-10 per cent, the effect on the electricity and coal industries would be minimal. However, there would be an obvious effect on the oil industry, which would be more noticeably over the medium and long-term. More importantly, the livelihood of the country rests on the energy industry, and must be treated with the utmost caution.

China's electricity industry has been financed partially through foreign debt, primarily in US dollar and Japanese yen, and in the form of long-term loans. According to China's current system of national accounting, discrepancies created by a changing exchange rate will translate directly into losses for the current financial period. This will, however, only show up on the industry's financial reports before repayment of the loan begins and not the corporation's cash flow. The electricity industry which suffers from big foreign exchange losses would benefit greatly from a *renminbi* revaluation.

As for the investments in new facilities in the electricity industry, an appreciating *renminbi* is of limited usefulness in lowering costs. This is because **thermo-electric generators**(热电发电机) that have below 300,000 kilowatts of capacity are all produced domestically, and the fuels they use are procured domestically.

On the other hand, this would mean a drop in costs for oil industries, which rely more heavily on imports. Take Shennan Electric as an example. It has imported over 600,000 tonnes of heavy oil and 60,000 tonnes of light oil each year. If the *renminbi* were to rise 5 per cent, this company could reduce its costs by over Rmb60m.

Overall, experts recommend that the electricity industry should try to pursue the opportunities of an appreciating *renminbi* by readjusting their financing mechanisms. Under one possible scenario, these corporations should delay the construction or purchase of new investments, to take advantage of cost savings after a future appreciation.

The influence on the coal industry is considerably smaller. Because exports currently account for a relatively small proportion of the domestic coal industry—only 4.5 per cent—there would not be much of an effect on the industry's overall profits. Moreover, China's major listed coalmakers don't hold any foreign currency debt and so would not be influenced by a fluctuating exchange rate. However, international coal prices could become more competitive with a revaluation, and coastal areas may take the lead in choosing import coal fuels. Experts conclude that an appreciation of less than 10 per cent would have a negligible effect on domestic coal price competition.

The coal industry is advised to closely follow developments in supply and demand, and carefully adjust the proportions of foreign sales accordingly. Under a possible change in coal prices, they should be careful to expand production capacity.

In contrast to the coal industry, the domestic oil products industry still lacks the capacity to set prices, with a relatively large dependence on imports. The market follows price changes abroad and is influenced by changes in the US dollar. Should the *renminbi* appreciate it would directly cause domestic crude oil prices to fall, and exert downward pressure on the once high profits in the industry.

In the refined-oil industry the price of crude oil is subject to international forces but the sale price of the end product of refined oil is controlled by China's government. An appreciation of the *renminbi* will lower the cost of international crude imports for the refinery industry and thereby lend some help to raising profits. Since the prices of finished oil-products are determined with a fixed mechanism, and selling prices are interrelated with international prices, if the price of refined oil products drops lower than the price of the drop in crude it would engender a substantial benefit to China's refined oil industry.

China's main petrochemical imports are **synthetic rubber and synthetic resin**(合成橡胶与合成树脂), while the chief exports are more basic industrial chemicals. If the *renminbi* appreciates, the profits of chemically engineered products will be squeezed, with the only products avoiding influence being those that are under non-tariff protections such as import quotas. The present imports for synthetic rubbers, resins, fibres and other **intermediate products**(中间产品) are larger than the exports. A *renminbi* revaluation would lower import prices for these items, creating more competition in the domestic market, resulting in price pressures at home.

A Classification of industry influences

When asked how she thought an appreciating *renminbi* would influence domestic industries, Professor Hu Jian, chair of the Beijing University Center for Chinese Finance, replied, "This problem is too big to be answered in one or two sentences." Indeed. To discuss this issue first requires that we set up a classification of various industries and businesses that could be affected, and identify a range of specially designated circumstances under which we can observe the diverse responses to a *renminbi* revaluation.

First of all, those businesses that engage in foreign trade or hold foreign capital will certainly feel a much stronger influence that those that are not involved. Those with foreign trade or foreign capital will also experience a more direct effect from a revaluation, while those without must consider that a revaluation would affect the entire state of the economy, changing the environment of outside competition, which is an influence in itself.

As for foreign trade, says Harvest Fund Management analyst Dr Li Ji, the influence of a revaluation works both ways. For industries like textiles, TVs, electronics and others, a *renminbi* appreciation would mean a reduction in exports, but at the same time would reduce import costs on components and machine equipment. Because the need of intermediate products for industry will be lessened, imports like machinery, transportation facilities, textiles, chemical products and others that influence key domestic import and export industries will be decreasing along with the exports.

But for the oil and natural gas, steel, aluminium, copper and other staple raw materials a large effect would be felt in the short- and medium-term as prices for these are fixed in US dollars. In the short-term this means these materials and products would be priced lower due to a rise in the *renminbi*, bringing along with it two major effects: a fall in the sales of companies that produce these raw materials and lower costs for those industries that require purchase of these raw material for use in production. At the same time we must consider the effect that the international price of raw materials will have on China's national demand. Lower prices bring with it increased demand, which could cause an increase in the price of some parts of the international raw material trade, ultimately offsetting the negative influence of a rising *renminbi*.

However trade companies can be further separated according to whether they engage in general trade or in processing trade, with a decidedly different effect on each. A rising *renminbi* will cause a consequent rise in the prices of export products and a drop in international price competitiveness which would bring about a crisis especially for small and medium businesses that engage in general international trade.

Dr He Fan, assistant to the director of the World Economic and Political Research Institute at the China Academy of Social Sciences, says that the influence of appreciation on **finished products**(成品) must be analysed in more specific detail. The processing trade can first be further divided by whether the imported components are paid by foreign investors or local companies. Currently, these two forms together account for 55 per cent of China's exports, while added by the import of machine equipment from abroad, they account for nearly 60 per cent of imports.

Looking even closer at the imports of raw materials and investment products among these trade enterprises, the ratio still has room to rise. The profit of companies that engage in the assembly of products from imported materials is mostly fixed, and would not be fundamentally influenced by a change in the exchange rate. However, their purchasing power will rise, allowing them to purchase a greater amount of imports. In Professor He's estimation, the

Part Ⅲ CURRENCIES

positive and negative sides should be given equal weight, but the net effect remains to be fully determined.

Professor He also says that there is still a relationship between the influence of an appreciating *renminbi* and the corporations' ability to set prices abroad. China has a set of export products that make up a large share of the international market, leading many to rely on the competitiveness of their manufacturing costs. This group of manufacturers has a very strong ability to set prices abroad, and the revenues from exports will actually rise with the stronger *renminbi*.

In other words, Chinese industries and companies which have the ability to set prices abroad stand to gain from a rise in the *renminbi*'s value. However, this is only true if their ability to set prices stems from their own advantage, such as through competitiveness or product superiority, and not based on a reliance on low prices to make a tiny profit.

(*FROM*: http://yaleglobal.yale.edu/display.article id = 6044 &page = 1)

1. What does the author of the passage think of the overall effect of the *renminbi* appreciation on China's economy.
2. Summarize the possible effect of the *renminbi* appreciation on each Chinese main industry as mentioned in the passage.

FURTHER READING

HK DOLLAR, MACANESE PATACA, NEW TAIWAN DOLLAR

HK dollar

The Hong Kong dollar (currency code HKD) is the currency of the Hong Kong Special Administrative Region of the People's Republic of China, and has been the currency of Hong Kong since 1937. It is normally abbreviated with the dollar sign $, or alternatively HK $ to distinguish it from other dollar-denominated currencies. It is divided into 100 cents.

The Hong Kong dollar has been pegged to the US dollar since 1983.

The Basic Law of Hong Kong and the Sino-British Joint Declaration provide that Hong Kong retains full autonomy with respect to currency issuance. Currency in Hong Kong is issued by the Government and three local banks under the supervision of the territory's de facto central bank, the Hong Kong Monetary Authority. Bank notes are printed by Hong Kong Note Printing Limited.

The Hong Kong dollar is accepted in southern parts of mainland China and Macau as well as some shopping malls in Singapore. Hong Kong people often call a Hong Kong dollar 蚊. This term possibly originated with the first syllable of "money". In written Chinese, however, Yuan(圓 or 元) is used, particularly in cheques and commercial documents.

The Hong Kong dollar has been pegged to the United States dollar since 17 October 1983 at HK $7.80 per U.S. dollar through the currency board system. A bank can only issue a Hong Kong dollar if it has the equivalent exchange in U.S. dollars on deposit. The currency board system ensures that Hong Kong's entire monetary base is backed with U.S. dollars at the linked exchange rate. The resources for this backing are kept in Hong Kong's Exchange Fund, which is among the largest official reserves in the world.

As of 18 May 2005, in addition to the lower guaranteed limit, a new upper guaranteed limit was set for the Hong Kong dollar at 7.75 to the USD. The lower limit will be lowered from 7.80 to 7.85 in five weeks, by 100 pips each week. (One pip is the smallest measure of price move used in forex trading.) For instance, if the currency pair EUR/USD is currently trading at 1.3000 and then the exchange rate changes to 1.3010, the pair did a 10-pip (smallest units) move. The pip is the smallest measure regardless of the fractional representation of the currency exchange rate. Thus, 1.3000 to 1.3010 is the same move in pips terms as 110.00 to 110.10. The Hong Kong Monetary Authority indicated this move is to narrow the gap between the interest rates in Hong Kong and those of the United States. A further aim of allowing the Hong Kong dollar to trade in a range is to avoid the HK dollar being used **as a proxy for speculative bets**(成为投机赌注的替代品) on a Yuan (*renminbi*) revaluation.

Nowadays, banknotes of legal tender in local circulation include six denominations of $10, $20, $50, $100, $500 and $1,000. The issue of $5 note was discontinued after 1975 when the government replaced it with the $5 regal coin.

History

Regal coins

As Hong Kong was established as a **free trading port**(自由贸易港口) in 1841, there was no local currency existing for everyday circulation. Foreign currencies such as **Indian rupees**(印度卢比), **Spanish and Mexican Reales**(西班牙、墨西哥里亚尔), Chinese cash coins and British currency were employed as substitutes. Coins particularly issued for Hong Kong did not appear until 1863 when the first regal coins of Hong Kong, i.e. coins with the portrait or Royal Cypher of the reigning monarch, were issued. They were produced by **the Royal Mint, London**(伦敦的英国皇家造币厂) and comprised the silver ten cent, the bronze one cent and one mil, the last being one-tenth of a cent.

Silver trade dollars

Foreign currencies continued to circulate along with home denomination, but the majority of these were not up to standard for government payments. Owing to the fiscal loss, the Hong Kong Mint, which was located at Sugar Street established in 1866 was closed two years later. Minting machines were sold to Jardine Matheson, which in turn sold them to the Japanese Government. The Government started producing Japanese yen in Osaka with the equipment bought. As a stand-in for the regal dollar coins, silver trade dollars from the USA, Japan and Britain were used.

The Trade Dollar of the USA minted between 1873—1885

Hong Kong dollar

From 1895, legislation was enacted in attempts to coalesce the coinage. With the release of one-dollar note pursuant to the One-Dollar Currency Note Ordinance of 1935, the Government acknowledged the Hong Kong Dollar as the local monetary unit. It was not until 1937 that the legal tender of Hong Kong was finally unified. The history of local coinage is thus only one hundred and thirty years old. A sum of six coins of different shapes and metal contents with denominations of ten, twenty and fifty cents, one, two and five dollars, have been made available for general exchange in Hong Kong.

It is improbable that paper money was in local circulation as a medium of exchange for daily use prior to the establishment of the Oriental Bank, which was the earliest bank to open in Hong Kong, coming into operation in 1845. Other banks began to set up and issued their own banknotes. However, such notes were not accepted by the Treasury for imbursement of government dues and taxes but were still good enough for transmission in mercantile field. Under the Currency Ordinance 1935, banknotes in denominations of $5 and above issued by the three authorized local banks, namely the Mercantile Bank of India Limited, Chartered Bank of India, Australia and China (Standard Chartered Bank), and The Hong Kong and Shanghai Banking Corporation, were all declared legal tender.

Japanese Military Yen

Japanese Military Yen bill used in occupied Hong Kong during World War II

During the Japanese occupation, Japanese Military Yen were the only means of everyday exchange in Hong Kong. When the JMY was first introduced in December 26, 1941, the exchange rate between HKD and JMY was 2 to 1. However, by October 1942, the rate was changed to 4 to 1. After exchanging for HKD, the Japanese Military purchased supplies and strategic goods in neutral Macao. On 6 September 1945, all JMY was announced to become void. The issue of local currency was then resumed by the Hong Kong Government and the authorized local banks after the emancipation.

1941 年

Part III CURRENCIES

1945 年

Currencies for handover

Starting in 1997, prior to the establishment of the SAR, coins with Queen Elizabeth II's portrait were gradually withdrawn from circulation, and now most of the notes and coins in circulations feature Hong Kong's Bauhinia blakeana flower or other symbols. Coins with the Queen's portrait are still legal tender, but are being **phased out**(逐渐淘汰).

Because the redesign was highly sensitive with regard to political and economic reasons, the designing process of the new coins could not be entrusted to an artist but was undertaken by Joseph Yam, Chief Executive of the Hong Kong Monetary Authority, himself who found in the bauhinia the requested "politically neutral design" and did a secret scissors and paste job.

New designs

After a less-than-successful trial from 1994 to 2002 to move the 10-dollar denomination from the banknote format (issued by the banks) to the coin format (Government-issued), the 10-dollar banknotes are currently the only denomination issued by the SAR Government and not the banks. The older 10-dollar bank notes issued by banks are, although rare and being phased out, still circulated.

Hong Kong coinage

Hong Kong coins

The Government issues coins of $10, $5, $2, $1, 50 cents, 20 cents and 10 cents. Until 1992 these coins were embossed with the Queen's head. In 1993 a programme was initiated to replace the Queen's Head series with a new series depicting the bauhinia flower. Commemorative coins and coin sets are sometimes produced for special occasions, for example the opening of the Hong Kong International Airport.

Hong Kong banknotes

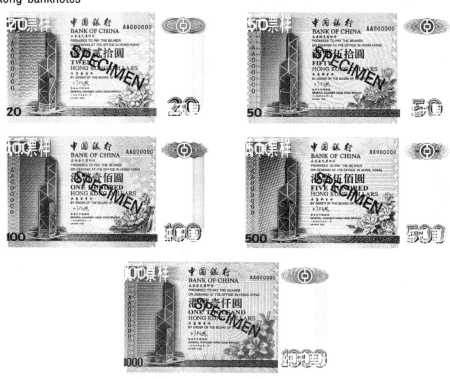

1993 年

1994 年

2001 年   2002 年

2003 年   2003 年

The Government, through **the Hong Kong Monetary Authority** (HKMA)(香港金融管理局), has given authorization to three commercial banks —**The Hong Kong and Shanghai Banking Corporation Limited** (HSBC)(香港上海汇丰银行有限公司), **Standard Chartered**(渣打银行), and **the Bank of China**(中国银行). The HKMA acquired the note printing plant at **Tai Po**(大埔,位于新界) from the **De La Rue Group of the UK**(英国德拉鲁集团公司) on behalf of the Government. The plant has been operating under the name of HKNPL since then. Currency notes in everyday circulation are $10, $20, $50, $100, $500 and $1,000. In 2002, the HKSAR Government issued a new ten dollar note (which is printed directly by the HKMA, and not through the banks) in recognition of a continuing demand among the public for a note in addition to the coin. Various security features are incorporated in genuine Hong Kong banknotes.

Linked exchange rate system

The primary monetary policy objective of the Hong Kong Monetary Authority is to maintain exchange rate stability within the framework of the linked exchange rate system through sound management of the Exchange Fund, monetary operations and other means deemed necessary.

The important underpinnings of the linked exchange rate system include the strong official reserves of Hong Kong, a sound and robust banking system, fiscal prudence and a flexible economic structure.

(FROM: http://encycl.opentopia.com/term/Hong_Kong_dollar)

Macanese pataca

The pataca is the monetary unit of Macau (currency code MOP; 澳門圓), made up of 100 avos. Monetary policy is managed by the Monetary Authority of Macao. The abbreviation MOP $ is commonly used.

The name "pataca" is derived from formerly popular silver coin in Asia, the Mexican peso (eight reales), known in Portuguese as the pataca mexicana. Another version of the pataca was also used in Portuguese Timor, now East Timor, until 1957, when it was replaced by the escudo. The Chinese name for the currency is yuan (圓), which is the same word for Chinese yuan, New Taiwan dollar, and Hong Kong dollar.

History

The pataca was introduced in 1894 as a unit of account. It was initially equivalent to the Mexican peso, Spanish dollar, Hong Kong dollar and replaced the Portuguese real at a rate of one pataca for 450 reis.

The pataca has been the legal tender in Macau for over a century. **The Banco Nacional Ultramarino**(BNU；大西洋銀行) has been the banknote-issuing authority since 1905. Pataca banknotes have been circulated in Macau since January 27, 1906. Pataca coins were first issued in 1952. However, owing to the small market demand in Macau, the second issue was postponed until 1967. The 1952 coins were bronze 5 and 10 avos, cupro-nickel 50 avos and 0.72 silver 1 and 5 patacas.

1952 年

In 1980, the Macau Government transferred the exclusive right to issue patacas to the Instituto Emissor de Macau (IEM). The BNU became the IEM's agent bank and continued to issue banknotes. On agreement with the BNU on October 16, 1995, **Bank of China**, **Macau Branch**(中國銀行澳門分行), became the second note-issuing bank. The authority to issue patacas was transferred to the Monetary Authority of Macao (AMCM).

Coins

Banknotes

At the time of the first issuance, the only denominations were 1 pataca, 5 patacas, 10 patacas, 25 patacas, 50 patacas, and 100 patacas, with the 20-cent coin from Canton Province. Later, Macau began issuing 5 avos, 10 avos, and 50 avos in February 1920. Not until 1942 did Macau issue smaller denominations like 1 avo, 5 avos, and 20 avos.(阿沃,澳门硬币：分)

1952 年:10 分

On August 8, 1988, BNU issued a 1000 pataca banknote, the highest value banknote yet. Because 8 in Chinese (Ba) is similar to **"getting rich"** (Fa; 發), this unique date which occurs only once per century gives the note a special meaning. Another feature is the replacement of the Coat of arms of Portugal with Banco Nacional Ultramarino's logo, symbolizing the fact that Macau would become part of the People's Republic of China.

1995 edition

1996 edition

1999 edition

2001 edution

2008 edition

1981 年

1991 年

1992 年

1996 年

1999 年

2001 年

The pataca comes in banknotes of 10, 20, 50, 100, 500 and 1000 patacas. Banknotes are issued by the Banco Nacional Ultramarino and the Bank of China. The current series of BNU banknotes was issued in 2005, while the Bank of China notes were last issued between 1995 and 2003. The physical sizes of the banknotes are "coincidentally" the same as that of Hong Kong banknotes. On December 20, 1999, the day Macau was retroceded to China, banknotes of all values (except for 10 patacas) by both banks were reissued with that date.

(*FROM*: *http*:*//encycl. opentopia. com/term/Macanese_pataca*)

New Taiwan dollar

The New Taiwan dollar (currency code: TWD and common abbreviation: NT $), or simply Taiwan dollar, is the formal currency in Taiwan since 2000, although it has been in circulation since 1949. Originally issued by the Bank of Taiwan, it is now issued by the "Central Bank of China".

Although the formal English word for the currency is dollar, in Mandarin it is known as yuan (as with Chinese numerals, this character has two forms—an informal form 元 and a formal form 圓 used to prevent alterations and accounting mistakes). Colloquially, it is called a kuài. Subdivisions of a yuan are rarely used, since practically all products on the consumer market are being sold at whole units of yuan.

History

1976 年

An NTD note is issued by the Bank of Taiwan in February 1988. It was taken out of circulation on July 1, 2002, as it had been replaced by a new NTD note on July 2, 2001 issued by the "Central Bank of China".

1949 年

1972 年

The New Taiwan dollar was first issued by the Bank of Taiwan on June 15, 1949 to replace the Old Taiwan dollar at a 40,000-to-1 ratio. The first goal of the New Taiwan dollar was to end the hyperinflation which had plagued Taiwan and China's mainland due to the civil war. A few months later, the government under the Kuomintang was defeated by the Chinese communists and retreated to Taiwan.

Even though the Taiwan dollar was the de facto currency of Taiwan, for years the old Chinese Nationalist yuan was still the formal currency of Taiwan. The Chinese Nationalist yuan was also known as the **fiat currency**(法幣) or the **silver yuan**(銀元), even though it was decoupled from the value of silver during World War II.

According to the laws, the exchange rate is fixed at 3 TWD per 1 silver yuan and has never been changed despite decades of inflation. Despite the silver yuan being the primary legal tender currency, it was impossible to buy, sell, or use it, so it effectively did not exist to the public.

In July 2000, the New Taiwan dollar became the official currency and is no longer secondary to the silver yuan. At the same time, the "Central Bank of China" began issuing New Taiwan dollar banknotes directly and the old notes issued by the Bank of Taiwan were taken out of circulation.

Part III CURRENCIES

In the history of the currency the exchange rate as compared to the United States dollar (USD) has varied from over 40 TWD per 1 USD in the 1960s to about 25 TWD per 1 USD around 1992. The exchange rate has been around 33 TWD per 1 USD in recent years.

BACKGROUND KNOWLEDGE

1 Basic Law of Hong Kong《香港特别行政区基本法》

The Basic Law of the Hong Kong Special Administrative Region of the People's Republic of China, or simply Hong Kong Basic Law, serves as the constitutional document of the Hong Kong Special Administrative Region (HKSAR) of the People's Republic of China (PRC). It was adopted on April 4, 1990 by the Seventh National People's Congress (NPC) of the People's Republic of China, and went into effect on July 1, 1997 (replacing the Letters Patent and the Royal Instructions) when this former colony of United Kingdom was handed over to the PRC.

The Basic Law was drafted in accordance with the Sino-British Joint Declaration on the Question of Hong Kong (The Joint Declaration), signed between the Chinese and British governments on December 19, 1984. The Basic Law stipulates the basic policies of the PRC towards the Hong Kong Special Administrative Region. As agreed between the PRC and the United Kingdom in the Joint Declaration, in accordance with the "One Country, Two Systems" principle, socialism as practised in the PRC would not be extended to Hong Kong. Instead, Hong Kong would continue its previous capitalist system and its way of life for a period of 50 years after 1997. A number of freedoms and rights of the Hong Kong residents are also protected under the Basic Law.

The source of authority for the Basic Law is somewhat controversial, with most Chinese legal scholars arguing that the Basic Law is a purely domestic legislation deriving its authority from the Constitution of the People's Republic of China, and with some legal scholars arguing that the Basic Law derives its authority directly from the Sino-British Joint Declaration. The argument is relevant in that it affects the amount of authority that the PRC has to change the Basic Law, and the ability of the Hong Kong courts to challenge PRC domestic legislation.

2 Sino-British Joint Declaration《中英联合声明》

The Sino-British Joint Declaration, formally known as the Joint Declaration of the Government of the United Kingdom of Great Britain and Northern Ireland and the Government of the People's Republic of China on the Question of Hong Kong, was signed by the Prime Ministers, Zhao Ziyang and Margaret Thatcher, of the People's Republic of China (PRC) and the United Kingdom (UK) governments on 19 December 1984 in Beijing.

The Declaration entered into force with the exchange of instruments of ratification on 27 May 1985, and was registered by the PRC and UK governments at the United Nations on 12

June 1985. In the Joint Declaration, the PRC Government stated that it had decided to resume the exercise of sovereignty over Hong Kong (including Hong Kong Island, Kowloon, and the New Territories) with effect from 1 July 1997, and the UK Government declared that it would hand over Hong Kong to the PRC with effect from 1 July, 1997. The PRC Government also declared its basic policies regarding Hong Kong in the document.

In accordance with the "One Country, Two Systems" Principle agreed between the UK and the PRC, the socialist system of PRC would not be practiced in the Hong Kong Special Administrative Region (HKSAR), and Hong Kong's previous capitalist system and its way of life would remain unchanged for a period of 50 years. The Joint Declaration provides that these basic policies should be stipulated in the Hong Kong Basic Law.

3 Bauhinia blakeana 洋紫荆

It is an evergreen tree, in the genus Bauhinia, with large thick leaves and striking purplish red flowers. The fragrant, orchid-like flowers are usually 10-15 cm across, and bloom from early November to the end of March. This unique endemic flower is special of Hong Kong's **ecosystem**(生态系统). It is referred to as bauhinia in non-scientific literature though this is the name of the genus. It is sometimes called **Hong Kong orchid tree**(香港兰).

The shape of a Bauhinia double-lobed leaf is similar to a heart, 7-10 cm long and 10-13 cm broad, with a deep cleft dividing the apex. Local people call the leaf **chungmingyip**(聰明葉, lit. "clever leaf"), and regard it as a symbol of cleverness. Some people use the leaves to make bookmarks in the hope that it will assist them to study well.

It is usually sterile (does not produce seed), suggesting a hybrid origin, probably between Bauhinia variegata and Bauhinia purpurea, though this is still a matter of debate. Propagation is by cuttings and air-layering, and the tree prefers a sheltered sunny position with good soil.

It is named after Sir Henry Blake who was British Governor of Hong Kong from 1898 to 1903. An enthusiastic botanist, he discovered it in 1880 near the ruins of a house on the shore of Hong Kong Island near Pok Fu Lam. The first scientific description of the Hong Kong orchid tree was published in 1908 by S. T. Dunn, superintendent of the Botanical and Forestry Department, who assigned it to the genus Bauhinia and named it after Sir Henry Blake.

Bauhinia blakeana was adopted as the floral emblem of Hong Kong by the Urban Council in 1965. Since 1997 it has become the floral emblem for the Hong Kong Special Administrative Region of the People's Republic of China, and appears on its flag and its coins; its Chinese name has also been frequently shortened as 洋紫荊 (洋 means "foreign" in Chinese, and some may consider this would be deemed inappropriate by the PRC government). A statue of the plant has been erected in Golden Bauhinia Square in Hong Kong.

Although the flowers are bright pinkish purple in colour, they are depicted in white on the Flag of Hong Kong.

The endemic plant of Hong Kong was introduced to Taiwan in 1967. In 1984 it was chosen to be the city flower of Chiayi City(嘉義市), in southwestern Taiwan.

KEY TO THE EXERCISES

Part I EVOLUTION AND OPERATION OF THE INTERNATIONAL MONETARY SYSTEM

CHAPTER 1   THE GOLD STANDARD ERA, 1870—1914

I . **Translate the following expressions into Chinese.**
1. 建立在金本位制基础上的国际货币体系
2. 参加国
3. 严重偏离固定汇率
4. 自动调节机制
5. 达到国际收支平衡
6. 各国央行对跨国境黄金流动量的反应
7. 履行(他们的)职责兑换流通券
8. 确保全民就业
9. 经济政策对外部目标的依赖性
10. 试图调整对内对外收支的目标

II . **Give the Chinese meaning of the following plurals.**
   1. 国际储备(额/量)   2. 黄金流通量   3. 净进口(量)   4. 资金外流量   5. 国内资产

III . **Translate the following paragraphs into Chinese.**
1. 然而,研究表明各国经常反道而行之,他们制止黄金的流动,也就是说,当外国储备升高时他们售出国内资产,而当外国储备下降时,他们购买国内资产。政府对私人黄金出口的干预也破坏了该体系。第一次世界大战前平衡自动的国际收支调整情形常常与现实不相吻合。
2. 金本位制按惯例与三条规则有关联。第一条规则是每个参加国其国内货币价格以黄金来确定。由于每一货币单位的黄金含量是固定的,所以汇率也是不变的。这叫做铸币平价。第二条规则是黄金须自由进出口。第三条规则为顺差国,即得到黄金的国家应允许其货币量增加,而逆差国,即失去黄金的国家则允许其货币量减少。
3. 经历持续黄金输出的央行为了避免不能履行其兑换现钞的职责而趋于减少其国内资产的拥有量。这样国内的利率会提高,资金会从国外流入。而获得黄金的央行取消自己黄金进口的动机要弱得多。其主要动机在于与"贫瘠"的黄金相比,有利可图的国内资产具有巨大的获利性。
4. 因为是根据黄金储备而确定货币的价格,在金本位制国家内部的价格水平在 1870 年到 1914 年间并未像第二次世界大战后时期那样上涨。但是,全国的价格水平在短时期内出现了像通货膨胀和通货紧缩相互交替时期的不可预见的波动。

IV . **Read the passage and fill in the blanks with the words or phrases given below.**
   1. financial transactions   2. record   3. payments   4. investment purposes   5. immediate transactions

6. capital account   7. visible account   8. broking   9. non-commercial items   10. dividends   11. bank advances   12. bonds   13. an overall balance   14. net errors and omissions   15. net overflow

CHAPTER 2　THE INTER-WAR PERIOD（1918—1939）AND THE BRETTON WOODS SYSTEM（1944—1973）

Ⅱ. Translate the following expressions into Chinese.

1. 支付了大规模军费开支的一部分
2. 加速了伦敦作为世界一流金融中心的衰落
3. 被迫奉行经济紧缩的货币政策
4. 中止了英镑对黄金的可兑换性
5. 缺乏适当的调节机制
6. 在出现严重失衡时允许汇率的弹性
7. 见证了导致局势不稳的大规模资本流动
8. 开始磋商备用安排款
9. 指预先批准国际货币基金组织某成员国的未来借款
10. 用于干预外汇市场以阻击游资的流动
11. 积累了对欧洲大量的国际收支盈余额
12. 主要用美元支付其赤字额
13. 导致大量影响金融稳定的资金从美元流出到更强势的货币
14. 将黄金价格涨升到每盎司38美元
15. 即使是跌了价仍承受着巨大的抛售压力

Ⅲ. Translate the following paragraphs into Chinese.

1. 它们(这些发达国家)认为,货币贬值表示一个国家经济不景气(疲软),而货币升值则会削弱一个国家的竞争能力。
2. 在严重失衡状态下,发达国家不愿改变其货币面值作为一项政策有两个重大影响。首先它使布雷顿森林体系失去了大部分的弹性功能和国际收支失衡的调节功能。其次,仍与第一点有关,这些发达国家在严重失衡时不情愿改变其货币的面值为投机商们提供了极好的单向赌博的机会,因此,也就大大地提高了国际资本流通的不稳定性。
3. 国际货币基金组织的条款也提倡经常账户货币的可兑换性,仅因为是布雷顿森林体系的设计者们希望为自由贸易提供方便,同时,避免私人资本流动可能收紧政策制定者所面临的外部约束。
4. 1947至1971年间作为最为重大的改革机制而引入布雷顿森林体系的是特别提款权(SDRs)以补充国际黄金储备,外汇储备以及国际货币基金组织的储备净值。特别提款权有时也称为纸黄金,在国际货币基金组织的账户里作为会计分录。
5. 尽管采取了多种政策但收效极其有限。这些政策包括提高短期利率以阻止短期资金的外流,降低长期利率以刺激国内生产,干预外汇市场,以及一系列直接控制资金外流的措施。
6. 总之,布雷顿森林体系崩溃的直接原因在于20世纪70年代初美国国际收支的巨大赤字及其美国贬值美元的无能为力。因此,布雷顿森林体系缺乏一种合适的各成员国都愿意并且能够用做策略的调节机制。后来美国的国际收支赤字持续无变,这就破坏了人们对美元的信心。结果,在调节、流通和信心相互关联的种种难题中找到了布雷顿森林体系崩溃的根本原因。

KEY TO THE EXERCISES

CHAPTER 3 MANAGED FLOATING SINCE 1973 AND THE EUROPEAN MONETARY SYSTEM

Ⅰ. Decide whether the following statements are true(T) or false(F).
1. T 2. F 3. T 4. F 5. F 6. T 7. T 8. T 9. F 10. F

Ⅱ. Translate the following expressions into Chinese.
1. 有责任干预外汇市场以消除短期汇率的波动
2. 制定专门的规则以管理浮动,防止竞争性的汇率贬值
3. 不断一体化的欧洲日益强大
4. 被指责对全球范围的环境造成破坏
5. 被确定为各成员国货币的加权平均值
6. 当一个成员国的币值波动达到其许可幅度的75%时
7. 1979年至1987年间,欧洲货币体系内部出现了十一国再结盟
8. 采用单一货币后承担经济调整的压力
9. 考察从金本位制时期到现在为止的国际货币体系的运作
10. 正如价格—货币—流动机制所要求的
11. 以大幅波动汇率为特征的
12. 向各成员国提供借贷款以修复其暂时的国际收支失衡状态

Ⅲ. Translate the following paragraphs into Chinese.
1. 同时人们一直趋向脱离基于黄金的国际货币体系。随着《牙买加协定》的生效黄金的作用大为降低,黄金的官方定价被取消。按配额付给国际货币基金组织的黄金的六分之一返还给了各成员国,另一六分之一由国际货币基金组织拍卖给私人买家,拍卖所得款项用于帮助发展中国家;国际货币基金组织保留其余的三分之二。最终,黄金不再充当国际货币体系的记账单位。自1974年起,国际货币基金组织一直以特别提款权而不是用美元来衡量所有的储备额和其他官方的交易量。
2. 自1979年3月始,欧共体九个国家中的八个(除了英国)加入了欧洲货币体系的汇率机制,其目标之一是为该体系实现成员国内更大规模的货币一体化,包括其终极目标。
3. 随着金融和经济的不断独立,发展中的国际金融体系很有可能需要更加密切的合作。经济力量更加均享的结果之一是三个货币贸易集团的悄然出现:以美元为基础的美元集团,以日元为中心的日元集团和以欧洲本土贸易为核心的欧元集团。
4. 1989年6月,以欧洲委员会主席雅阁·德勒斯为首的委员会推荐了一个过渡到单一货币的三步走方案。第一步包括扩大汇率机制成员国。第二步涉及缩小汇率的上下限,同时把对宏观经济政策调控由国家控制改由一个欧洲中央权威机构控制。第三步将建立一个欧洲央行体系来替代各国央行并用一种欧洲货币替代各国的货币。

Ⅳ. Read the passage and decide whether the statements followed are true(T) or false(F).
1. F 2. T 3. F 4. T 5. F 6. T 7. T

Part Ⅱ ORGANIZATIONS

CHAPTER 4 THE INTERNATIONAL MONETARY FUND (IMF)

Ⅰ. Decide whether the following statements are true(T) or false(F).
1. T 2. T 3. F 4. F 5. T 6. F 7. T 8. F 9. F 10. T

Ⅱ. Translate the following expressions into Chinese.
1. 类似于世界央行而能够根据意图创造新的储备或一个更为有限的借款机构
2. 为能够在国际范围使用流动资产制作了美国式的规划/蓝图
3. 我们的任务是去发现每个国家都能认可、任何国家都不讨厌的一种公共测度，一个通用标准，一条共同规则。
4. 债务国和债权国都应改变其货币政策
5. 优先发展经济，提供短期资金以帮助国际收支
6. 推行减少在新兴市场国家发生危机的频率的政策
7. 由于这两个职位会很快面向来自世界任何地方的合格候选人，该标准日益受到质疑
8. 完全依据其在世界经济中所占相对量/值来指定配额
9. 加入IMF时必须全额缴纳其认缴额
10. 分配给每一个成员国的基本票数

Ⅲ. Translate the following paragraphs into Chinese.
1. IMF追踪全球经济趋势与经济表现，当发现即将发生的问题时对其成员国发出警告，为政策对话提供论坛，并向政府提供应对经济困难的专业知识。
2. 凯恩斯的提案应该是要确立一种世界储备货币（他觉得可以称之为"班科"），该货币由一个可以创造货币和有权在更大程度上（考虑到当时英国的通货紧缩，可以理解）采取行动的中央银行管理。
3. 这样的市场缺陷，与国际收支融资一起，为官方融资提供了正当理由，否则很多国家只能通过采取会对国家和国际经济繁荣产生负面影响的措施来调整严重对外收支失衡。
4. 作为IMF的最高决策机构，理事会由一名理事长和每个成员国的候补理事长组成。理事长由成员国选出，通常为财政部长或央行行长。

Ⅳ. Read the passage and choose the correct answer.
1. D 2. C 3. A 4. D

CHAPTER 5　THE WORLD BANK

Ⅰ. Decide whether the following statements are true(T) or false(F).
1. F 2. T 3. T 4. F 5. T 6. F 7. T 8. F 9. T 10. F

Ⅱ. Translate the following expressions into Chinese.
1. 贷款目标从基础设施扩展到社会服务和其他行业
2. 搜集潜在借款国的信息，使银行能够更快处理贷款申请
3. 通过逐步淘汰95%的臭氧消耗化学品以中止臭氧消耗对地球大气的破坏
4. 包括审批贷款额和抵押金、新政策、行政预算、国家援助战略以及借款和财务决策
5. 鉴于当今可用的资源和技术，这种情况在道义上不可接受
6. 用量化的、直观的、浅显易懂的术语聚焦中心使命
7. 持续致力于增加各国穷人和弱势群体的福利
8. 气候变化的负面影响也有可能不均衡地殃及那些最贫穷国家
9. 调和了减少贫困、推动共享繁荣所需的快速经济发展和高效管理环境之间的矛盾
10. 实施政策改变的同时向困难国家提供援助以减轻通货膨胀和财政失衡

Ⅲ. Translate the following paragraphs into Chinese.
1. 当马歇尔计划于1947年实施的时候，许多欧洲国家开始接受其他来源的援助。面对这一竞争，世行将其重心转移至非欧洲国家。直至1968年，世行贷款专门用于产生效益的基础设施的建设，如

海港、公路系统和发电厂,这样资金借入国能够获得足够的收入偿还贷款。
2. 20世纪80年代,世行着重满足第三世界贷款需要,以及致力于第三世界国家经济重组的结构调整政策。联合国儿童基金会于20世纪80年代后期报道说世行的结构调整项目对数千万亚洲、拉丁美洲和非洲儿童的健康、营养和教育层次的下降负有责任。
3. 消除贫困和促进共同繁荣也非常清晰地涉及非货币化的福利方面的进步,包括教育、健康、营养和获得必要的基础设施,同时也涵盖加强经济、社会、政治等所有社会阶层的发言权和参与机会。
4. 在不到一代人的时间内在全球范围有效消除极端贫困,要达到这样的目标是一项雄心勃勃的努力,需要发展中国家持续的高经济增长率,以及在每一个发展中国家将发展更有效地转化为减贫。

CHAPTER 6 ASIAN DEVELOPMENT BANK

Ⅰ. Decide whether the following statements are true(T) or false(F).
 1. T 2. F 3. F 4. F 5. T 6. F 7. T 8. T 9. F 10. T

Ⅱ. Translate the following expressions into Chinese.
 1. 一个建立于1966年8月22日的地区性开发银行,目的是促进亚洲国家的经济发展
 2. 一个具有亚洲本质特征的金融机构,促进地区经济增长和协作
 3. 使用它的记录从私营部门调动额外的发展资源
 4. 一场严重的金融危机侵袭了该地区,使得亚洲巨大的经济收益蒙受损失
 5. 响应了20国集团领导人的呼吁,增加多边发展银行的资金来源,以支持全球金融危机中发展中国家的增长
 6. 将大量增加的重要的而且高质量的知识从经验转化到决策者、设计者和实施者手中
 7. 行动的自主性,避免利益冲突,隔离外部影响,机构的独立性
 8. 批准自我评估以缩短学习周期

Ⅲ. Translate the following paragraphs into Chinese.
 1. 从创建时的31名成员,亚洲开发银行现有67名成员国,其中48名来自亚洲和太平洋地区,19名来自地区外。亚洲开发银行高度模仿世界银行,有着相似的加权表决体系,票数根据成员国资本的认缴款额比例分配。
 2. 20世纪70年代,亚行的援助项目扩展至教育和公共卫生,以及后来的基础设施和工业领域。70年代后半期亚洲经济开始增长,激发了对于更好的基础设施的需求,用以支撑经济增长,亚行集中于修建道路与供电。
 3. 紧随第二次石油危机,亚行继续支持基础设施建设,特别是能源项目。亚行也增加了对于社会基础设施项目的支持,涉及性别、小额信贷、环境、教育、城市规划和健康问题。
 4. 就普通资本来源而言,成员国认购资本,包括已缴纳和可赎回资本,50%为初始认购的已缴纳比例,5%为1983年的第三次总增资,2%为1994年的第四次总增资。
 5. 自我评估由负责设计和执行国家战略、规划、项目或者技术援助行为的部门实施,由若干手段构成,包括项目执行情况报告、中期检查报告、技术援助或项目完成报告以及国家组合评估。
 6. 自1978年评估开始以来,亚行的运营评估已经有所改变。初始时评估重点是在项目完成后评估项目所达到的预期经济和社会效益的程度。现在,运营评估贯穿整个项目周期,而且在整体上影响着亚行的决策。

Ⅳ. Read the passage and choose the correct answer.
 1. B 2. C 3. D 4. B 5. C

Part III CURRENCIES

CHAPTER 7 THE FEDERAL RESERVE SYSTEM

Ⅰ. Decide whether the following statements are true(T) or false(F).

1. F 2. T 3. F 4. F 5. T 6. F 7. T 8. F 9. T 10. T

Ⅱ. Translate the following expressions into Chinese.

1. 无论是公共的还是私营的，获得流通性是为了防止银行挤兑

2. 给银行提供流通性以解决短期的急需，这些急需是由于季节性的存款波动或者不可预见的取款造成的

3. 描述为"政府内的独立"，而不是"独立的政府"

4. 须经国会修订或废止

5. 提供各种支付服务，包括托收支票，电子转账，分发和接收钱币

6. 全面监控美国的银行体系

7. 一旦他们的任期届满

8. 成员资格每2年到3年轮流

9. 就其管辖范围内的所有事务为董事会建言献计

10. 也会有意代表公众的利益

Ⅲ. Translate the following paragraphs into Chinese.

1. 偶遇下列情况，大量的银行客户取现，该行需要他行给予帮助以持续营业，这就是银行挤兑。银行挤兑会导致大量的社会和经济问题。联邦储备体系担当着试图预防或最小化出现银行挤兑的可能性，一旦银行挤兑真的出现，联储将会是银行最终借贷者。

2. 联邦储备系统作为美国的中央银行，既担当结算银行又担当政府银行的角色。作为决算银行，它帮助确保支付系统安全有效的运行；作为政府银行，或财政机构，联邦储备处理各种金融交易，涉及数万亿美元。

3. 通过影响金融市场的环境实现储蓄机构在联邦储备银行所持有的余额，联邦储备系统以此推行美国的货币政策。通过实施公开市场操作，强迫储备金要求，允许储蓄机构持有减少的清算余额；通过贴现窗口放贷，联邦储备系统强有力地控制着联邦储备银行的需求和供应以及联邦基金利率。通过其联邦基金利率的控制，联邦储备系统能够培育与货币政策目标一致的金融和货币环境。

Ⅳ. Read the passage and choose the correct answer.

1. B 2. D 3. B 4. C 5. D 6. B 7. A 8. A

CHAPTER 8 THE EUROPEAN CENTRAL BANK &THE EUROSYSTEM

Ⅰ. Decide whether the following statements are true(T) or false(F).

1. F 2. T 3. F 4. F 5. F 6. F 7. T 8. T 9. F 10. F

Ⅱ. Translate the following expressions into Chinese.

1. 确保币值随着时间的推移而保持不变

2. 设计了到1980年完成的三步走方案

3. 清除内部障碍使人员、货物、资本和服务在欧洲内部能自由流动
4. 加强了各成员国经济与货币政策的融合(以确保物价稳定和财政良好运行)
5. 成了规模更大更具独立性的经济体系的一部分
6. 就以购买力平价表示的国内生产总值而言
7. 国内的以及跨国的合并与收购(并购)
8. 选择极大的资本市场为其企业融资并使用新的金融工具以保护自己免遭各类金融风险,从而加强投资资金的管理
9. 具有独立法人资格的超国家机构
10. 主要再融资业务最小的买入汇率以及边际贷款便利和存款便利的利率
11. 规定各国央行主管和执行委员会成员的职务稳定
12. 为自身利益承担外汇储备管理业务并作为欧洲央行的代理
13. 依照行长委员会制定的方针和作出的决定在欧元区贯彻货币政策
14. 强调了其承诺以提供足够的安全系数以预防通货紧缩危险
15. 整个单一货币区央行流动性平均分布状态以及短期利率的均一水平
16. 一系列的金融政策手段,如公开市场业务,常用工具和准备金规定(法定存款准备标准)
17. 在特设的基础上控制市场中的流动性并且操控利率
18. 要求信贷机构在对各国央行储备账户上保持最低的准备金
19. 用于欧元区国家之间及国家之内以及其他几个欧共体国家使用欧元结账的全部交易活动
20. 2008年单一欧元支付区的启动

Ⅲ. **Translate the following paragraphs into Chinese.**

1. 在加入欧盟前须具备的条件即哥本哈根(入盟)标准。标准要求各预期入盟的国家(1)设立稳定的机构确保民主政治、依法治国、人权以及尊重保护少数民族,以及(2)设立发挥功能的市场经济,同时具备应付竞争压力的能力,以便能够承担成员国的义务,包括实现政治的、经济的以及货币联盟的目标。

2. 20世纪80年代下半期,经济和货币同盟的设想在1986年的《单一欧洲法案》中得以重提,由此而创设了单一市场。但是人们意识到,只有在成员国内引入单一货币才能完全获得单一市场的利益。1988年欧洲委员会下令德洛尔委员会考察实现经济和货币同盟的途径。1989年《德洛尔报告》引导了《欧盟条约》的磋商,该条约确立了欧洲联盟(欧盟)并且修订了成立欧洲共同市场的条约。条约于1992年2月在马斯特里赫特签订(所以有时称作《马斯特里赫特条约》)并于1993年11月1日生效。

3. 希望将欧元用作其货币的国家必须达到高度的"稳定融合"。融合度的评估基于《马斯特里赫特条约》的几项标准,标准要求一个国家具备下列条件:
   - 物价高度稳定;
   - 公共财政状况良好;
   - 汇率稳定;
   - 低而稳定的长期利率。

4. 自2004年来加入欧元的12个成员国中的9个国家以及瑞典作为"部分豁免"的成员国,这些国家没有符合采用欧元全部要求。享有部分豁免是指某成员国可豁免某些,但不是全部正常申请开始进入欧洲货币联盟第三进程的规定。它包括将货币政策的职责转换为欧洲央行管理委员会的全部规定。

5. 有效的对外交流是央行工作的基本内容。交流有助于提高货币政策的有效性和可信度。为了提升

公众对货币政策和央行其他活动的理解,欧洲央行必须公开透明。这是欧元系统在其对外交流中主要的指导原则,这种交流包括欧洲央行和各国央行之间紧密的合作。

6. 与第一代一样,第二代泛欧自动实时全额结算快速转账(泛欧自动转账)系统用于央行业务的结算、大笔欧元银行间转拨以及其他欧元的支付。该系统提供即时处理、用中央银行货币结算,并即时结算。不过,不同于其第一代系统(在第一代系统中全部支付由各国中央银行各自处理),新系统使用一个单一共享平台,全然不受央行的干扰。该平台使得提供一个高效而协调的服务成为可能。而且,由于规模经济效应,它实现低费用和低成本高效益。第二代系统没有支付金额的上下限。

Ⅳ. Read the passage and fill in the blanks.
1. EC, CFSP 2. foreign, immigration, judicial 3. Treaty of Lisbon

CHAPTER 9　HISTORY OF RENMINBI（RMB）

Ⅰ. Decide whether the following statements are true(T) or false(F) according to the text.
1. F 2. F 3. T 4. T 5. F 6. T 7. T 8. F 9. F 10. F

Ⅱ. Translate the following expressions into Chinese.
1. 根据硬币的形状命名
2. 有其特设的印钞工艺研究部门负责设计纸币并改进防伪技术
3. 导致了严重的黑市货币交易
4. 正面是龙的图案,反面是日晷
5. 签署一个双边的外汇结算协定
6. 被贬值以反映真实的市场价格,并且提升中国出口的竞争力
7. 使中国政府能从1997年到2005年盯住每美元8.27元人民币
8. 变为参照一揽子外币的以市场需求为基础的管理浮动汇率
9. 购买力平价
10. 一美元2006年相当于约3.462元人民币,2007年约3.621元,2008年约3.798元

Ⅲ. Translate the following paragraphs into Chinese.
1. 人民币由一家国营公司制造——中国印钞造币总公司,总部设在北京。该公司通过全国的印刷、制版和铸币的网络体系生产纸币和硬币后分送各地。纸币印制机构设置在北京、上海、成都、西安、石家庄和南昌;铸币机构分布在南京、上海、和沈阳。另有保定、昆山二家机构负责生产用于印制纸币的高级纸张。

2. 第一套人民币纸币于1948年12月由中国人民银行发行,大约一年后中国共产党取得了解放战争的胜利。当时仅发行纸币取代了在共产党控制地区流通的各种货币。新政府的首要任务之一是结束国民党统治后期全国的恶性通货膨胀。

3. 人民币作为官方称呼的首次记录是在1949年6月。1950年开始设计第二套人民币后先前的人民币被追溯定名为"第一套人民币"。

4. 第二套人民币于1955年发行。当时与西方货币的汇兑价格定得不切实际,而且制定了严格的汇兑规定。1978年中国经济改革开放,建立了双轨制的货币体系,人民币仅在国内使用,外国人必须使用外汇兑换券。

5. 美元对人民币银行间外汇市场每天的交易价格允许在中国人民银行公布的央行平价0.3%的窄幅浮动;后来,2007年5月17日发布的公告该浮动幅度增加到0.5%。中华人民共和国规定一揽子外币主要受控美国美元、欧元、日本日元、韩国韩元,而由英国英镑、泰国泰铢、俄罗斯卢布、澳大利亚澳元、加拿大加元以及新加坡元组成的一揽子占较小的比例。

KEY TO THE EXERCISES

Ⅳ. **Read the passage and answer the questions.**
1. The effect is intricate and difficult to accurately predict. Due to the costs and profits that vary with each industry, economists to a large extent have different estimates. The best prediction can be made after considering every angle as much as possible. For individual industries, it will clearly favour some, and cause worry for others.
2. (1) Textile: the textile industry would be in a difficult situation more than any other industries. It would see its profits from exports reduced. Some uncompetitive small-and-medium-sized companies would then likely face bankruptcy, causing possible job losses for a large number of workers who are from low or medium income families, thus could possibly trigger even greater social problems.
   (2) Real-estate: a possible *renminbi* appreciation would cause a still-adjusting housing sector to confront the enormous pressures brought on by the massive influx of hot money. It seems that regardless of the method, the health and continued development of the real estate sector will soon face an unprecedented challenge.
   (3) Banking: for China's banking industry, the greatest risk associated with a revaluation is the possibility of deflation. In the battle around *renminbi* revaluation it is the stream of foreign hot money that poses the greatest risk to damage China's economy. As foreign capital withdraws the bubble of prosperity will rapidly burst, causing bankruptcy of many investors.
   (4) Energy industry: the effect on the electricity and coal industries would be minimal. However, there would be an obvious effect on the oil industry, which would be more noticeably over the medium and long-term.